Civil War Stories
Tales of Everyday Soldiers and Civilians
Volume II

Greg M. Romaneck
with
Erin Elizabeth Romaneck

HERITAGE BOOKS
2008

HERITAGE BOOKS
AN IMPRINT OF HERITAGE BOOKS, INC.

Books, CDs, and more—Worldwide

For our listing of thousands of titles see our website at
www.HeritageBooks.com

Published 2008 by
HERITAGE BOOKS, INC.
Publishing Division
100 Railroad Ave. #104
Westminster, Maryland 21157

Copyright © 2008 Greg M. Romaneck

Other books by the author:
A Civil War Reenactor's Guidebook

Cover design by Kyle M. Romaneck

All rights reserved. No part of this book may be reproduced or transmitted in any form or by any means, electronic or mechanical, including photocopying, recording or by any information storage and retrieval system without written permission from the author, except for the inclusion of brief quotations in a review.

International Standard Book Numbers
Paperbound: 978-0-7884-4599-6
Clothbound: 978-0-7884-7181-0

Introduction

     The Civil War divided the American nation for four long and bloody years. The results of the Civil War helped shape American history not only in those distant days but also in our own era. As the post-war years rolled along quite a few Civil War veterans chose to record their experiences for posterity. A raft of memoirs poured out in the decades that closed the 19th century. In our own era, thousands of books have been published about this divisive conflict. Americans just do not seem to be able to get enough reading material when it comes to the Civil War.

     What follows are snapshots of Civil War life as the common soldiers who fought it and civilians who steadied the homefront experienced it. Throughout the book readers will have the opportunity to revisit the words and deeds of Northern and Southern soldiers and civilians who lived through one of the most important phases in American history. Civil War soldiers experienced deprivation, struggle, loss, loneliness, trauma, and death. The Civil War was a conflict in which over 600,000 men died. Such devastation could not help but leave its mark upon not only the individuals who fought but also the nation at large.

     In the stories that follow readers will encounter the words and deeds of common soldiers and civilians. In some selections the focus rests upon some of the banes and bonuses that soldiers lived with. Other chapters center upon conflict and the clash of battle. Civilian memoirs reveal the impact warring armies had upon those who they encountered and those who waited at home for word to come of distant loved ones. Many of the entries are primarily drawn from the writings of the veterans and family members themselves. However, in each selection, the author's hope is that readers will finish their reading with a deeper appreciation for the sacrifices made by Civil War soldiers and civilians. If that goal is achieved then the work that has gone into this book will have proven worthwhile.

GMR

Dedication: This book is dedicated to my family for all the love and patience they have shown me. Thank you Jane for being a wonderful wife. Thanks also to my daughter, Erin, and my two sons, Kyle & Colin, for being such inspiring people.
Finally, I wish to extend thanks to my mother and my late father for giving me a childhood that was secure and loving. GMR

TABLE OF CONTENTS

Part I—Soldier's Stories

1. The Civil War Letters of Mr. & Mrs. Moxley — 1
2. General John Basil Turchin: A Life of Service & Misfortune — 7
3. Edwin Hale Lincoln: A Union Drummer Boy — 13
4. Women Soldiers in the Civil War: The Tricks of Their Secret Lives — 19
5. Gallinippers: A Bane to Civil War Soldiers — 33
6. One Irish Brigadier's Experience — 39
7. Si Klegg's Civil War — 43
8. Henry Hunt's Artillerists & Pickett's Charge — 49
9. Joseph Garey: A Keystone Rebel — 67
10. Webb Baker: An Illinois Soldier's Story — 73
11. Carrying the Flag: Charles Whilden & the 1st South Carolina — 77
12. Lucius Barber's Civil War — 85
13. Albert Cashier: An Uncommon Civil War Soldier — 95
14. William Wiley's Civil War — 103
15. The Hawk Brothers — 111

Part II—Civilian Stories

1. Hannah Ropes: Civil War Nurse — 123
2. Illnesses of the Civil War Era: A Brief Compendium — 133
3. Simple Remedies of the Civil War Era — 139
4. Civilians and the Antietam Campaign — 145
5. Agnes Lee: A Child of Good Fortune — 169
6. Tillie Pierce: A Union Girl at Gettysburg — 173
7. Harriett Dada: The Story of a Union Nurse — 187
8. Views of Childhood During the Civil War — 193
9. Fanny Kemble's Rebellions — 209
10. Mary Loughborough's Cave Life in Vicksburg — 215
11. Women Spies of the Civil War — 223
12. Louisa May Alcott's Life & Times — 235
13. A Gentrified View of Plantation Life — 245
14. Harriet Jacobs' Life as a Slave — 253
15. "Dear Emma": Letters to and from the Homefront — 263

The Faded Stone – A Simple Poem — 271

Part I:
Soldier's Stories

1

The Civil War Letters of Mr. & Mrs. Moxley

Marriage is an institution with a long and vibrant history in the annals of human society. In marriages people of infinitely unique temperaments come together in an emotional and physical partnership that involves the most complex of loving & delicate negotiations. Every marriage is a unique merger that takes its changing form from the inner and external attributes of the people involved. It is all too easy to, when studying history, overlook the fact that people who were married in the past experienced many of the same issues that current couples encounter. Issues of trust, financial disagreement, longing, misunderstanding, discord, and loving harmony can come and go in even the soundest of marriages. Such realities did not just recently come into being in human cultures. No, married couples have been coping with the joys and vicissitudes of matrimony for as long as recorded history has existed and beyond.

The Civil War years were no exception to the reality that many married people will experience waves of happiness and dissatisfaction in their lives. What blurs this historical truth is the absence of tremendous quantities of primary source information about the state of marriage during the years of America's Civil War. While there are many soldier's memoirs and compilations of men's letters from the front each detailing a particular person's wartime experiences, there are very few extant accounts of marriage attitudes. Many soldiers were somewhat remiss in terms of their willingness or ability to save the letters from their spouses. Women tended to live a more passive life on the homefront so their observations were sometimes less compelling than men fighting at the front. Also, many women, particularly in the South, were less literate than their husbands. Thus, for a variety of reasons there is a relatively small treasure trove of information about how husbands and wives corresponded with one another during the tumultuous war years. For this reason the published letters of Emily & William Moxley offer people interested in social history a fascinating glimpse into the nature of one Civil War marriage.

For slightly less than one year William Morel Moxley served as an officer in the Eighteenth Alabama. During that time Moxley rose from the elected rank of captain to major in an infantry regiment that was to have a bloody and storied history. During his time in the Confederate army William Moxley never saw combat. He spent most of his enlistment stationed in or near Pensacola & Mobile. When the Eighteenth marched north to Corinth and beyond, Moxley was absent from duty as the horrific battle at Shiloh took place. William Moxley's letters do not recount great military exploits, spellbinding studies in command, or the ins and outs of camp life. What they do reveal, along with the many correspondences from his wife Emily, is an outline of how one married couple coped with the separation inherent in war. In this way the correspondence of this couple stands out as a simple and unvarnished look at the inner workings of a Civil War marriage.

In looking at the story told by the letters of William and Emily Moxley several themes emerge that shed some light on at least one Civil War era marriage and its conformation. The Moxley's come across the pages of their letters as a deeply devoted couple. Throughout these correspondences the reader is constantly struck by how honestly in love they were with each other. On September 1st, 1862 William describes his feelings for his wife and family in language that is repeated frequently throughout his letters, "If I should be killed in battle I want you to be close enough to see that {I} died for you & my children. It is for you and them I live & for you & them I am willing to die. My dear, you may be satisfied you always have the first place in my heart, and my children next. I am anxious to see you. I think while I am writing this sentence that you and the children may be talking about me." (27)

In a similar vein, Emily Moxley laces her letters with a steady and loving stream of best wishes, hopes, and dreams of reunion. Also in September Emil Moxley opens a letter to her beloved husband in this manner, "It is now 8 or 9 oclock (sic) and I am siting (sic) at my table, trying to write to the object of my heart. For all the pleasure I see is in writing to you or reading a letter, and then I cant (sic) write one or read with (out) crying, but it is a satisfaction to me if {I} do cry. I had rather write to you than eat when I am hungry. The worst, I never know when to quit when I commence." (28) Then, in what smacks of a typical wifely chit Emily added, "That is not the case with you. Your letters are too short to suit me." (28)

In many of the Moxley letters this chord of affection is frequently struck. Back and forth the letters flow, each of which incorporates some mention of loneliness, painful absence, and loving wishes. In reading these passages in this set of letters the reader may well better appreciate the realities of loss that dogged millions of Americans during the war years. In the Moxley's, and their sad separation, is the world of marriages split by war that is such a sad element of human history.

Another theme that runs through many of the Moxley letters is that of health and wellness. The Civil War was fought at a time when disease was not only the great predator in the armies but also in civilian life as well. During William Moxley's service Emily became pregnant and was called upon to cope with her pregnancy without her husband's presence and support. At the front, William Moxley often became ill with colds and respiratory infections. Thus, many times the Moxley's delve into the subject of health in a way that reminds readers of how tenuous life was in that bygone era. For example, at one point Emily both attempts to comfort her husband while also taking him to task for not caring for himself while ill, "Dear William you don't (sic) know the uneasy hours I have spent since I heard that you was sick. I have not had a night sleep since, but all that I can do is to grieve. I go to bed but not to sleep much but to cry and study about my poor Husband that is lieing (sic) on his cot and no one to nurse him as I would do, or at least they would not do it as willingly as I would. Oh, what a pleasure it would be to me to be with you now. I never was so uneasy in my life as I am now. You don't (sic) know how I feel, for I think that you (would) lie and die before you let me know that you was sick." (35)

Interestingly & tragically, in March of 1862 it was Emily Moxley that was to be struck down by the hard hand of illness. On March 13 Emily and her baby died during childbirth. They were buried in Spears Cemetery, Pike County, Alabama. A few weeks later William Moxley wrote home to his eldest son and sadly said, "I write you a few lines to let you know that you have a

Father who loves you dearly with your little Sisters & Brothers. George, I have often told you to be a good boy, mind your Mother, and take care of your Sisters & Brothers. George, I cant (sic) say so any more. Your dear Mother is gone now, George. Mind your Grand Pa & Ma and every person that teaches you to do right. George, you are the eldest. As you have no Ma, always take care of your little Brothers & Sisters. Be good to them & be a good boy. If your Pa should die or get killed in Battle, then you would have neither Father nor Mother to advise you." (137)

    Reflecting on these sad words one can only imagine how it must have felt to lose a spouse without any recourse or capacity to return home and ease the burden of grief & travail for one's children. William Moxley remained in service but was no longer the same man. When the time came for Shiloh he was reported as present for duty but not at the front. Was this a matter of courage, stamina, or simply a broken heart? No one will ever know, but what can be surmised from the Moxley letters was that they loved one another, lost that love to untimely death, and left a depressed survivor behind who left the army shortly after Shiloh.

    The Civil War letters of the Moxley's tell a simple yet profound story. It is the everyday story of a country physician serving as an infantry officer and his poor wife back home. Many of the couple's letters discuss the fine points of harvesting crops, financial affairs, neighborhood gossip, monetary woes, and the numbing sadness of separation. Married people who have been separated from their loved ones will understand the tone of these letters despite the fact that they were scribed by a couple over 140 years ago. Readers who peruse these entries will come away saddened by the human tragedy that came to the Moxley family. Like so many unknown people, the lives of William & Emily Moxley were filled with the drama that makes up common life. In these resurrected letters one can appreciate the cost that war can exact from its participants. One need not fall in battle to have a tragic wartime death. In peeking into the lives of the Moxley's readers are given a great opportunity to establish an acquaintance with two common people who lived lives that modern folk should be able to identify with.

Source

Curtrer, Thomas W. (ed.). *Oh What a Lonesome Time I Had: The Civil War Letters of*
Major William Morel Moxley, Eighteenth Alabama Infantry, and Emily Beck
Moxley. Tuscaloosa, AL: University of Alabama Press, 2002.

2

General John Basil Turchin: A Life of Service & Misfortune

By the end of the Civil War it was common practice for armies on the march to literally devastate the countryside through which they traveled. General William Tecumseh Sherman's minions burned, destroyed, and looted so many Southern homes that their March to the Sea became legendary & infamous. In the Shenandoah Valley the forces of Philip Sheridan were given instructions to leave that once prosperous region so barren that even a crow flying overhead would need to bring its own rations. Yet, while such total war techniques seem self-explanatory to modern readers, they were not the norm earlier in the war.

During the first two years of the Civil War a great debate surged up among Northern commanders, politicians, and the public in regards to the harshness with which the war should be prosecuted. In the early phases of the war Confederate property, inclusive of slaves, was seen as sacrosanct by the majority of West Point trained Union commanders. Leaders such as George B. McClellan and Don Carlos Buell gave strict orders that men under their command were to refrain from hard foraging, looting, or any other mode of desecration of southern property. These dictates extended to the return of fugitive slaves who had sought liberty and succor at the hands of the invading Federals.

Union officers did not universally accept this gentlemanly approach to warfare. Indeed, there was a cadre of generally non-professionally trained Union generals who looked at war in a far different way. For these men the war could not be won unless Union troops fought it in a way that brought the South to its knees. That goal could only be accomplished when Union soldiers took their gloves off and made the war painful for the Confederates.

Chief among these advocates of hard war was one Russian immigrant to Illinois, John Basil Turchin.

General John Basil Turchin was a latecomer to the issues leading up to the Civil War. Born in the Don Cossack region of Russia on January 30, 1822 as Ivan Vasilievitch Turchaninov, this Federal commander was to become an epicenter for the debate over how the Civil War should be waged. Turchin served in the Czarist army for a number of years and participated in several military campaigns inclusive of the Crimean War. Politically, Turchin was opposed to the repressive czarist regime and finally chose to leave military service and emigrate to America. In 1856 Turchin arrived in America along with his wife Nadezhda.

Once in America the Turchaninov's chose to Americanize their names and became John & Nadine Turchin. Both of the Turchin's also became staunch Republicans and fierce opponents of the slavocracy that they saw the antebellum South to be. The Turchin's saw slavery as no different than the oppression of the Russian peasantry that they had witnessed in their homeland. John Turchin never wavered in his critical view of the southern aristocracy and "their struggle to preserve slavery…Their lamentations of oppression by the North, and their declaration of their right to be free, jar discordantly with their firm determination to hold millions of blacks in bondage." (12)

Throughout their lives the Turchin's would work to oppose such oppression despite the fact that such actions were not always universally profitable to them. Indeed, it was because of his strongly held core values that John Basil Turchin chose to immediately volunteer his services to the Union after Fort Sumter was fired upon. Turchin saw the coming of war as an inevitability and one that afforded free men an opportunity to rid the nation of the stain of slavery. Interestingly enough Turchin became one of two men competing for command of the 19th Illinois. Eventually, because of his extensive command experience in the Russian army Turchin was chosen over his competitor for that command. That competitor was Ulysses S. Grant, a man under whose overall command Turchin was to eventually carry out a very hard war indeed.

As a regimental commander the then Colonel Turchin was an advocate of drill, discipline, and soldierly understanding. Turchin had served in the ranks of the Russian army for many years and there had seen the ways in which haughty officers could demean common soldiers. Throughout his career Turchin was aware of the need to maintain the well being of those whom he was entrusted to command. In future years this attitude was reflected in the way Turchin's subordinates referred to him. One of Turchin's men from the 19th later described his commander in this way, "He was like a father and called us his boys." (19)

Throughout his career as a Union officer John Basil Turchin fought against not only his Confederate foes, but also the dishwater style leadership of commanders who misread the total nature of the war. Under the command of Don Carlos Buell, Turchin rose to a brigade command and also nearly lost his military career due to his being labeled a brigand rather than a gentleman officer.

In May of 1862 Turchin's brigade entered into the city of Athens, Alabama. There, after experiencing the ruination of guerrilla warfare in the region, Turchin's men indulged in harsh foraging, looting, and destructive behavior that would have been seen as the norm during later years of the war. However, in 1862, prior to the Emancipation Proclamation and the clear necessity of "destructive war" these actions were deemed criminal. In one of the more interesting segments of this comprehensive biography, author Chicoine traces the court martial that was staged by Union officers to punish the actions of a foreign born colleague whom they saw as having crossed the line of acceptable conduct.

Because of the Athens affair, a court martial was convened and Colonel John Basil Turchin was charged with a breach of military conduct resulting in wanton destruction of civilian property. A tribunal was convened under the supervision of General James Garfield. After weeks of testimony wherein Turchin served as his own counsel two opposing results occurred. First, Turchin became a national symbol behind which the advocates of harder warfare could rally. Second, despite deporting himself in a reasonable & dignified manner that won over many of the members of the tribunal, John Basil Turchin was found guilty.

The court martial members recommended that Turchin be dismissed from the service but also advocated for clemency on the part of the army commander, General Buell. Simultaneously, John Turchin's name was approved by a narrow margin in the United States Senate for promotion to the rank of Brigadier General.

While Abraham Lincoln was signing off on this promotion General Buell ignored the advisement of clemency and dismissed John Basil Turchin from his command.

Left without a command but with great political capital General Turchin returned to Chicago. There he became an active symbol for a more radical approach to both the waging of the war and the way in which slavery should be viewed. Papers such as the Chicago Tribune used Turchin as an example of how the nation was being led astray by soft hearted leaders who were doomed to fail, "Colonel Turchin has had, from the beginning, the wisest and clearest ideas of any man in the field about the way in which the war should be conducted." (99) With such political backing and at a time when President Lincoln was looking for a more aggressive approach to the waging of the war, it was only a matter of time before General Turchin returned to the field.

Once back in command of a brigade in the Army of the Cumberland, General Turchin demonstrated great bravery and skill as a leader. At places such as Chickamauga, Missionary Ridge, and during the Atlanta Campaign Turchin consistently modeled outstanding leadership. Indeed, at Chickamauga General Turchin was among the most important Union commanders on that bloody field.

Chickamauga was one of the few Civil War battles in which the utter destruction of one army by its opponents nearly was possible. The mismanagement of the Federal army by Union Commander General Rosecrans resulted in the artificial creation of a gap in the line that was promptly and fortuitously exploited by Confederate General Braxton Bragg. As a result at one point in the battle the majority of the Union army was splintered and driven from the field in disorder. All that stood in the way of complete destruction was the Union wing under the command of General George Thomas. Thomas stemmed the Confederate advance but was eventually cut off from his lines of retreat by advancing Confederates. In that precarious circumstance Thomas ordered Turchin's brigade to "charge to the rear." Under the brave command of John Basil Turchin the Confederate line was breeched and an avenue of retreat was opened. This attack allowed General Thomas to withdraw under the cover of darkness and retreat intact to Chattanooga. One of Turchin's regimental commanders described this successful attack in this way, "The success of this regiment and brigade is not owing to its discipline and efficiency alone, but to its confidence in the skill of the brigade commander." (XI)

At Missionary Ridge General Turchin's brigade was one of the first to advance up the rocky slopes to eventual victory. In the Kennesaw Mountain battle, Turchin again displayed vigor and skill as a commander. It was only a severe case of heat stroke that, in August of 1864, felled John Basil Turchin and debilitated him to such an extent that he had to resign his commission and return to civilian life. There, having served nobly for a cause that he supported with all his heart, John Basil Turchin watched from a distance as the Union armies slowly ground down their foes and eventually prevailed.

In later years the Turchin's led an impoverished life. General Turchin attempted several careers inclusive of real estate speculation, railroad management, and writing. While Turchin's account of the Chickamauga battle was a critically acclaimed book, it netted him a very small profit. Turchin's efforts as a businessman generally failed not so much due to his own incapabilities but rather because of his small amount of investment capital. General Turchin was denied a military pension under the technicality that he had been convicted and discharged by a court martial. Despite all evidence to the contrary that he had been reinstated the fact that he had once been discharged barred him from a pension.

By the turn of the 19th century John Turchin became increasingly prone to bouts of dementia. Turchin was eventually placed in a state asylum where he died in 1901. Nadine Turchin, who leaps out of the pages of history as a vibrant and fascinating companion to General Turchin, lived on until 1904. She too was denied a widow's pension as her marriage, which took place in Russia, was not accepted as valid. Only in the last months of Nadine Turchin's life was that decision reversed. However, the bitterness of the military hierarchy's treatment of both Nadine Turchin and her beloved husband must have irked this strong spirited woman to her grave.

In the end John Turchin remained a steadfast advocate for freedom and reform in his adopted homeland. The Turchin's came to America in search of liberty and opportunity. They arrived as the nation was on the cusp of civil war. During the war

John Turchin nobly served the cause of freedom. His actions were not universally understood or appreciated by either citizens of the North or South. However, as a Union commander John Basil Turchin never lost sight of not only the political goals of the war bit also his role as a leader of men.

To the end of his service as a Union officer General John Basil Turchin looked at war not as a game but as an endeavor to win. Throughout his life Turchin remained a humble man blessed with a spouse who possessed wit, determination, and courage. Near the end of his life John Turchin looked back on his achievements in the war and, instead of aggrandizing his efforts, declared, "the greatest hero during these long, anxious hours and the savior of our army was the soldier…if at any time a monument should be reared up to the memory of the Army of the Cumberland, the soldier should be the crowning and dominant figure of it." (189)

Source

Chicoine, Stephen. *John Basil Turchin and the Fight to Free the Slaves.* Westport, CT:
    Praeger, 2003.

3

Edwin Hale Lincoln: A Union Drummer Boy

In 1934 Edwin Hale Lincoln, then Vice Commander-in-Chief of the Grand Army of the Republic (G.A.R.) rose to address an audience in New York City that had gathered at a dinner hosted by the United Daughters of the Confederacy. At the time Edwin Hale Lincoln was eighty-six-years-old and his wartime service was a distant but still lively spark of memory. As Lincoln began to speak he looked at his audience and said, "We should remember that Lee, too, was an American....Crossed today are the swords of Grant and Lee, with the memory of Lincoln above them as a benediction and the battle flags are furled. We have gone far since Appomattox. We have a united country and we are living in harmony beneath a common flag. We can afford to forget the strife and what was behind it and remember the acts of devotion on both sides, the courage, the intrepidity, the sacrifices, the chivalry that were in those hearts of oak and nerves of steel." (68-69)

Many years had passed since that same speaker had served as a drummer boy in the 5th Massachusetts Infantry at the mere age of fourteen. But, the passage of those years brought Edwin Hale Lincoln to a point of forgiveness and reunion. In this way, Lincoln's short but memorable wartime service followed by long term involvement in veteran's affairs are representative of his nation's pathway to, through, and following the Civil War. In addition, Edwin Hale Lincoln's short diary of his year served as a drummer boy serves as a fine resource for those individuals wishing to learn more about the life of a Civil War drummer boy.

Edwin Hale Lincoln's diary reveals a number of things about that intrepid youth and his time in military service. To begin, Lincoln chose to enlist at the age of fourteen because he felt a deep and abiding loyalty to the cause of Union. Lincoln was allowed to ultimately enlist in the 5th Massachusetts at such a tender age because of the presence of his cousin, Jarius Lincoln, who served as a sergeant in Company E of the regiment. Once Edwin Lincoln was mustered in as a musician he went along with the 5th as it spent virtually all of its nine-month enlistment in or near New Bern, North Carolina.

One of the things that make the writings of young Lincoln so fascinating is the fact that very few youngsters his age left behind any written record of their military service during the Civil War. Young Lincoln not only did so but also wrote in such an adept manner that in many instances his words are hard to recognize as those of a boy rather than a mature adult. Throughout his short diary Lincoln comes across as a thoughtful and observant youngster. For example, in November 1862 Lincoln's unit marched from New Bern to Morehead City, North Carolina. In describing one of his first experiences in camp Lincoln noted that, "We marched about ¾ of a mile through sand to our camp. We are now in the midst of a hailstorm. Our tents are those of the Sibley pattern. There are 18 of us in one of these. They are about 15 ft. in diameter + 50 in circumference. The 2nd night, after we came here, the whole Reg't were all ordered to be ready to march at 4 the next morning…We are on the outskirts of the City. We are nearly surrounded by swamps. Every Company has seven Tents. 1 for the Capt. + Lieuts, 1 for the Sergeants, 5 for the men." (9-10)

This eye for detail was common throughout Lincoln's diary and bespeaks his ability to observe and recount his life in the army. However, such an eye for detail did not prevent camp life from taxing even so stoic a writer as young Edwin Lincoln. Time and again Lincoln recounted waking up after tough night's sleeping only to find that, "This morning we had quite a frost. There was frost on the ground and the ground was very hard. There was ice on the swamps." (9-10) On another night Lincoln was cursed by the ill effects of rain, "Towards midnight the storm broke fresher and fierce. The water filled the trench around our tent + it began to flow into the tent. It finally covered about 1/3 of the tent floor. P.S. we had the ground for our floor." (12)

Another interesting, and contrasting, aspect of the wartime diary of this youngster is the fact that boys will be boys. Despite the careful and well-educated aspect of Edwin Hale Lincoln's

writings he still was a lad rather than an adult. As a fourteen-year-old Lincoln was prone to immature actions and misadventures. Those realities come across at several junctures of Lincoln's diary. While out looking for firewood near Fort Totten, North Carolina young Lincoln came across a souvenir he could not resist. While scrounging in the brush Lincoln made a startling discovery, "I found a cannonball a 32-pounder. I put it in the wagon + had it brought to the tent. I buried it all but the top + left that sticking out of the ground." (13)
Fortunately this unexploded ordinance did not end or maim Lincoln's life but its presence did cause him to sarcastically note, "It must be pleasant to have those flying around a fellows' head." (13)

    Just before Christmas in 1862 Lincoln also betrayed his natural immaturity and rambunctiousness while he, and some of his comrades, were foraging for supplies at a nearby farm. In Lincoln's own words, "Leaving my Reg't, I went to see if I could not "forage a bit." I found some cornmeal in a shed back of the house. I should think that there was over a bushel. Going out into the garden I saw more than a dozen beehives ripped open and the men at working (sic) breaking open more. Honey was plenty. However toward the last I got a bee into my mouth who stung under my lip. It swelled out to over three times the original size." (18)

    In looking at incidents such as this one can almost see the natural playfulness and curiosity of a young teenager. Sadly, those normal inclinations were at work in a war zone wherein the potential cost of playfully bringing an artillery shell back to camp or unobservantly foraging could be death and destruction Further, although Edwin Hale Lincoln and the 5th Massachusetts were destined to see only skirmishes rather than full scale battles, that fact did not immunize the unit from losses.

    Camped in swampy land in North Carolina led to a constant stream of sickness, disability, and death. In fact, about halfway through his term of service Lincoln was transferred to the regimental hospital as an assistant to the surgeon. In that capacity Lincoln was able to observe at close range the debilitation that disease created in the Civil War. Or, as Lincoln noted in one diary entry, "Soldiers are buried here nearly every day. We can here (sic) the volleys that are fired." (12)

Life in the 5th for Edwin Hale Lincoln was a combination of new horizons, hard work, boredom, and premature responsibility. Camp life was full of rainy days, drill, inaction, and labor. Even the Sabbath was not immune to the demands that the army placed upon its enlisted members. In January 1863 Edwin Lincoln wrote, "How different the Sabbaths out here are, when compared with those at home! Here there is scarcely any difference in the noise and bustle. We have the customary Inspection every morning. At home all is quiet on Sunday." (23)

The natural boredom of camp life sometimes led Lincoln to partake of gossip. Much like his older comrades-in-arms Lincoln took i8n camp rumors and embroidered them to meet his understanding. Near the end of his diary Lincoln records his take on a camp rumor having to do with the raising of a new Massachusetts regiment, "They are now raising a negro regiment in New Berne. I understand that it is to have negro officers. The negroes enlist very fast. As soon as they are enlisted they are uniformed and sent into camp. A negro regiment the 54th Mass. Is expected here every day." (41-42)

Unfortunately these references to the historic 54th Massachusetts are just about the last few words entered into Edwin Hale Lincoln's diary. Approximately one month after writing that sentence, in July 1863, Lincoln and the 5th were sent home to Boston. There, back in their home state, the men of the 5th were mustered out of service. While many of the men who served in the 5th reenlisted with other regiments, Edwin Hale Lincoln did not. Lincoln's wartime service was over but his life still held many fascinating aspects

In later years Lincoln led a colorful and public life. In the 1870's Lincoln began what was to be a sixty-year-long career as a naturalist photographer. Indeed, Lincoln became on of the leading American photographers with a specialty in wildflowers and trees. In addition Lincoln became heavily involved in his local G.A.R. post. Over the years Lincoln rose to state and then national office within the G.A.R. and remained involved in that organization until his death.

On a personal level Edwin Hale Lincoln married, divorced, remarried, and raised five children one of whom died while in the American army during World War One. Throughout his life Edwin Lincoln held firm to the lessons he had gleaned from his Civil war service. Lincoln remained a steadfast comrade to his fellow veterans. He expressed his intellectual curiosity in his art and life. Finally, on October 15, 1938 Lincoln was struck and killed by an automobile driver while crossing a street. At the age of ninety Lincoln had come a long way from his camp experiences as a scamp in North Carolina during the Civil War. However, through his now available diary, modern readers can revisit that time of military service and learn about the life of one Civil War veteran amongst the millions who served in that distant but still memorable conflict.

Source

Marty, Karl & Drickamer, Lee C. (editors). *Drummer Boy: The Civil War Diary of*
 Edwin Hale Lincoln. Raleigh, NC: Ivy House Publishing Group, 2005.

18

4

Women Soldiers in the Civil War: The Tricks of Their Secret Lives

In the late 1880's when Mary Livermore, a former Civil War nurse and soldier's aid coordinator, heard the speculation that more than four hundred women "bore arms and served in the ranks" of the Union army she recorded in her memoir that although she could not "vouch for the correctness of the estimate," she felt confident that "a larger number of women disguised themselves and enlisted in the service, for one cause or other, than was dreamed of."[1]

While there is no accurate way to actually determine the number of women who donned male attire and went to war as soldiers, scholars of creditable repute have come to some conclusions. Most recently historians Deanne Blanton and Lauren M. Cook, in their comprehensive work *They Fought Like Demons: Women Soldiers in the Civil War,* note, "Approximately three million soldiers served throughout the Civil War. While no one will ever know exactly how many of these soldiers were women, extant documentation suggests they only numbered in the hundreds."[2] Given that tiny number of women soldiers these two capable writers note, "Clearly, the service of these women did not affect the outcome of battles and campaigns, and the service of women did not alter the course of the war. Their individual contributions and exploits are fascinating but are not the primary reason for their historical significance."[3] The primary significance of these women warriors rests in the fact that, "Women soldiers of the Civil War merit recognition because of the fact that they were there and because they were not supposed to be. They deserve

xix―――――――――――――――――

[1] Tsui, Bonnie. *She Went to the Field: Women Soldiers of the Civil War.* The Globe Pequot Press, 2003, pp. 1
[2] Blanton, Deanne & Cook, Lauren M. *They Fought Like Demons: Women Soldiers of the Civil War.* Vintage Books, 2002, pp. 205-206
[3] Blanton & Cook, pp. 206

19

remembrance because their actions made them uncommon and revolutionary, possessed of a valor at odds with Victorian and, in some respects, even modern views of women's proper role."[4]

Given this unusual role for a mid-nineteenth century woman, the image of a Civil war soldier serving while disguising her gender remains a gripping one. As a result of in our own era, a small percentage of Civil War reenactors is made up of women portraying soldiers. In many cases the women who don military clothing and march or ride out onto the recreated battlefields do a very creditable job of portraying a Civil War soldier. In other instances, the self-evident truth of the living historian's gender and soldierly bearing make that impression at best inaccurate, and at worst discomfiting. In a paradoxical manner the ability of female living historians to blend in or not with their male reenacting counterparts is a perfect recreation of the primary dilemma faced by distaff soldiers of the Civil War. How could they make their disguise appear and remain believable?

Given the fact that women did successfully maintain military impressions in the Civil War it is appropriate to highlight some keynote points that assisted in the development & maintenance of those alter egos. Imagine living, breathing, eating, drilling, and fighting alongside thousands of men while you attempted to suppress not only gender but also most aspects of your personality. While the number of distaff Civil War soldiers was not huge, the very fact that they existed at all underscores their intrepid nature. Those women in soldier's garb remain a puzzling and inspiring aspect of the Civil War. Although no sound historian or student of the war would go so far as to say that the contributions of female Civil War soldiers was of paramount value, the fact that they existed at all is memorable. Yet, it should also be remembered that while in some cases the contribution of woman warriors was minor, in others it represented not only great sacrifice but also even death. But the question remains—how did those women pull off such a seemingly improbable outcome? What follows are clues to the successful endeavors of those long ago women soldiers.

---
xx————————————————

[4] Blanton & Cook, pp. 206

Maintain a Believable Disguise

In 1911 State Senator Ira Lish backed his automobile out of the driveway of his home in the rural community of Saunemin, Illinois. Unfortunately, Senator Lish struck his hired handyman, Albert Cashier, severely injuring the elderly fellow. During a medical examination of Mr. Cashier the consulting physician discovered that Albert was, indeed, a woman. This fact stuck all who eventually realized the reality of Albert Cashier's gender as remarkable. Not only was Cashier's disguise a contemporary befuddlement but also a historical one as well. For, Albert Cashier, who in reality was Jennie Hodgers an Irish immigrant who came to the United Sates just prior to the Civil War, had proudly served "his" country for nearly four years as a Union soldier in the 95th Illinois.[5]

While Albert Cashier's unmasking has historical interest, it also presents key lessons to modern women intent upon portraying a Civil War soldier. Albert Cashier was able to maintain her disguise for nearly fifty years. For most of the Civil War Albert Cashier lived, marched, fought, ate, and simply passed time with male soldiers without discovery. In 1914 when, in light of the revelations regarding Albert Cashier's gender, hearings were held to ascertain the validity of "his" ongoing military pension, a number of Albert's former comrades in the 95th Illinois came forward to testify on her behalf. Those veterans' commentaries are enlightening in terms of how successful Albert Cashier was in disguising her true persona.

As part of Albert's defense her counsel asked fellow members of her unit to testify as to her service. None of the veterans questioned in Albert's review hearing had any prior idea that she was a woman. Several of Albert's comrades from the 95th remembered that she had been "shy and hard to know." One Illinois soldier noted that, "Cashier was very quiet in her manner and she was not easy to get acquainted with." Another veteran from the 95th explained how it was possible for Albert to conceal her identity during the war, "When we were examined at induction we were not stripped. We were examined on the same day. All

xxi─────────────────

[5] Romaneck, Erin Elizabeth. *Civil War Stories: Tales of Everyday Soldiers & Civilians*. Unpublished Manuscript, pp. 82-83

that we showed was our hands and feet. I never did see Cashier go to the toilet nor did I ever see any part of his person exposed by which I could determine the sex. He was a very retiring disposition and did not take part in any of the games. He would sit around and watch but would not take part. He had very small hands and feet."[6]

Every veteran who testified at Cashier's hearing was surprised to discover that she was a woman. When asked to identify Albert from pictures of her as a soldier and as a male civilian, Robert D. Hannah of the 95th expressed his surprise, "About two weeks ago I learned that Albert D.J. Cashier is a woman. I never suspected anything of that kind. I knew that Cashier was the shortest person in the Co. I think he did not have to shave. There has never been any doubt in my mind since it came out that Cashier was a woman but that it is so. I have not seen Cashier since a few years after the war. I am not able to identify the right hand figure in the double picture you show me. It has been too long ago, and fifty years make too many changes in a person for me to identify the right hand figure. I have no doubt about the left hand figure being the picture of Albert D.J. Cashier."[7]

Among the primary lessons of these historical facts was that it was essential that any woman who wished to maintain an authentic impression of a soldier had to develop a believable material interpretation. Such a woman's uniform had to disguise their gender in an effective way. Hairstyles were adopted that concealed the reality of the person's gender. Make-up and any other vestiges of femininity were not permissible. In all regards, a woman soldier was required to look like a man and be able to pass muster as such both with comrades in arms and the general public while also maintaining a low profile.

Proficiency in Drill

"When you think of me think where I am. It would make your hair stand out to be where I have been. How would you like to be in the front rank and have the rear rank load and fire their

---

[6] Wiley, Bell. *The Life of Billy Yank: The Common Soldier of the Union.* LSU Press, pp. 338.
[7] Military & Pension Records of Albert Cashier, National Archives, pp. 5

guns over your shoulder? I have been there my Self."[8] In this way Lyons Wakeman of the 153rd New York described one aspect of his training as an infantryman. In reality, Lyons Wakeman was Sarah Rosetta Wakeman, a young woman who had chosen to enlist in the Union army after previously working as a canal boatman in the pre-war years. In this comment, and throughout Private Wakeman's letters home to her family, a theme is revealed—being a soldier meant mastering the drill.

Throughout her letters Sarah Rosetta Wakeman revealed a trait that was common among many of the recorded women soldiers of the Civil War. For Sarah, and her female compatriots, it was essential to master drill in order to maintain the believability of their disguise. A poorly drilled soldier drew attention from officers and others. Such attention could easily lead to scrutiny, discovery, and ultimate banishment from the unit. Therefore, women soldiers had to become proficient in the machinations and facings inherent in Civil War drill.

Drill was an innate reality in the lives of Civil War soldiers. As Lyons Wakeman noted in a letter written in October 1863, "We are adrilling (sic). Company drill in the morning and a battalion drill in the afternoon. For my part I like to drill. I think a Skirmish drill is the prettiest drill that ever was drill. I have got so that I can drill just as well as any man there is in my regiment. When Colonel Davis gives a order I know what the regiment is agoing (sic) to do just as well as he does."[9] In another entry Wakeman simply states, "I like drill first rate."[10]

For any daring female who either anticipated or carried out a male soldier impression, the words of Lyons Wakeman must have been taken to heart. Drill was a basic fact-of-life for Civil War soldiers. Being adept at all elements of drill demonstrated a commitment to military service that was essential for women who wished to remain in cognito during their military service. A woman soldier who was a laggard in drill would draw negative attention to her, become obvious to observers, and quickly fall prey to the inquiring eyes of contemporaries. Knowledge &

---

[8] Burgess, Lauren Cook (Ed.). *An Uncommon Soldier: The Civil War Letters of Sarah Rosetta Wakeman, 153rd Regiment, New York Volunteers, 1862-1864,* Oxford University Press, 1994, pp.26-27
[9] Burgess, pp. 48
[10] Burgess, pp. 25

proficiency in the use of a musket, cavalry sword, or artilleryman's garb was a necessary survival skill not only in combat but also in regards to continuing a woman's military existence.

Demonstrate Sturdiness & Toughness

Civil War soldiers lived rough-and-ready lives. They slept outdoors in all sorts of weather. On the march they slogged through mud, waded streams, ate dust, and endured blistering heat. Food was often non-existent or abominable. Medical care was intermittent and often of low quality. All in all, the life of a Civil War soldier in the field was tough and required a sturdy disposition.

Among the women who undertook the role of a Civil War soldier in the actual conflict many of them demonstrated a level of toughness that was striking. Elvira Ibecker, alias Charles Fuller of the 46th Pennsylvania, was noted for "his" ability to both drink whiskey and chew tobacco. Confederate Melverina Peppercorn also chewed tobacco and later recalled being able to spit its juice more than ten feet. Loretta Velasquez, who adopted a Confederate officer identity, learned to smoke cigars while in military service. Martha Parks Lindley of the 6th U.S. Cavalry learned to smoke a clay pipe while serving as a soldier.[11]

In regards to toughness Lyons Wakeman comes to the forefront as an example of how at least one woman withstood the bullying that sometimes occurred in units. In January 1864 another member of her company, who was a noted troublemaker and bully, prodded Wakeman into a scrap. Latter Sarah Rosetta Wakeman described the outcome of that fight in one of her letters home, "Stephen Wiley pitched on me and I give him three or four good cracks and he put downstairs with him Self."[12]

Another way in which women soldiers demonstrated their toughness was in terms of language. No woman wishing to be accepted as a man could be shocked by the rough soldier's language that was heard in camp and on the field. Any sort of prissy or sissified attitude would quickly draw suspicion and

---
[11] Blanton & Cook, pp. 53
[12] Cook, pp.60-61

unwanted attention. Therefore, some women soldiers became quite adept at bandying about the profanities that are part and parcel of being a soldier. One woman soldier, Ella Reno, was jailed for two weeks as punishment for cursing out a superior officer. Three Confederate women who were discovered to be female while imprisoned at Cairo, Illinois were described as "reckless and profane with their profane and vulgar comrades." In another instance a guard at the Carroll Prison in Washington, D.C. described two female inmates in this way, "They are a tough couple and talk worse than any degraded witch possibly could. They are impudent and can beat any private in the oath uttering line."[13]

Women who adopted a male impression needed to be able to fit in with the guys. They had to be capable of shouldering the burdens of their job. Likewise, they could not be outwardly uncomfortable when men discussed things that were profane or lascivious. The life of a soldier was hard and hardening. Therefore, it was essential for a female in uniform to emulate women such as Confederate Melverina Peppercorn who could shoot as well as the twin brother she enlisted with and was "as strong as a man." A woman wishing to remain in the ranks must have adopted an attitude similar to Albert Cashier who one comrade described as able to "do as much work as anyone in the company." And finally, a successful distaff soldier had to learn from the example of an unnamed woman who enlisted in the 1rst Kentucky Infantry (US) and was described by a contemporary journalist in this manner, "She performed camp duties with great fortitude, and never fell out of the ranks during the severest marches."[14]

Develop a Soldierly Bearing

In 1882 at a pension hearing on behalf of Sarah Edmonds who served in the war under the alias Frank Thompson, one of her comrades-in-arms from the 2nd Michigan Volunteer Infantry said the following, "More than one member of the company can attest…Frank's manly bearing, soldierly qualities, kindness, and

---
[13] Blanton & Cook, pp. 53
[14] Blanton & Cook, pp. 53

devotion to the sick deserve to be recognized in a liberal and substantial manner."[15]

This ability to become a good comrade while demonstrating a soldierly bearing was essential for women who hid their gender identity while serving in the Union and Confederate military forces. At the heart of military service rests this sense of comradeship. For women soldiers of the Civil War perhaps no skill was more important than that of being able to demonstrate such a soldierly demeanor.

At the time of her enlistment in the Confederate army Loretta Velasquez was determined to be "as good a man as any of them."[16] In a similar vein Sarah Wakeman reported her first winter camp experiences in this way, "The weather is cold and the ground is froze hard, but I sleep as warm in the tents as I would in a good bed."[17] In a post-war article a reporter described former Union soldier Martha Lindley as "a good soldier…and never shirked any of the unpleasant duties of the men at the front."[18] Lindley herself modestly described her efforts as a Union cavalryman, "I did the best I could in the service of my country…Although I am only a woman, I think I can say without egotism that there were worse soldiers than I in the service."[19] Confederate Jane Perkins was much more bold than Lindley when, in June of 1864 after her capture, she defiantly told a Union provost marshal at Point Lookout Prison that she "could straddle a horse, jump a fence and kill a Yankee as well as any rebel."[20]

This type of mental toughness and commitment to the role of being a soldier was essential to becoming a successful male impersonator in the military ranks. In order to carry that sort of impression off a woman must have had both mental and physical conditioning that met the demands of the job at hand. Women soldiers of the Civil War were committed to their personal and national causes. They were often stoic even in the face of death. One need only recall the image of Sarah Wakeman who was felled by chronic diarrhea during the ill-fated Red River Campaign of

---

[15] Tsui, pp. 7
[16] Tsui, pp. 29
[17] Burgess, pp. 21
[18] Blanton & Cook, pp. 75
[19] Blanton & Cook, pp. 75-76
[20] Blanton & Cook, pp. 76

1864. Alone in a hospital bed in New Orleans, Sarah Wakeman slowly withered away. At no point did she reveal her female identity. In the end she died and was buried in New Orleans without military or hospital staff realizing that he was a she.[21] It was this type of bravery and commitment that allowed Lyons Wakeman to exist as a military recruit. It also was the sort of commitment to the role of a soldier that was required of those often misunderstood but nonetheless brave women who maintained the disguise of a man and served in the war.

Perform Realistically in Combat

In August 1863 Sarah Rosetta Wakeman wrote to her parents about the possibility of impending combat, "I don't know how long before i shall have to go into the field of battle. For my part i don't care. I don't believe there are any Rebel's bullet made for me yet. Nor i don't care if there is. I am as independent as a hog on ice. If it is God will for me to fall on the field of battle, it is my will to go and never return home."[22]

This spirit was not uncommon among Civil War soldiers in general, and those female ones in particular. Looking back at the performance of Albert Cashier one of her sergeants in the 95th Illinois said, "He might be the littlest Yankee in the Company, but by golly, he darn sure carries his share of the fight!"[23]

At Cold Harbor in 1864 the Union Army of the Potomac suffered one of it bloodiest repulses. Yet, the Federals did manage to capture a few Confederate prisoners in that engagement. Among these Rebel captives was one artillery NCO who turned out to be a woman. This female cannoneer was described by one of her captors in this fashion, "We did capture a full-fledged artillery woman who was working regular at the piece, she was very independent and saucy as most Southern ladies are."[24]

Women soldiers were in battles and became casualties. In some cases women soldiers paid the highest price a soldier can be

---

[21] Funkhouser, Darlene. *Women of the Civil War: Soldiers, Spies, and Nurses.* Quixote Press, 2004, pp.54
[22] Burgess, pp. 42
[23] Dawson, Lon. *A.K.A. Albert D.J. Cashier.* Illinois Veterans Home, 1999, pp. 11
[24] Blanton & Cook, pp 22

asked to contribute—death. In a letter home a member of the 1st Minnesota Artillery wrote home to his sister and recounted the following anecdote, "One of the members of the 1st Kansas Reg't died in the Hospital...After death the somewhat startling discovery was made by those who were preparing the body for burial, that their companion beside whom they had marched and fought for nearly two years was a woman. You can imagine their astonishment. The Reg't is camped near us and I went to the Hospital and saw her. She was of pretty good size for a woman with rather masculine features. She must have been very shrewd to have kept her secret so long when she was surrounded by several hundred men."[25]

    The fortitude shown by the women soldiers of the Civil War noted above provides several lessons to be learned regarding the issue of how did women carry out the role of "fighting men," In battle women in the ranks had to be as well drilled and versed in regards to maneuvers, safety, and weapon handling, as was the norm for their unit. Distaff soldiers had to maintain a fitness level adequate to allow them to cope with the rigors of weather, effort, & the elements that were a part of their world. Finally, in combat, women had to cope with wounds, death of comrades, flight, and steadfastness in the way in which their male counterparts did. Dangers existed in many aspects of Civil War life. Nowhere was that potential risk greater than in combat. Women who wished to participate in that combat experience must have had the skills and attitudes necessary to both maintain a realistic persona and behave in a responsible manner on the field of battle. Without those attitudes discovery or death would become all too predictable.

Understand the Historic Motivations Involved

    In many ways a modern woman wishing to become a military Civil War reenactor or make a career in the actual military shares some of the same motivations that her historic predecessors held. Among these were and are patriotism, a search for comradeship, an independent spirit, and a yearning for adventure.

    In 1861 Sarah Edmonds felt a powerful inner drive to volunteer and serve in the Union army. In later years she

---

[25] Blanton & Cook, pp. 99-100

described her feelings at that pivotal time in her life, "The great question to be decided…what can I do? What part am I to act in this great drama?"[26] Sarah Edmonds decided to don male clothing and join the army in pursuit of what she described as "an entirely new kind of life."[27] Edmonds also was not content "to stay home and weep" while her male counterparts sacrificed everything for a cause she believed in.[28]

Once in service many women soldiers developed deep and abiding friendships with their comrades. In camp, on the march, and while in combat women soldiers bonded with the men with whom they shared the dangers and vicissitudes of military life. In her experience Sarah Edmonds lived to see one of her closest friends slain in battle. Afterwards Sarah Edmonds described her feelings, "There was a strong bond of sympathy existing between us, for we both believed that duty called us there, and were willing to lay down even life itself, if need be, in this glorious cause. Now he was gone, and I was left alone with a deeper sorrow in my heart than I had ever known before."[29]
Friendships such as the one shared by Sarah Edmonds and another member of her regiment would have been virtually impossible in civilian society. Therefore, this type of comradeship often became a defining part of a woman soldier's experiences in the war.

In the 1860's, as now, there were women who chose to join the army out of a deeply felt sense of patriotism. Yes, in the Civil War, as in contemporary military service & reenacting, there were women who initially volunteered because they thought the experience might be adventurous, glorious, or fun. After that initial naïve belief was drowned by the realities of actual war or the hardships of wearing Civil War uniforms on hot summer days, other motivations were necessary to maintain a woman in the ranks. None was or is more powerful than belief in a cause.

While she was serving, Sarah Edmonds described why she chose to fight and remain in service, "Perhaps a spirit of adventure was important, but *patriotism* was the grand secret of my

---
xxix

[26] Tsui, pp 10
[27] Garrison, Webb. *Amazing Women of the Civil War*. Rutledge Hill Press, 1999, pp. 13
[28] Tsui, pp. 11
[29] Tsui, pp. 19

success."[30] Thus, a woman may well have been motivated to become a Civil War soldier as an act of homage to beliefs held as dear in the 1860's as they are today. Such emotions remain as a testament to the love felt for their homeland that lay so close to the heart of many women soldiers of the Civil War & in our won day and age. An independent spirit was another reason why women volunteered to fight in the Civil War. One need only read the following section of one of Sarah Rosetta Wakeman's letters to see that she possessed an indomitable and quite independent will, "I don't want you to mourn me for I can take care of my Self and know my business as well as other folks know them for me. I will Dress as I am a mind to for all anyone else (cares), and if they don't let me Alone they will be sorry for it."[31] At a later date Sarah Wakeman described herself as "tough as a bear."[32] There is little doubt that Lyons Wakeman was well served by his actual female personality hidden beneath the folds of her sack like uniform.

Concluding Thoughts

In a variety of ways women soldiers in the Civil War stand out despite their relatively insignificant incidence. In an age when women were considered virtual property it was striking to find a small band of them so powerfully motivated that they adopted the role of a combat soldier. In fact, when several women were discovered in the ranks, they were considered insane and were treated as such.[33]

Yet, despite the relatively small number of documented female Civil War soldiers, their contribution at a time when women's liberation was more than a century away, stands out as revolutionary and exceptional. As Blanton & Cook note in their pivotal study of women soldiers, "By simply changing a set of clothes, changing a name, changing a hairstyle, and adopting a male alias, many women found that they could easily bypass all of

---
XXX

[30] Tsui, pp. 20
[31] Burgess, pp. 31
[32] Burgess, pp. 58
[33] Romaneck, pp. 83

society's barriers to creating a decent, comfortable, and independent lifestyle for themselves."[34]

    Given the powerful stories that have been uncovered by journalists and historians regarding the small cadre of women soldiers whose identities were ultimately uncovered during or after the Civil War, there is little doubt that the draw of such adventuresome hearts can be very powerful indeed. However, it was in their ability to merge into the male world of military life that distaff soldiers of the Civil War showed their greatest mettle. It was in their ability to successfully amalgamate the soldierly qualities necessary not only to remain undiscovered but also to fulfill the duties of a soldier that the women who donned blue and gray demonstrated their greatest accomplishment. At some decisive point these women warrior decided to take to almost sacrilegious step of becoming a man of war. After such a watershed decision the hard work of carrying out their desires became a daunting reality. Once the die was cast it became time to select an authentic and discrete uniform, learn the drill, perform well on the field of battle, become a good comrade, act in a soldierly manner, understand their motives, and serve with honor. These were the traits shared by the women who fought in the Civil War. These also were the traits that continue to make those distaff soldiers of the Civil War worthy of notice and respect.

---

[34] Blanton & Cook, pp. 39

5

Gallinippers: A Bane to Civil War Soldiers

"Confound the mosquitoes! I used to exclaim every minute. They were the pests of the South, and of summer, and, like the Thane of Cawdor, did murder sleep!"[1] Thus did J. H. Brown, a correspondent working for the New York Tribune during the 1862 Federal siege of Port Hudson, describe the irritating and seemingly omnipresent pest that plagued troops in the 1860's. Mosquitoes or gallinippers as Civil War soldiers sometimes referred to these hearty biting adversaries were a bane in the existence of campaigners then and now. In a very real sense when a person goes into the field, garden, or backyard on wet spring weekends or during hot and humid summer days only to be assaulted by the buzzing hordes of mosquitoes they relive an experience that any Civil War veteran could identify with. Yet, in order to put that irritating and persistent experience in perspective perhaps a brief look back at the viewpoints of veterans on this pestilential topic might be enlightening.

During the early stages of the Civil War troops fresh from home entered camps that quickly became less than sanitary. Coming from a variety of climates young recruits from temperate places like Michigan, Wisconsin, and Minnesota to often stifling areas in the east or south had a significant adjustment to make. Swiftly, these camps became overcrowded and pestilential heaps. The odiferous combination of sewage, garbage, and slops

---

xxxiii————————————
[1] Miller, Gary, Historical Natural History: Insects and the Civil War, American Entomologist 43, 1997, 227-245.

produced what one soldier described as "an olfactory sensation which has yet to be duplicated in the Western Hemisphere."[2]

The contaminated atmosphere of the early war camps led to a plague of vermin inclusive of seemingly countless mosquitoes. One Confederate snorted that these diminutive creatures "seem resolved to take me dead or alive."[3] A Federal private stationed at Beaufort lamented that he understood why there was slavery in the South as it would take hundreds of slaves to keep off the mosquitoes. This sad soldier went on to denigrate his new home by stating, "this most god forsaken spot…mosquitoes, sand fleas, and the thousand and one bugs that infest us that Lt. Col. Allison says God Almighty could not find a name for it."[4]

Trying to live any sort of normal life could be quite improbable when the gallinippers were out and about. A Pennsylvania man recorded in his diary, "Went on picket at five o'clock in the evening. Got no sleep at all that night on account of the mosquitoes being so bad. No other news."[5] A New York volunteer camped near Charleston agreed with his Pennsylvania comrade in arms and described picket duty in this way, "Our worst picket duty is on the borders of the swamp. The myriads of stout ringtailed mosquitoes rush upon the detail the moment it arrives and jab their bills in the chuck up to the head…Even overcoats are no protection from the torturing rascals, who pierce through everything. Sleep is of course impossible with such a ravenous horde of bloodsuckers singing and biting and buzzing…getting up your sleeves and trouser legs, crawling slyly down your neck or dashing into your ears or throat, wearing a fellow's life out with coughing, slapping, pinching, and scratching."[6]

Soldiers who could do little about their fate as bait for thriving gallinippers often resorted to stoicism and resignation. The buzzing foes became the fodder for exaggeration. Tall tales

---
xxxiv

[2] Robertson, James, Soldiers Blue and Gray, University of South Carolina press, Columbia, SC, 1988, 153.
[3] Ibid., 153.
[4] Mitchell, Reid, Civil War Soldiers, Touchstone, New York, NY, 1988, 93-94.
[5] Miller, Gary @ http://entomology.unl.edu/history_bug/civilwar/gallnippers.htm, 1
[6] Ibid., 1.

sprang up about the size and strength of these tiny irritants. While one Rebel claimed to be more afraid of mosquitoes than Yankee bullets he also swore that these insects were of a "ponderous size-almost able to shoulder a musket."[7] Another Confederate, serving in a Tennessee regiment in the Mississippi lowlands, made the following comparison between the flying vermin of his home state and those of his new locale, "The Mississippi river fellow is far larger, has a longer and sharper bill…and though he sings the same tune, he sings it with far greater ferocity."[8] This same lad also noted that the while Tennessee mosquitoes could only muster squads, the Mississippi brand came after you in regiments.[9] For one Northerner the persistence of mosquitoes came out in a statement that can be appreciated to the present day, "The strife went on without intermission, day and night; the musquitoes relieving each other punctually, and mounting guard every five seconds…We never took up a book or commenced any manuscript but the musquito attacked us in force, and showed the most desperate determination to drive us from our labor or our love."[10]

    Sadly, these sometimes humorous accounts of warfare with mosquitoes generally resulted in literally thousands of visits to the various hospitals that dotted the landscape of Civil War America. While some troops attempted to make use of mosquito bars to avoid these voracious pests those protective measures were aimed at comfort and not health. At the time of the Civil War there was no connection made between the hungry mosquitoes and the dread malaria that tormented all too many soldiers. Referred to as fever and ague or the shakes, malaria was to victimize over one million Federal soldiers during the war's course.[11] Malaria was also a significant problem for the Confederate forces as well. However, mortality from malaria appears to have been somewhat slighter in the southern armies than their northern cousins.[12] Yet, whichever side's accounts you read you will probably find entry after entry that refers to the

---

[7] Wiley, Bell Irwin, The Life Of Johnny Reb, LSU Press, Baton Rouge, LA, 1994, 249.
[8] Ibid., 249
[9] Ibid., 249.
[10] Miller @, Ibid., 2.
[11] Ibid., 2.
[12] Ibid., 2.

coming of mosquitoes to places such as Vicksburg, the Peninsula, or New Orleans, and the subsequent outbreak of what the doctors often referred to as "intermittent fever."[13]

Indeed, so widespread was the incidence of ague in Federal forces visiting the Southland that one noted Civil War scholar was moved to state, "If the men in blue could have been synchronized the South might have been shaken into submission."[14]

With mosquito-borne ague present in virtually every military department in the South, and incidence rates sometimes reaching 100%, the control of this disease became a major concern to the medical corps of both sides. Attempting to prevent this scourge puzzled physicians and led to reliance upon traditional and oft-times addlepated explanations of what caused malaria. Among the many theories in vogue at the time of the war were sleeping in damp blankets, swift climate changes, foul drinking water, miasmas, the effects of camp crowding, and gaseous fumes from rubbish piles.[15]

While each of these causative theories was in error, as it overlooked the common mosquito, they did result in unexpected benefits. Locating camps as far away as possible from stagnant water avoided mosquito breeding grounds. Another preventative measure used to combat foul vapors was the building of bonfires. While these roaring fires did little to alter the state of the atmosphere they did create a manmade fog that drove off mosquitoes. The digging of ditches and canals was viewed at the time as an invitation to the shakes and was a situation to avoid. Once again, a misunderstood byproduct of this injunction against stagnant water was the elimination of places that would increase the mosquito hatch. Thus, the greatest planned avoidances of malaria were not connected to its actual cause but did result in some lowering of the risk.[16]

Despite the absence of medical knowledge about malaria's cause doctors were armed with an effective post-infection treatment. Quinine was known to combat the fever,

---

[13] Wiley, Bell Irwin, The Life of Billy Yank, LSU Press, Baton Rouge, LA, 1992, 134.
[14] Ibid., 134.
[15] Adams, George Worthington, Doctors In Blue, LSU Press, Baton Rouge, LA, 1996, 218.
[16] Ibid, 218

chills, and exhaustion attendant to ague. This bitter medicine was so widely used that within the Union armies fully 19 tons of quinine sulfate were consumed during the war.[17] As early as 1861 the Sanitary Commission, after investigating the widespread incidence of malaria in Federal units, advised the administration of preventative doses of quinine to all troops heading south.[18] Unfortunately, the standard dosage of quinine at the time was one to two grains a day to be taken in combination with an ounce of whiskey. This dosage level was adequate enough to kill most mature parasites in the bloodstream but was inadequate to assure total elimination and, hence, the disease frequently reoccurred. Therefore, while quinine was partially effective in limiting the effects of malaria, it rarely did a complete job.[19] Ultimately fully 25% of all Union soldiers fell victim to this hidden aspect of the mosquito hordes.[20] Totals for Confederate troops are unknown but could be assumed to be comparable. One problem that plagued Confederate efforts to combat malaria was the Federal blockade.

With limitations on source of quinine Confederate physicians had to scrounge for alternate treatments. The Confederate Surgeon General's Office improvised anti-malarial concoctions that contained a mixture of willow, poplar, dogwood bark, and whiskey. This potion seemed to be modestly effective but the inclusion of plants such as poplar and willow, from which aspirin was originally derived, may have proven somewhat beneficial in terms of fever control.[21]

Those troops who were unfortunate enough to contract particularly virulent forms of intermittent fever often literally wasted away while in the hospital. In *Hardtack & Coffee* John Billings of the 10th Massachusetts Battery told the sad tale of this type of wasting death when he recounted the following epitaph, "I can see some of my old comrades now, God bless them! Sterling fellows, soldiers to the core, stalwart men when they entered the army, but, overtaken by disease, they would report to sick-call, day after day, hoping for a favorable change; yet, in spite of medicine and the nursing of their messmates, pining away until at

---
xxxvii

[17] Miller @, Ibid., 2.
[18] Adams, Ibid., 218.
[19] Ibid., 218-219.
[20] Wiley, Billy Yank, Ibid., 134.
[21] Miller @, Ibid., 3.

last they disappeared—went to hospitals, and there died."[22] Billings went on to lament this type of prolonged and saddening death as "one of the saddest pictures that memory brings me from Rebellion days."[23]

Looking back at the pestilential experiences of veterans of both the blue and the gray it is easy to imagine their despair at coping with so miniscule a creature as the mosquito. In our own age reenactors, picnickers, hikers, and anybody who goes outside on a warm day can identify with those veterans who waged the Civil War. Thus, the next time you are standing a lonely picket post at a reenactment or gardening in your back yard and mosquitoes are tormenting you, remember the life of the true warriors of that conflict. As you swat an errant mosquito recall the fact that Union and Confederate soldiers did battle with these pests as well. By slapping down one of these bloodsucking kamikazes you can achieve a level of understanding seldom matched in our efforts to grasp the Civil War experience. In that sense the long enduring "Gallinipper" stands out as a helpful tool at improving our ability to bridge the gap between an intellectual interest in the Civil War soldier's experience and its reality.

xxxviii———————————————
[22] Billings, John D., Hardtack & Coffee: The Unwritten Story of Army Life, Bison Books, Lincoln, NE, 1993, 175.
[23] Ibid., 175.

6

One Irish Brigader's Experience

In the pantheon of Civil War units perhaps none has received greater attention than the Irish Brigade. Made up primarily of immigrant soldiers of Hibernian descent the Irish Brigade fought at some of the toughest engagements of the entire Civil War. Bearing the green flags of Ireland the Irish unionists fought for a nation that in many ways rejected them as perceived social misfits. Brave hearted men the soldiers of the Irish Brigade carried banners decorated with a golden harp, a sunburst, and a wealth of shamrocks that bore the Gaelic motto, "Faugh, a Ballagh" or "Clear the Way." Led by General Thomas Francis Meagher, a political refugee who fled to the United States to avoid British "justice", the Irish Brigade stood out then and now as one of the most colorful Union fighting units.

Given the fact that the Irish Brigade continues to have such a draw on the attention of Civil War buffs and scholars it is interesting to note that very few memoirs by unit members have been published. Over the years only a select few primary source publications have come to light dealing with life in the Irish Brigade. Within those publications it is even more compelling to realize that virtually no scholarly attention has been paid to resurrecting the memoirs of any common soldier who served in that brigade. Thus, it is doubly impressive that William McCarter's memoir, *My Life In the Irish Brigade*, has received attention.

Private William McCarter enlisted in the 116th Pennsylvania in August of 1862. This Irish unit was amalgamated into General Meagher's brigade shortly thereafter and became a part of General Hancock's division in the Second Corps of the Army of the Potomac. Private McCarter only served with the 116th for about four months. However, his record of those experiences, culminating in his participation and wounding at the ill-fated Fredericksburg Battle, provide readers with a vivid look into life in the Irish Brigade.

As noted above, William McCarter chose to enlist in defense of the Union at a time when Irish immigrants were looked down upon by many other Americans. In an era when "Know Nothings" were a vibrant social and political force men like William McCarter could easily have become Copperheads due to the discrimination they faced. Yet, despite the prejudice that did exist in a broad band of American culture, William McCarter elected to enlist in the Federal force. McCarter later described his reasons for joining the Union Army as "my love for my whole adopted country, not the North nor the South, but the Union, one and inseparable, its form of government, its institutions, its Stars and Stripes, its noble, generous, brave, and intelligent people ever ready to welcome, and to extend the hand of friendship to the downtrodden and oppressed of every clime and people." (IX)

Once mustered in Private McCarter threw himself into becoming a good soldier. The 116th merged with the Irish Brigade just after the Battle of Antietam. While many rookie replacement units that brigaded with veterans were met with resentment due to their newness, the men of the 116th received a warm greeting from the Irish Brigaders. In his subsequent memoir, which he penned in 1879 at the request of his immediate family, McCarter was to recount not only the chronology of events that made up his term of service but also the human face that history sometimes loses track of.

My Life In The Irish Brigade is a book that allows readers to capture a sense of what life was like in a unit that saw hard service while also developing a strong sense of unit identity. The author offers tidbits of information about topics such as interacting with hostile Confederate civilians, food preparation, the nature of picket duty, and a host of other military minutiae. In addition, McCarter, due to his outstanding writing abilities, became attached to upper echelon officers of the Irish Brigade. In this capacity McCarter served men such as General Meagher and came to have close observations of the unit commander's personality and leadership style. However, it is when describing the Fredericksburg Battle that McCarter's prose achieves its most memorable moments.

Leading up to Fredericksburg Private William McCarter had already participated in skirmishes at Charlestown and near Falmouth. McCarter had seen death firsthand but none of these experiences prepared him for the bloody assault that his unit was to take part in on December 13th. As part of General Burnside's grand attack on Marye's Heights the Irish Brigade, inclusive of William McCarter, was destined to launch one of the most spectacular and ill-conceived actions of the entire war. After only a few hours of battering away at the Confederate position behind a stone wall the Army of the Potomac was ground to a halt. In McCarter's brigade 45% of the assault troops fell either killed or wounded. Among those men was William McCarter.

Originally ordered by General Meagher to stay behind as a clerk and not take part in the attack, McCarter disobeyed his commander and joined the other lads in his unit. He observed the slaughter that had preceded his unit's assault both in the environs of Fredericksburg and on the cold and windswept slope that led up to the infernal stonewall. Already wounded by a shell splinter while waiting in the town, McCarter advanced up the slope with a blood-drenched boot. Once on the firing line, McCarter was amazed by the impossibility of the task he and his comrades confronted. The Confederate position was virtually impregnable and McCarter and his comrades fully realized it. As men fell all around him McCarter had his cap's visor shot off and was struck in the shoulder and ankle by spent balls. Eventually, McCarter was struck in his right shoulder as he rammed a round home into his musket. McCarter's reaction to being wounded is interesting as he noted, "At first, I thought that the man in the rear immediately behind me in the second line or one of the men in the front or first line by my side had accidentally struck my elbow with the butt end of a musket. For my feelings then were exactly like those produced by being suddenly hit in that way or knocking my elbow a hard blow against a brick or stone wall." (179)

In reality, what had happened was that the Confederates had shot down McCarter. He then faced an all too familiar and menacing proposition. As his regiment withdrew McCarter was left exposed on the slope amidst shot and shell coming from a variety of directions. Using his blanket roll and the body of a comrade as a barrier McCarter survived a bitter night. Later, when in hospital, McCarter's blanket roll revealed several dozed Confederates rounds that had been stopped by its thick folds. Ultimately, as McCarter vividly describes in this outstanding memoir, he was able to make his way back to the rear where he sought and received medical care.

In describing the way in which his wound was tended McCarter provides readers an insider's perspective on Civil War medical care. In his memoir McCarter pulls no punches. The horrors of Civil War hospitals operating in the midst of a bloody battle are clearly delineated. Indeed, throughout this well crafted book the author delivers a graphic account of the horrors of war in his descriptions of dead and dying soldiers and civilians. As such, McCarter's story is a relatively unvarnished look at Civil War combat and its concomitant human costs.

In the end, William McCarter did survive the war. The shot that struck McCarter down ended his military career and its wound took years to heal. However, the experiences William McCarter had during his time in General Meagher's brigade permanently affected him. Years later, in 1885, McCarter chose to settle in Fredericksburg where he resided for nearly two years. He then went on to work as a government clerk in the military pension bureau. Finally, McCarter died in 1911 at the age of seventy-one. He left behind both a family that loved him and a literary legacy of his time spent in the Irish Brigade. Written with a steady and skilled hand this book remained obscure until its re-publication a few years ago. Readers with an interest in the Irish Brigade, or the life of common soldiers of the Civil War, will find McCarter's words to be very powerful. This is a book dealing with both a famous unit and one man's experience of the Civil War. It is also a book that tells the story of war and all its grim realities.

Source

Kevin E. O'Brien (Ed.). *My Life In The Irish Brigade: The Civil War Memoirs of Private*
   William McCarter, 116th Pennsylvania Infantry. Campbell, CA: Savas Publishing
   Company, 1996.

7

Si Klegg's Civil War

In October 1885 readers of the *National Tribune,* a widely circulated Union veterans publication, opened the pages of that journal to find the first installment of a new serialization dealing with wartime experiences. The series featured a fictionalized Federal volunteer named Josiah (Si) Klegg and his sometimes humorous service. Written by Wilbur Fisk Hinman, the story of Si Klegg quickly became one of the most popular fictional accounts of Civil War service ever penned. After running for approximately a half year in serialization Si Klegg's adventures were then published in book form. Although Hinman's work is rather obscure in our own era it was widely read and accepted by veterans as both entertaining and accurate.

Wilbur Hinman, the creator of Si Klegg, was a veteran himself. A member of the 65th Ohio, Hinman had served for over three years. During that time Hinman rose to the rank of major and fought at places such as Stone's River, Chickamauga, Missionary Ridge, Atlanta, Spring Hill, Franklin, and Nashville. Hinman suffered a severe wound at Chickamauga and lay in a hospital bed when he heard the news of the death of his closest "pard", Wilbur Hulet. Drawing from his own experiences, Hinman set out in his writing to tell the story of the average soldier. In Si Klegg, Hinman hoped to create a sometimes comic but also dedicated figure. In this task Hinman succeeded as Si Klegg offers modern readers a fantastic glimpse of what actual veterans of the Civil War thought about their service. Si Klegg's oft times bumptious behavior is counterbalanced by the valuable insights Hinman affords readers on topics related to the daily life of combat soldiers in the Civil War. Readers with any interest in understanding or recreating an accurate image of a Civil War soldier will do well to read this amazing fictional account. Buried within its approximately 700 pages are literary nuggets of gold regarding camp life, the reality of marching, equipment do's and don'ts, as well as the psychological effect of military service.

For Hinman, and his fictional counterpart Si, enlistment in the Union army was a somewhat naïve action. Si Klegg is recruited and goes off to serve with no understanding of what he is getting into. When first outfitted in a misshapen and ill-fitting uniform Si is in his glory. He reflects to himself that, "No five-year-old boy was ever prouder when he laid aside his pinafore and donned his first pair of breeches than was Si when he arrayed himself in the habiliments of a soldier. It mattered little that the trousers were several inches too long, and the blouse so small that it embraced him like a corset." (12) Si was a soldier and, like so many actual youths that joined the respective armies of the Civil War, he had virtually no idea what lay before him.

In the reality of service Wilbur Hinman made and lost one friend above all others. Wilbur Hulet was the "pard" that shared the bonds of military comradeship most closely with the creator of Si Klegg. Indeed, this book was dedicated to, "My "pard" who fell at Chickamauga…We slept under the same blanket and drank from the same canteen." For Si Klegg, his closets bonds are with "Shorty", a veteran soldier who takes the youngster under his proverbial wing. This theme of comradeship is one that runs throughout Si Klegg's adventures. It is Shorty who helps Si understand the intricacies of culling his initially overloaded knapsack. Shorty teaches Si the way to sleep in a thunderstorm. Under Shorty's tutelage, Si learns that wily members of other companies will steal one's belongings. All in all, the bonds of service with Shorty, and many other members of his company, lead Si Klegg to realize that "few ties on earth are as strong as those that bind the hearts of men who so long marched and fought and suffered together." (674) This theme of comradeship is one that modern readers would do well to emulate not only as a part of their daily life but also as an avenue for renewal.

One area that Hinman's work is of most benefit to a modern day Civil War aficionado is in his many discussions of equipment and their usage. As noted above, Si attempted to march off to war with a pack that was fitter for a mule than a man. It was the cruel reality of the march that led Si, and many real life Civil War soldiers, to dump the valued but irrepressibly punishing comforts they hoped to transport on their backs. After several days of brutal marching under the weight of his dreams Si finally concedes to the fact that he can only carry so much. He culls his belongings and begins the transformation into a veteran who carried only what he had to in order to survive. As Si notes after dropping items such as a quilt made by his mother, a weighty framed picture of his beloved, and several towels, "Si had learned his first practical lesson in making himself a soldier. It had come to him through much pain and tribulation. Two or three million men were taught by the same educator—Experience. Precepts and theories went for naught. The shrinkage of the knapsack was the first symptom of the transformation that changed the raw recruit into an effective soldier, ready at any moment for a fight or a foot-race." (163) Over the course of his service Si, and possibly those historians who strive to understand the departed veterans, learned that, "What a man carried on his back he was always sure of, and this was the only kind of transportation that he could depend upon." (589)

      Another piece of equipment that Si grew to depend upon was his haversack. Initially, the grease-laden instrument from which he was supposed to draw his sustenance repelled Si. Young Klegg looked at his haversack and saw "a receptacle for chunks of fat bacon and fresh meat, damp sugar tied up in a rag—perhaps a piece of an old shirt—potatoes and other vegetables that might be picked up along the route." (52) Under the grinding circumstances of the march a soldier's haversack swiftly "took on the color of a printing house towel." (52) Si notes that the sight and odor of a soldier's haversack would grossly offend the more fastidious tastes of civilians. However, "the educated taste of the veteran soldier disdained all such squeamishness." (52) For Si and his pards, "When the regiment halted he would drop by the roadside, draw his grimy and well greased haversack around in front of him, and from its dark and odorous recesses bring forth what tasted better to him than the daintiest morsel to the palate of an epicure. It was all getting used to such things." (52)

      Of course, Si was also acquainted with that oft-times futile attempt at homemaking known as the shelter or dog tent. Si spent many a night huddled under or in his shelter half. At one point Si settles in and waxes lyrical over the old shelter tent, "Under ordinary conditions of weather they furnished comfortable shelter. True, a hard rain would beat through them, and trickle in baptismal streams over the inmates; a furious wind would sometimes play sad havoc with the fragile structures, tearing them from their fastenings and sending them flying through the air in wild confusion. A visitation of this kind at night, with the accompaniment of copious rain, was somewhat calamitous in its effects upon both the comfort and the tempers of those so rudely unhoused; but it is only an incident in the soldier's life that passed away with the morrow's sunshine." (590) Si concludes his thoughts on the realities of dog tents by noting, "Next to the hardtack and the "grayback," no feature of army life will dwell longer or more vividly in the memories of the veterans of the war than the Pup Tent." (590)

Looking back at his wartime experiences Wilbur Hinman, and his fictional self in the form of Si Klegg, were amazed at the travail mankind can both create and withstand. Civil War service was grinding in nature. Many men simply broke down under the weight of daily existence under tough conditions. In a hard minded but realistic moment Si reflects on the type of men who could and could not withstand the pressures of service, "A few months of active campaigning, without decimation by battle, always weeded out the two classes of those who were but an encumbrance to an army. There were the men of whom it might be said the spirit was willing but the flesh was weak. They were ready to do and dare, but physically unable to endure the fatigues and hardships of service. The other class was composed of those who could march and eat well enough, but were deficient in "sand." Every company had such men at first, but they did not stay long." (385) This wastage of men, linked to the horrors of combat, moved Si to comment, in true veteran's style, "Ye who around peaceful firesides enjoy the fruits of that four year's struggle know little of the fearful cost." (458)

At the conclusion of Si's story the narrator attempts to put the young man's service in perspective, "Si Klegg was but an atom of the mighty army; but it was the united efforts and sacrifices of a million such as he that withdrew the rebellion and saved the nation from dismemberment." (674-75) In this sentence lies the true value of the service given by Civil War veterans. The nation we live in today was formed by the real life Si Klegg's, north and south, as much as by the hands of any other Americans.

In *Corporal Si Klegg And His Pard* Wilbur F. Hinman offered readers of his age a retrospective look at Civil War soldiers that was grounded upon the rock of his own experience. Despite the fact that Hinman's work failed to achieve the lasting popularity of a work such as John Billings' *Hardtack and Coffee* there is little doubt that it was accepted by its readers as having the ring of truth. Thus, modern readers who wish to enhance their understanding of the life and times of common Civil War soldiers will do well to peruse Hinman's work. This is a fine story and one that will enrich those who take the time to read it.

Source

Hinman, Wilbur F., *Corporal Si Klegg And His Pard,* Ashburn: VA: J.W. Henry
        Publishing, Inc., 1997.

8

Henry Hunt's Artillerists
&
The Repulse of Pickett's Charge

Artillery played a significant role in numerous Civil War battles. However, one would be hard pressed to think of a more dramatic application of gunnery science than that demonstrated by the Federal gunners at Gettysburg on July 3 1863. On that hot summer day the artillerists of the Army of the Potomac were to serve their nation in a way that directly affected the eventual outcome of the war. Under the command of Henry Hunt, one of the preeminent artillerists of that or any other age, the Union gunners were an elite force. Once the men of General Lee began to cross the deadly space leading up to Cemetery Ridge they came to fully realize the capacity of the Federal guns and the men who manned them. The repulse of General Pickett's ill-fated charge has come down to us as an almost mythical event. Yet, the role of artillery and the Federal gunners at Gettysburg in turning the tide of battle is one that is often underestimated.

There have been many books and articles written about the Gettysburg battle. However, the contributions of Federal artillerists are but a tiny fraction of that massive total of published data. What follows is a concise look at the work of these stalwart gunners on the third day of fighting at Gettysburg. The material in this piece is drawn from a wonderful little book entitled *Double Canister At Ten Yards* by David Shultz. A former artilleryman himself, Shultz does a wonderful job of describing the nature of the July 3 fight with a specialized focus upon the Union gunners. That day was one that played out in a way that the Chief of Artillery for Meade's force might have predicted. Yet, the tortuous events of that day had all the elements of a stage play.

EARLY MORNING

When Henry Hunt arose at 4:30 in the morning on July 3 his first thoughts were related to seeing to the necessary reorganization of the Army of the Potomac's artillery force. The previous two days had resulted in significant damage to the Union gunners and their hardware. Fighting along McPherson's Ridge, in the Wheatfield, at the Peach Orchard, and on Little Round Top had taken a toll of both men and ordnance. A 44 year old career soldier, Henry Hunt was responsible for making sure that Union infantry would have the artillery support they needed to fend off what Federal leaders predicted would be a Confederate smash at the center of their line. In order to accomplish this task Hunt knew that some reorganization and refitting of his men and their guns was in order.

Throughout the previous night Hunt had worked on the logistical details encompassed in his amazingly responsible assignment. Later, Hunt stated, "The night of July 2 was spent devoted in great part to repairing damages, replenishing ammunition chests, and reducing and reorganizing such batteries as had lost so many men, equipment and horses, as to be unable efficiently to work the number of guns assigned…By daylight the next morning this duty had been performed as good as possible, and, when it was found impossible to reorganize, the batteries were withdrawn and replaced by others from the Artillery Reserve. The work was completed by daylight of the third."[36]

By one o'clock that afternoon Hunt was to have helped craft a massive artillery defense system. At that time there would 175 guns along the entire Federal line. Of these 132 would be between Little Round Top and Cemetery Hill. A further 95 pieces were stationed behind the center of the Union line in reserve awaiting the call to battle.[37]

However, in the morning hours Hunt faced the daunting task of making sure these arrangements were in good order. The executive meeting of General Meade and his Corps Commanders

---

[36] David Shultz, *Double Canister At Ten Yards: The Federal Artillery And The Repulse of Pickett's Charge*. (Redondo Beach, CA: Rank And File Publications, 1995), 2-3.
[37] *Ibid.*, 3.

the previous evening had left little doubt that the Union Army faced the probability of yet another Rebel attack. Hunt felt that it was likely that Lee would strike at the Federal center. In his distributions of men, guns, and ordnance Hunt predicated his actions on this belief. He strove to develop a defensive cordon that would maximize the destructive power of the Federal guns. Hunt summarized his thoughts about what the Federal force would face in battle in the following way:

> It was of the first importance to have our line in the best possible
> condition to meet *the assault*, to which the cannonade would be a
> mere subordinate preliminary; and with that view to subject his troops
> from the first moment of their advance and whilst beyond musketry
> to a heavy concentrated cross fire of artillery in order to break their
> formation, check their impulse, and bring them in as disordered a
> condition and with as much loss as possible to the point of attack,
> and my orders were given specially with this view.[38]

MORNING INSPECTIONS

After a quick breakfast Hunt set about inspecting his artillery line. As he rode along the line he noted the losses that several batteries had experienced. Along the Federal left near the Peach Orchard sector Union batteries had suffered significant casualties. Infantrymen detached from their regiments generally reinforced the seven batteries along that part of the line. This was also true in the Union center where fully one third of the men serving in Woodruff's 1st U.S. Battery I were II Corps infantrymen.[39] On the right of the Federal line, on the face of

---

[38] *Ibid.*, 4.
[39] *Ibid.*, 9.

Little Round Top, Rittenhouse's Battery D, 5th U.S. included 40% infantry volunteers.[40]

As the morning unfolded Hunt made arrangements to withdraw and replace from the reserve units that were too broken up to fight effectively. He also noted that artillery fire from the Confederate line was drawing counter-battery rounds from his men. Sometime between 8 and 9 o'clock Hunt paused near an angle in the stone wall that marked the position of Lieutenant Alonzo H. Cushing's 4th U.S. Battery A. Cushing's six 3-inch Ordnance Rifles were engaged with Confederate gunners across the field. While the smoke of the Rebel guns could be plainly seen their actual position was masked. While the Federal Chief of Artillery spoke to Cushing a Rebel shell caused a nearby explosion. Cushing's First Sergeant, Frederick Fuger, later wrote this description of that moment:

> The morning was all quiet until (approximately) 8:00 a.m. when the enemy
> opened upon our position, exploding three chests close by. General Hunt,
> Lieutenant Cushing and myself were standing close by the number three limber
> when it exploded. General Hunt had marked out to me on a piece of paper the
> directions to find the reserve train. We all scattered and the general could not
> be found.[41]

Sensing that the early morning bombardment was the beginning of a softening up attempt by the Rebels, Hunt gave orders that battery commanders replenish their limbers and caissons. He also was concerned that gunners limit their long-range fire so that ample ordnance would be available once the anticipated infantry assault stepped off. Hunt's longitudinal plan was to smash the Confederate attack before it could ever reach the Federal lines. His work throughout that day was based upon that premise.

lii————————————————
[40] *Ibid.*, 14.
[41] *Ibid.*, 10-11.

In order to assure maximum destructive force once the Confederate infantrymen began their advance Hunt dedicated a great deal of time to passing on a cautious firing demeanor to his men and officers. Hunt met with Lieutenant Colonel Freeman McGilvery, Commander of the Artillery Reserve, and admonished him to not engage small bodies of men or waste ammunition on Confederate guns that were not clearly visible. "Artillery," Hunt declared, "should be used only against large bodies of men, rarely against small groups, never in cannonading individuals, which is too often done, especially if they are riding white horses."[42] Hunt continued on down the Federal line admonishing individual battery commanders to ration their fire and hold back for the big attack that was coming.

REARRANGING THE LINE

At about noon, Hunt once again checked in at Meade's headquarters to ascertain any changes in the thinking of the army commander. After a brief conference Hunt set out to check on the status of units on the Federal right. He paused for a moment in the vicinity of what now is the Visitor Center at the Gettysburg National Battlefield Park and reflected on what he saw, "Our whole front for two miles was covered by enemy batteries already in line or going into position. They stretched in one unbroken mass from opposite the town, to as far south as the Peach Orchard. Never before on this continent had such a sight been witnessed." [43]

Noting some activity near the Angle, Hunt once again visited Cushing's Battery. Near the Copse of Trees Hunt stood with Cushing and two other artillery officers. At the same moment Confederate gunners, using the Copse of Trees as a sighting in point for counter-battery fire, observed a knot of mounted officers. At that point they began to direct their fire on Hunt and his comrades. Shells landed near Hunt once again and exploded several ammunition chests. Faced with this fire Hunt withdrew and started down the line again for yet another inspection.[44]

liii————————————————

[42] Fairfax Downey, *The Guns At Gettysburg*. (NY: David McKay Company, Inc., 1958), 119.
[43] *Ibid.*, 121.
[44] Shultz, 17-18.

As Hunt continued along the line heading toward the Cemetery Hill segment he ran into a rifled battery that seemed to be awaiting orders. This group was Captain Andrew Cowan's 1st Battery, New York Light Artillery. Cowan was a 22-year-old battery commander who had originally enlisted as an infantry private. Eventually he transferred to artillery where he had risen through the ranks to battery command. Hunt directed Cowan to move his guns about 100 yards west in a position behind the center of the Union position. Cowan was then given detailed instructions as per counter-battery fire.[45]

After Hunt left Cowan he had to run a gauntlet of Confederate fire. Shells were periodically landing all along this part of the line. One Federal battery commander described this moment by stating, "Men, horses, mules and wagons were moving everywhere, at top speed. Enemy shells plowed the earth and exploded to the point that nowhere was safe."[46] Despite this type of environment Hunt continued on with his inspection ride ending up in the vicinity of the 11th Corps.

THE CONFEDERATE BOMBARDMENT

Once he reached the Cemetery Hill sector Hunt met with the artillery commander for that area, Major Thomas Osborn. Oliver O. Howard, commander of the XI Corps and Major General Carl Schurz, joined these two artillerists as they discussed the probable events of the day. While the four officers spoke the Confederate fire in that area seemed to intensify. This marked the beginning of the large-scale preliminary bombardment that Lee's artillerists staged prior to the infantry advance. Although generally inaccurate, the Rebel shells did occasionally find their mark. One solid shot struck a six-horse artillery team stationed near Hunt killing or mortally wounding all the animals. The officers glanced at the horses and continued their conversation. Moments later, a shell landed in the middle of a nearby New York regiment killing or wounding 30 men.[47] All in all, this part of the Federal front was becoming a hot place.

liv————————————————————
[45] *Ibid.*, 18.
[46] *Ibid.*, 23.
[47] *Ibid.*, 27.

While Hunt was postulating with XI Corps officers as to what Lee would do next, further down the line a mini-drama was unfolding. All morning Hunt had been chastising artillerists for firing too fast and too much. Hunt knew that the key was smashing the Confederate infantry assault and not wasting ordnance on an improbable artillery duel. However, from an infantry commander's perspective things looked slightly different. While Hunt spoke with Howard and his staff General Winfield Scott Hancock issued orders to Union gunners in the center of the line to begin to increase their fire. For Hancock it was imperative that the morale of his infantrymen be maintained. Hancock believed that by having the Union guns stand relatively idle a message was sent to the infantrymen that their officers were preparing to give up the position. Faced with a massive cannonade of his position Hancock demanded return fire from the Federal gunners. Hence, while Hunt was calling for deliberation, Hancock demanded an intemperate rate of fire.[48]

    While still in the XI Corps position Hunt began to think that a ruse might be in order. He felt that if the Union guns fell silent and appeared to withdraw they might lure the Confederates into believing that a withdrawal of ordnance was beginning. This lure might in turn result in the commencement of the dreaded yet anticipated infantry attack. With this thought in mind Hunt rode back along the front passing these new orders on to his gunners.

    As Hunt once again came into the vicinity of Cushing's Battery he was struck by what a change had occurred to that unit. Cushing stood by one of his Rifles hunched over, grasping his bleeding abdomen where he had been seriously wounded. Only three of Cushing's guns remained in service. Dead horses, wounded men, smashed limbers, and disabled guns dotted the position. That once proud unit was virtually smashed but Cushing stood by his guns and prepared to meet the Confederate onslaught.[49]

    After passing Cushing's spot on the line Hunt next encountered Perrin's Battery B, 1st Rhode Island Light. This unit was posted near the Copse of Trees and it had suffered greatly during the Confederate bombardment. Hunt ordered this unit out of line. Further south Hunt met the men of the 1st New York

lv

---

[48] Bruce Catton, *Glory Road.* (NY: Doubleday, 1952), 312.
[49] Champ Clark, *Gettysburg.* (Alexandria: Time-Life, 1985), 135.

Battery B under the command of Lieutenant Robert Rogers. Looking across the field at the Confederate line Hunt asked Rogers what he would do once the enemy advance began. Rogers looked back at his commander and calmly replied, "I'll hold my ground."[50]

As Hunt progressed from battery to battery he gave orders to cease fire and conserve ammunition for the attack. Ironically, following in his wake by a very few minutes was Hancock who provided contradictory commands. Although Captain John Hazard, Hancock's own II Corps artillery commander, disagreed with him he insisted that the return fire accelerate. Hancock continued to feel that his men's spirit might crack under the weight of the massive Confederate bombardment unless they felt supported by their own guns.[51]

THE CONFEDERATE ASSAULT

Eventually, at about 3:00, the Confederate artillery fire abated. With that profound silence the Union men looked across the field of battle to behold an amazing sight. Thousands of veteran Rebel infantrymen emerged from the trees opposite the Federal line. As these serried ranks began to move forward the Federals must have been awe struck. However, for the Federal artillerists their work was about to truly begin. This was the moment that the gunners had been waiting for and they were not going to waste a once in a lifetime opportunity.

Although there was still some Rebel counter-battery fire the Union gunners paid no attention to it. Their focus was to remain upon the Rebel foot soldiers throughout the assault. Major Osborn, of the XI Corps, looked at the Rebel host and stated, "The gunners on Cemetery Hill concentrated on the Confederate line now advancing, paying no attention at all to the enemy batteries still firing."[52]

All along the Federal line the gunners began to sight in on the advancing Confederates. Osborn's rifled pieces fired along the Rebel line using percussion shells, case shot, and solid shot to wreak havoc. The bounding solid shot not only caused fearful

lvi——————————————
[50] Shultz, 33.
[51] Clark, 135-136.
[52] Shultz, 37.

injuries it helped to break the spirit of some of the Rebels. Imagine marching in ranks while a nearby comrade's head is torn from his body and then think about continuing that forward lurch. Huge holes began to open in the Rebel fronts as shells exploded in and about the infantrymen.

The Federal gunners were among the best in the world. Their ordnance was superior to their Confederate counterparts, as were their gunnery practices. The target before them was one they could hardly miss. However, their skill made the suffering of the Confederates memorable as it was applied with devastating effect. One Federal battery commander whose unit contained three 20-pounder Parrotts recalled, "I could sight down the entire length of their line, which stretched as far south as the eye could see, a perfect enfilading shot for my gunners...I watched my fire stop and break one column, all the men turning back in mass seeking cover in the woods."[53] Another battery commander commented, "Our practice was very good; every one of our case shot struck home and exploded in their ranks."[54]

The Federal gunners had learned their trade well. They were masters who had previously exacted a fearsome toll on Confederates at places such as Malvern Hill, Stone's River, and Antietam. Now, at Gettysburg, they were to serve their country in an unheard of manner. The effects of their professionalism were measured in sweat, toil, and blood. Major Osborn's calm assessment of the Federal artillerymen's performance on that day is very clear:

> By watching the effects of their fire the gunners soon had the exact range.
> The smoothbores fired solid shot and the rifles percussion shell, this was
> changed accordingly. Each solid shot or unexploded shell cut out at least
> two men. The exploding shells took out four, six, eight men, sometimes
> more than that, with twice that many turning back.[55]

lvii————————————

[53] *Ibid.*, 39.
[54] *Ibid.*, 39.
[55] *Ibid.*, 40.

All along the Federal front the gunners strove to shatter not only the bodies but also the will of the attacking force. One officer in a New Hampshire battery noted, "A grand attack was made by the enemy…and I commenced a rapid fire of case shot on…his advancing lines. I fired obliquely from my position upon the left of the attacking column with destructive effect, as that wing was broken and fled in confusion across the fields and back into the woods."[56] That particular battery fired 248 rounds in less than one hour to devastating effect upon the Confederate right.[57]

Union fire from both flanks had a terrible impact upon the Rebels. From Little Round Top one of Rittenhouse's shells tore along the Rebel front from right to left. That round cut through the Confederates like a scythe taking out thirty men.[58] On the opposite flank Captain Edwin Dow commanding the 6th Maine Light commented:

My battery was on the left and Pickett was aiming at our center.
My guns, and thirty of the other batteries around me, sent a hail
of shot and shell into their right flank. I tell you, the gaps we made
were simply terrible. But they closed up their lines, and closed up
and closed them up, till they got within a hundred yards of our line
in the center. I tell you, it looked bad from our position when the
Confederate line went at ours in the center.[59]

In the center, the advancing Confederates were also met with a fearsome array of firepower. However, General Hancock's insistence that the gunners fire during the Rebel preliminary bombardment left those batteries short of long range ordnance.

lviii————————————————
[56] *Ibid.*, 40.
[57] *Ibid.*, 40-41.
[58] *Ibid.*, 42.
[59] *Ibid.*, 46.

These cannoneers had to wait patiently as the Confederate infantrymen approached their posts.
Once they were within range of their guns the central Union batteries began to fire canister rounds at their foes. Still—the Confederates came on.

For General Hunt the climax of the battle was approaching. He must have sensed the dire elements involved in a failure to hold the line. He rode toward the Copse of Trees intent on helping orchestrate a Union victory. As he approached that spot he ordered Captain Cowan to bring his guns forward to that part of the line. Cowan responded swiftly and his pieces were drawn into line near Cushing's remaining three guns. One crew overshot their mark and came in on Cushing's left. Cowan, amazingly calm in the circumstances politely asked Cushing, "Is my piece crowding you sir?" Cushing, possibly through teeth clenched in pain, replied, "Your piece is fine where it's at. I see it causing no problems." As Cowan returned his attention to his guns he heard Cushing yell, "Forward to the wall!" Cushing then moved his guns up to the stone wall and had his men stack canister rounds for rapid fire.[60]

Further down the Federal line the men of Rogers' Battery were also firing at the Confederates who were at the fence line of the Emmitsburg Road. Rogers' two 10-pounder Parrott Rifles were being mostly served by infantrymen of the 15th Massachusetts due to casualties among the cannoneers. These foot soldiers were ramming whatever they could find down the rifled barrels inclusive of cups, rocks, bayonets, nails, and spoons in an effort to slow down the Rebels. Meanwhile, General Alexander Hays put the nearby men of his division through the manual of arms while under fire to calm their nerves and steel their courage.[61]

As the Confederate troops attempted to scramble over the fences along the Emmitsburg Road they were met with a blistering canister fire. Many Rebels were struck down while clambering over these rail fences. Their bodies remained dangling and strewn along the fence as a grim reminder of the ultimately vain sacrifice.

As the Rebel infantrymen advanced a few Confederate gunners ran their pieces out toward the Emmitsburg Road. These

lix――――――――――― ―――
[60] *Ibid.*, 48.
[61] *Ibid.*, 47.

artillerists began to fire at the Union soldiers near the Angle and the Copse of Trees. In Parson's Battery situated in that area a shell fragment struck one German driver. Parson later recalled, "He raised up six inches in the saddle and then settled back down, seemingly unhurt. The old German stood for a moment, wobbled, then fell dead."[62] He was but one of many Federal gunners to fall on that day.

HIGH TIDE

Still, despite the cannon and musketry fire directed toward them the Rebels advanced. Rogers' Battery fired double rounds of canister at their foes. In some cases Union troops moving along the line got in the way of Rogers' men as they fired. Several times Rogers' canister rounds took off the heads of wayward Federal infantrymen who blundered unknowingly into the path of their comrade's fire.[63] However, this was a result that could not be averted as the guns were called upon to fire at an emergency rate. Some battery commanders who ran low on canister rounds fired spherical case shot without fuses. These rounds became deadly solid shot that bounded through the Confederate lines, tearing gaps along the way.[64] One Federal section commander engaged in the central part of the line remembered the closing moments of the assault in this way:

When I saw this mass of men approaching our position, and knowing
that we had but one thin line of infantry to oppose them, I thought that
our chances for kingdom come, or Libby prison were very good. As the
enemy started across the field in such splendid array, every rifled battery
from Cemetery Hill to Round Top was brought to bear upon their line.
We, with the smoothbores, loaded with canister, and bided our time.

lx————————————————
[62] *Ibid.,* 50.
[63] *Ibid.,* 51.
[64] *Ibid.,* 52.

when arriving within five hundred yards we commenced to fire, and
the slaughter was dreadful. Never was there such a splendid target for
light artillery.[65]

As the Confederates made their final surge toward the Copse of Trees Lieutenant Cushing ordered his guns to fire double canister rounds. These discharges tore into the Confederates to great effect. However, Cushing was swiftly struck down and killed with command in his unit devolving to Sergeant Fuger. Fuger did his best to deal with the emergency facing him. He ordered the guns reloaded with multiple canister rounds and directly oversaw the firing of a triple round of canister from the gun Cushing had fallen near. Despite this terrible destructive force the Rebels surged around the guns and Fuger found himself in hand-to hand combat.[66]

Meanwhile, General Hunt, who was on the scene frantically attempted to pull more guns into what was becoming the apex of the assault. Hunt dispatched Colonel Warner of his staff to bring up reserve units. Warner stumbled upon the 5th U.S., Battery C of Lieutenant Gulian Weir. Upon finding Weir's unit Warner yelled, "Weir! Weir! Every battery is ordered to the front." Weir asked, "Where shall I go?" Pointing toward to center of the Federal position Warner said, "Go right up there, someone will show you where to go in." As Weir brought his men, guns, and horses forward he encountered a scene he would never forget, "I saw before me a small open plain, our men on either side. There was to the front several guns lying to the left, an open space to my front, and beyond this gap, a dense body of the enemy." Weir's men quickly brought their guns to bear on these gray and butternut clad foemen. Loading double canister, Weir's gunners fired at the Rebels at a range of less than ten yards. As the guns recoiled backwards crushing wounded artillerists of another battery their lethal loads literally disintegrated the attacking Rebels. The Confederates' remains lay strewn across the area in indescribable heaps of mangled flesh.[67]

lxi—————————————

[65] *Ibid.*, 52-53.
[66] Downey, 153-154.
[67] Shultz, 56-57.

South of the Copse of Trees Captain Cowan was so close to the Rebels that he heard an enemy officer yell, "take that gun". At Cowan's side one of his section commanders was struck down—shot through the lungs. Private McElroy, a veteran cannoneer, shouted back to Cowan, "Captain, this is our last round!" Cowan yelled back, "I know it Jake!" only to see McElroy cut down with three bullets to the face. As the men working the gun rammed home a load the Number 1 man, Private Gates, fell—shot through both legs. Cowan responded by ordering his men to fire at a range of twenty feet. Using double canister rounds, Cowan's gunners "blew the line to pieces" and "the officer was gone" to be buried with honors after the battle.[68]

As Cowan gave this lethal order General Hunt was near at hand. Mounted, Hunt fired his pistol at the Confederates to his front and yelled, "See 'em! See 'em!" At that moment Hunt's horse, Bill, was shot. As the animal fell Hunt was pinned beneath him. Cowan, who was engaged in having his men prolonge their pieces back ordered two of his cannoneers to free Hunt. These two men accomplished that task and Cowan, Hunt, and the men of that battery moved back a bit.[69]

Near Cowan's position the men of Rogers' Battery also had their hands full. One of the Parrotts manned by the Massachusetts infantrymen burst with an explosion so violent that it flipped the gun completely over crushing part of the crew. Rogers continued to have his other guns fire but some disruption to his line occurred. The Confederates surged toward Rogers' position. Double canister rounds slowed the Rebel advance but, ultimately, they reached the Federal line. Corporal Walter Brogan of Rogers' Battery remembered the scene in this way, "The enemy swept on over all obstacles and around our pieces, and for the first and last time in the history of Battery B, the hands of the foe were laid upon its guns. It was but for a brief moment. Sergeant Darveau fired his revolver at the foe as they came on, and when an officer planted his colors on a gun, exclaiming, "This is our gun", Sergeant Darveau seized the trail hand-spike, and struck him full across the forehead, as I blasted him with my revolver, killing him

lxii—————————————

[68] *Ibid.*, 57., George R. Stewart, *Pickett's Charge.* (Boston: Houghton Mifflin, 1987), 223, Henry Woodhead, (ed.), *Voices of the Civil War: Gettysburg.* (Alexandria: Time-Life Books, 1995), 125.
[69] Shultz, 57 & 1, Clark, 140-141.

on the spot…Darveau fell instantly riddled with bullets. Our infantry closed around our position and helped rescue our guns taking many prisoners."[70]

As the few remaining Confederates who had actually made it as far as the Union line paused for a few seconds to regroup they came under terrible enfilading fire from Federal guns further down the line. One Federal artilleryman later wrote of this moment, "This gave me an opportunity to enfilade their column with canister which threw them into great disorder, and brought them to a halt three times."[71] This was too much for any men and the Rebels began to fall back.

CONFEDERATE RETREAT

Seeing the dissipation of the Confederate tide Union gunners began to fire at the retreating foes. Captain Cowan ran his guns back up to the wall and exerted pressure on the fleeing Confederates. All along the line Union gunners continued to weigh into the enemy with ordnance. Eight batteries concentrated their fire against one Confederate battery that had moved up to support the Rebel assault. This unit was crushed near the Klingle Barn. General Hays, who had put his infantrymen through the school of the soldier under fire, joyously seized a captured Confederate battle flag and rode toward what had been Cushing's position dragging the banner behind him in the dirt.[72]

As the Union soldiers looked around they observed a sea of suffering. Bullets were still flying about and Lieutenant Gulian Weir wrote, "I remembered the distinct sound of enemy bullets striking the wounded and dead that laid about me."[73] Lieutenant Homer Baldwin, of Weir's Battery, wrote home to his parents four days later and described what he felt about the battle and its aftermath, "I never saw such a battlefield. On the 3rd every recoil of our guns would send them over the dead and wounded, and flashes of our pieces would scorch and set fire to the clothing of those that lay in front of us. I have seen many a big battle, most of

---
lxiii———————————————

[70] Shultz, 57-58.
[71] *Ibid.*, 58.
[72] *Ibid.*, 64.
[73] *Ibid.*, 65.

the big ones of this war, and I never saw the likes as this one. It was a glorious victory."[74]

For Captain John Burton of the 11th New York Independent Battery the end of the fighting brought an opportunity to look out at the results of victory. Burton later remembered that experience in this manner, "I walked a short distance to the right of our guns to look over the ground. Scarcely a square yard of this immense field in front of us but was covered with either dead or wounded." As Burton approached a wounded Confederate the man asked him if he would relay a message back to his mother. Burton provided the stricken man with paper and pencil and the soldier wrote, "Tell my mother I died trusting in the Lord." The man then signed the note—"John T. Burton, 38th Virginia Infantry". The irony of meeting a dying enemy in a helpless state with the same name as himself left a permanent mark upon Captain Burton's psyche.[75]

CONCLUSION

The battle was over—the Confederates had been driven back—the day was a Union victory. As these truths sank in the men of both Meade's and Lee's armies were struck by the magnitude of what they had wrought. On the Federal side, Gettysburg was an enormous relief. The war had hung in the balance across three July days. On the final day of battle the seemingly indomitable Confederate force was repelled. While later there were to be some feelings from President Lincoln and others that the repulse of Lee's forces should have been followed up with a swift counter attack that was not the prevailing feeling on the field of battle on July 3. Henry Hunt, that most capable of artillerists looked at the battlefield and commented:

A prompt counter-charge after combat between two small bodies
of men is one thing; the change from the defensive to the offensive
of an army is quite another. To have made such a change to the

lxiv—————————————
[74] *Ibid.,* 66.
[75] *Ibid.,* 66-67.

offensive, on the assumption that Lee had made no provision against
a reverse, would have been rash in the extreme.[76]

The battle had been fought at enormous cost. Within the Federal artillery, casualties were severe. Among Union cannoneers there were 54 missing, 592 wounded, and 113 dead.[77] Yet, despite these grave losses the men behind the artillery pieces had fought with courage and calmness. This spirit of professionalism flowed from General Hunt to every man in this proud branch of service. How could these gunners not have remained steadfast when led by a commander who was so cool under fire that, at the height of the assault on the Union center, he responded to the request of a young battery commander for more shells with, "Young man, are you aware that every round you fire costs two dollars and sixty-seven cents?"[78]

No soldiers could claim more credit for victory than the men who manned the Federal guns. Union artillerists, from General Hunt down to the humblest private, exerted a tremendous influence upon the day's results. With leadership of the highest order, outstanding equipment, superior drill, dedication, and professional coolness under fire, the artillerymen of the Army of the Potomac stood firmly and helped crush the brave and capable Confederate legions. Although the contribution of the Union gunners is sometimes overlooked in scholarly treatises it cannot be forgotten. Union artillerists turned the tide at Gettysburg. They set the stage for the Federal victory and continued to play a significant role across all theaters of battle for the remainder of the war. Those artillerymen's dedication to their duty helped shape the results of the Civil War.

---

[76] Ann Graham Gaines, *The Battle of Gettysburg In American History.* (Berkeley Heights: Enslow, 2001), 88.
[77] W.C. Storrick, *Gettysburg: Battle & Battlefield,* (NY: Barnes & Noble, 1993), 128.
[78] Fairfax Downey, *Sound of the Guns.* (NY: David McKay Company, Inc., 1955), 150.

9

Joseph Garey: A Keystone Rebel

Over the years literally thousands of books have been published that present the
diaries, memoirs, and letters that were crafted by Civil War veterans. In many cases readers of these reminiscences are able to gain a better understanding of both the war itself and the beliefs & experiences of the writers. Civil War soldiers poured their hearts, minds, and hopes into the written words they consigned to paper. Through recounting these writings readers can also come away with a deeper understanding of what the Civil War meant to the people who experienced it. Here, in *A Keystone Rebel*, readers will encounter a unique memoir in diary form that differs from most other books of its kind.

A Keystone Rebel encompasses the diary of Joseph Garey, a young man who was reared in Pennsylvania but who fought for the Confederacy. As such, Garey stands out as a somewhat unusual Civil War soldier. While it is true that Union states such as Missouri, Kentucky, and Maryland provided substantial numbers of troops to the Confederate force it is highly unusual to see a man from Pennsylvania donning the gray or butternut of the Confederacy. Further, as Garey's diary reveals, the author of this engaging work was a man who held a strange combination of values. Garey is no hero and the fact that he eventually deserted from the Confederate army and returned home to Pennsylvania prior to the war's end all points toward an apparent disconnect between his oft time stated love of the Confederate cause and Garey's actual performance as a Rebel artilleryman.

In Joseph Garey one meets a man whose pathway to and through war was uneven. As previously noted, Garey was a Pennsylvanian by birth. While Garey's exact point of emigration to Mississippi is unclear it is believed that it occurred around 1860. At that time the twenty-one-year-old Garey went south to live with his brother who was working as a physician in Cockrum, Mississippi. There, in Cockrum, Joseph worked as a grocery clerk and laborer. Living with his older brother and associating with people who held values far different than those commonly accepted back in Pennsylvania, Joseph Garey swiftly became an adamant secessionist.

On June 28, 1861, following the commencement of the Civil War, Joseph Garey signed up for a twelve-month tour of duty in the Confederate army. While Joseph never recorded the exact reasons for joining the army the fact that his elder brother volunteered as a member of the 4th Mississippi Cavalry certainly could have played a part. In the end, Joseph Garey chose the artillery and signed on as a charter member of the Pettus Flying Artillery. This outfit, originally named after the state governor, was swiftly relabeled as Hudson's Battery G and remained as such during the course of Joseph's service.

About one month after joining the service Joseph began to maintain a diary. During the first year of the war Garey was fairly dedicated to completing his diary on virtually a daily basis. Later, after 1862, Garey set his diary aside only to add a few entries for the latter phase of the war and a few disjointed entries during the immediate post-war era. However, it is the first year of the war that encompassed Garey's actual participation as a Confederate. In 1862, following the surrender at Vicksburg Garey and his comrades parted ways. Indeed, Garey deserted the cause he had held so dearly and never returned to his unit. Yet, during the first year of the war, if you judge Garey's ardor by his diary, one could scarcely find a more dedicated Confederate. In this way *A Keystone Rebel* brings to light the stark contradictions embodied by this paradoxical man.

In the diary that encompasses this enlightening book readers will encounter a writer who presents life in an artillery unit in a meaningful way. The diary entries that Garey left behind reveal the tedium, false rumors, scuttlebutt, drill, and sometimes horrible weather conditions that dogged not only Garey but also the vast majority of Civil War veterans. What is generally missing in these pages is any sort of comradeship, a quality that often rings true in many other memoirs.

Joseph Garey must have been a man of somewhat limited social connection. At no point during his hundreds of entries does he mention another soldier as a friend or close companion. Indeed, there is a great void in this book of any sense of personal responsibility or connection to fellow unit members. In this way Garey may strike readers as a somewhat cold and aloof man. While this judgment may be faulty it is interesting to note that Garey felt no compunction about deserting his unit after a year's service and the returning home to live with his parents in Pennsylvania in 1862. One can only wonder what Garey truly believed in and how audacious it must have seemed to neighbors and family members once he set foot back at home in the north.

One theme that does stand out in Garey's writings is that while he professed to hold the Confederate cause dear to his heart, he truly did not like being a soldier. There is a vast difference in tone when Garey is writing about the tedious reality of a soldier's life and when he is describing his activities on rest days or Sundays. For example, on one Sunday Garey described military life in the following way, "The morning is fine. Once more I welcome a day of rest, as I seldom welcomed it before I became a soldier. None know but those who have tried it, how tiresome it is to be constantly under restraint; the constant tramp; the same pound of duties, & the petulancy of officers, is enough to worry a martyr." (17) It is interesting to note that this exhausted reference to a soldier's lot was written about two months after Garey joined Hudson's Battery and at a time when the unit had never seen combat and had enjoyed relatively light service. Garey was not meant to be a soldier and one can only wonder why he chose the route he took.

Another factor that leaps off the pages of Garey's diary is his great ability to turn a phrase. Garey was a capable writer and his entries are very literary in form. Garey also was a fine observer of the people and landscapes that he encountered. Readers come away from some entries with a sense that Garey should have been a journalist. For example, on one occasion Garey set out to describe a pleasant morning, "Once more we hail the day of rest & for once in a long while it is a day of rest to us. The sun sheds his effulgent rays over the landscape, warming the fresh morning air, & creating buoyancy in our spirits, which even the sight of tents & the sound of the bugle try in vain to dispel." (23) Garey seemingly was not meant to be a soldier but should have been pursuing his hobby of poetry writing instead.

Life in Garey's unit was one of tedium. Hudson's Battery initially served primarily in the border regions of

Kentucky and Missouri. For Garey, and his unit comrades, there were no grand marches, sieges, or glorious battles. In fact, the unit's moral began to plummet early in the war as they vainly awaited their first battle. It was to be at Shiloh where Garey and his fellow battery members first encountered the enemy on the field of battle.

In the two-day struggle at Shiloh Garey's unit was to "see the elephant" and suffered accordingly. Garey describes the unit's involvement in the battle in this way, "Thus ended the fight of Sunday, our battery losing four men killed & twelve wounded. We also lost four fine horses & abandoned two pieces remaining upon the battle ground Sunday night." (85) Interestingly, Garey makes virtually no comments about what battle was like. Nor does he refer to any unit members by name who might have fought well or fallen on the field of battle. Indeed, Garey's diary entry for the days that he fought at Shiloh are only marginally longer than any others and lack any sort of detail about the battle. One is left with a feeling that Garey, despite months of recorded anticipation and frustration about not seeing combat, was unable to record the realities of what he came to know about war's grim visage. The entries for Shiloh, and later Vicksburg, remain strangely vague and non-descriptive.

In the end, Joseph Garey faithfully, albeit sadly, served the Confederate cause for slightly more than his original term of enlistment. As Garey's term of service was about to sunset new Confederate conscription acts extended the enrollment of twelve-month men to three years. Garey bitterly resented this and noted in his dairy that this act of governance was "very unjust & I fear will cause many to desert the army who have been free volunteers for the war." Perhaps that entry represented a thought process that Garey was applying to himself for that is exactly what he chose to do.

Following General Pemberton's surrender of his army at Vicksburg Garey was paroled. He then went back to his home in Cockrum and awaited exchange. Back in Cockrum Garey was more than half-hearted about his responsibilities and simply faded away from his unit and ultimately returned to his parent's home in Berlin, Pennsylvania. Joseph was carried on the rolls of Hudson's Battery as "missing" until January 1864 when he was officially labeled as a deserter. Strangely, Garey inserted a handful of diary entries during the time of his desertion and traced the campaigns within which Hudson's Battery participated. It was almost as if Garey simply did not possess the necessary strength to once again return to his adopted cause but wished that he did.

In the end, Joseph Garey and his published diary stand out in several ways. To begin, there are very few primary source books available that chronicle the experiences of Civil War artillerymen. Garey, while a reluctant cannoneer, was a member of a unit that saw service in some of the most important battles of the early war. Secondly, Garey was a northerner serving in the southern force. This anomaly makes him a very rare soldier indeed. Thus, reading his rationales for serving in the Confederate army makes for interesting and counterintuitive reading. Finally, Garey was a talented writer whose prose carried the undertone of a poet. Indeed, the editor of this engaging work has added a brief appendix that includes some of Garey's poetry. While these verses are somewhat rough-hewn they do provide a glimpse into the mind and spirit of a tough talking but very reluctant soldier. If there is a weakness in this book it rests in the author himself and not the content.

At the very end of Garey's diary, more than a year after Lee's surrender at Appomattox, he briefly touches upon the subject of his desertion. After blandly noting that he remained in Pennsylvania during the waning days of the Confederacy Garey ambiguously writes, "Who can tell what a day may bring forth." (103) Garey goes on to say, "Upon what trivial matters do sometimes even the destination of not only individuals hang but also nations." (103) Garey goes on to describe the victorious federalists as "usurpers" who suppressed the noble Confederacy, a state that, "lives alone in the hearts of those who thought to sustain her by thrusting themselves into the breach." (103)

In reading these words one can only scratch one's head. Joseph Garey was a man who felt so compelled to serve the Confederacy that he left his previous homeland behind to do so. After serving for a year he chose to wither away and hide in the north. Once the war was safely over he returned south and resided in the former confederacy until his death in 1884. There, safely ensconced in Dixie, Joseph Garey remained an adamant rebel until his dying days. Yet, in his diary and in his life, Garey deserted the cause he espoused and left no recorded memory of any personal connection to other soldiers with whom he served.

In reading *A Keystone Rebel* students of the Civil War are destined to encounter a paradoxical figure in the form of Joseph Garey. Garey was a man of apparently deeply held values but not of the internal mechanisms to connect his thoughts with his deeds. Yet, is it not reasonable to assume that not every Civil War soldier was a paragon of virtue? In Joseph Garey readers are reminded that in all historical times, even those turned to mythology by the false patterns that historical memory can sometimes create, people were uneven in their thoughts, deeds, and beliefs. Joseph Garey perceived himself to be a loyal Confederate even as he deserted and avoided the cause for which he had fought. How seemingly ironic but completely human Joseph Garey appears in this contradictory but important work. Likewise, how important it is to realize that the people who make up history were indeed flawed like all of us.

Source

David A. Welker, (Ed.). *A Keystone Rebel: The Civil War Diary of*
   Joseph Garey, Hudson's Battery Mississippi Volunteers. Gettysburg, PA: Thomas Publications, 1996

10

Webb Baker: An Illinois Soldier's Story

"I have seen some pretty hard times, went hungry a good many days, slept many a night on the ground with a stone for a pillow & went some nights without sleep. But that is nothing for a soldier…We don't look for easy times here." (46-47) Thus did young Benjamin W. (Webb) Baker describe his soldiering experience early on in the Civil War. Baker's thoughts are a sampling of the type of words he sent home on a regular basis in a series of literate and compelling letters. Those letters also serve as the backbone of understanding the perspective of a singular Illinois soldier as well as the life of his comrades.

Webb Baker chose to join the Union Army in August of 1861. Baker's unit, the 25th Illinois Regiment of Volunteer Infantry was made up of men from Coles County. These men of east central Illinois were destined to spend three years in service and march over three thousand miles, travel an additional seventeen hundred miles by boat or rail, and fight in numerous battles and skirmishes. At nineteen years of age, Webb Baker had little comprehension of the way in which the war would mark his life and those of his comrades.

Like so many young northern men of his age, Webb Baker felt compelled to put down his civilian life and march off to war. Baker, whose mother opposed his enlistment, wrote home shortly after mustering in and explained why he volunteered, "I ask forgiveness for going contrary to your wishes…(but) I feel that I have only discharged a duty which as a good citizen I owe my country, to my friends & to liberty itself. And now I ask your blessing as with my face to the enemy's land I go forward—as long as this arm has strength to wield a sword or handle a rifle; as long as these feet can carry me forward & these eyes can see to direct my steps I expect to march forward unless they (the Rebels) submit to the Constitution and laws…" (36)

As the days, months, and years passed Webb Baker's strong constitutional beliefs were mightily tested. The 25th fought at places such as Pea Ridge, Perryville, Stone's River, Chickamauga, Missionary Ridge, and Atlanta. In those tumultuous days more than 230 members of the 25th were to fall. Many others were wounded or disabled by their service. Baker, himself, was to receive three wounds and left the service with a permanently disabled arm. However, throughout all of the travails he underwent, Baker remained a steadfast and loyal soldier. On one occasion, on the eve of battle, Baker wrote, "I do not know how it might be. If there is a battle & I should fall, tell with pride & not with grief that I fell in defense of liberty. Pray that I may be a true soldier."

In Webb Baker modern students of the Civil War are presented with a common American soldier. Baker's letter's offer up nuggets of wisdom, information, and knowledge that help the reader to better understand the daily life of a singular veteran. Baker's comments about camp life, diet, marching, combat, and grief all serve to fill out the reader's grasp of the effects of the Civil War upon its participants. During the course of the war Baker suffered terrible deprivation but never lost hope. Even after sleeping out without any tentage for months he wrote, "There is a great deal of solid comfort in the wild rough life of a soldier. It is true there are a great many hardships to be endured, but those I expected to find, & in them I find pleasure in the tendency they have to develop the unselfish in one's character." (48)

Like so many American's of his day Baker was to experience dreadful loss during the war's course. Baker's younger brother, John, chose to ignore the advice of his sibling to forgo enlistment. John Baker mustered in with the 123rd Illinois and served with his brother in the Army of the Cumberland. At Perryville, on a dry fall day in 1862, John Baker was shot down and killed by the forces of Braxton Bragg. John's death was a bitter blow to Webb and he wrote home to his mother after personally burying his brother to share this dreadful news, "Oh mother, how can I say it! But I must! John is dead!!! He was killed on the battlefield on the 8th inst. In one of the hottest engagements of the war—he was shot in two places. The balls must have struck him in the same instant—one entered his left side at the waistband & passing through his heart came out under his right arm. The other struck him in the neck under the jaw & near the jugular vein & passed up into his brain...He evidently never moved after he fell, nor at all only to fall for his arms were as if he had been holding his gun to shoot...I send you a lock of John's hair. Everything was taken from his pockets but his Testament. John died like a man & a soldier at his post & in the front rank. Would I had died in his stead—my only, my true and noble-hearted brother." (109-110)

In Webb Baker and his recorded thoughts one can discern the essential soldier's experience of the Civil War. Baker fought through most of the major western campaigns of the war's first three years. Through Baker's letters readers are presented with both a symbol and a real epitome of the soldier's life in the war. Baker's personal sufferings, family losses, and physical pain are counterbalanced by the heartiness of comradeship and the purposeful motivation of his sacrifice. In Baker the reader encounters a man whose life and labors as a Union soldier come to life in broad strokes.

In the end, the efforts of Webb Baker, and his Federal comrades, resulted in a Union victory. For Baker, who was badly wounded at Chickamauga but did return to his unit just prior to the commencement of the Atlanta Campaign, the war ended in 1864. At that time the three-year enlistment of the 25th lapsed and Baker, like most of the unit's members, chose to return home. In later years, Baker went to college to expand his horizons. After five years of study at Illinois State Normal University Baker became a college instructor. At Normal, Baker also met Martha Francis Henry whom he courted, married, and raised a family with. Over the following years Baker was a successful teacher, minister, college president, and writer. Baker lived on until 1909 when he died and was buried at Oakwood Cemetery in Metamora, Illinois.

The letters Webb Baker wrote were carefully saved by his family. Shortly after his death a typescript version of them was created by one of Baker's children who had an eye toward seeing them published. This version of Baker's letters never was published save for a few samplings that were printed in a magazine in 1917 to serve as a spur to the enlistment of young men in the First World War. Baker's letters were then overlooked and lay buried among the belongings of a series of relatives. Ultimately, in 1998, the letters fell into the hands of Webb Baker's great-grandson. That person, Benson Bobrick, chose to use the letters as the foundation for a book and that book did them justice.

Benson Bobrick's *Testament: A Soldier's Story of the Civil War* is a book of great power and substance. It tells the story not only of Webb Baker but also the course of the war in the western theater. Its author has invested his personal expertise and a great deal of emotional energy as well. This is a book that readers will enjoy and remember as both a work of history and a personal testimonial. This "testament" has been made by a talented writer on behalf of his long gone, and nearly forgotten relative. As such, *Testament* has what fine writing requires—a good story and emotional depth of character. It is a book well worth reading, written about a person worthy of recounting.

Source

Benson Bobrick, *Testament: A Soldier's Story of the Civil War,* New York, NY: Simon & Schuster, 2003.

11

Carrying the Flag: Charles Whilden & the 1st South Carolina

All too often history is written from the perspective of "great men." Powerful leaders, brilliant generals, and statesmen tend to dominate the annals of history. In reality, the vast majority of the human saga, recorded or otherwise, has been staged by common folk. It is the great mass of men, women, and children who create & live the motions of history. This is true of each epoch in the human story and the American Civil War is no exception to that historical rule. In this spirit it is refreshing to see a recent book compiled by a noteworthy Civil War historian that focuses upon not only a singular but also an improbable figure.

Charles Whilden is not a name that brings with it instant recognition. Private Whilden was one of the more than three million Americans who bore arms in the Civil War. In this way his experience is far from unique in the annals of Civil War history. However, as stellar Civil War historian Gordon Rhea recently discovered in his research and writing, if you delve beneath the surface the story of Private Charles Whilden of the 1st South Carolina Infantry is stirring indeed.

Born in South Carolina and reared in Charleston, Charles Whilden spent much of his adulthood working in rather tedious and mundane venues. A member of a mercantile family, Charles worked with relatives in a variety of capacities within the family business. For period of years just prior to the commencement of the Civil War Charles served in a secretarial position on an army post in Santa Fe. But, when word traveled west of the coming of secession Charles' loyalty to his family, hearth, and home in Charleston summoned him home.

In 1861 Charles Whilden was thirty-seven years old. He was not in peak physical condition and years of sedentary work had not helped him to maintain a dynamic physique. In addition to the normal infirmities of age Charles also suffered from a significant medical disability. Charles was epileptic and underwent infrequent but significant seizures. Still, despite his age and infirmities, Charles repeatedly attempted to enlist in the Confederate army. Regrettably, for Charles, his attempts at enlistment were ultimately rebuffed due to his illness. In the words of one of his great-nieces years after the close of the war, "He enlisted a number of times, but when he had an (epileptic) attack he would be discharged. Then he would go somewhere else and enlist again." (72)

As the first three years of the war passed Charles remained in Charleston with his family. There, Charles continued to work with his brothers in the retail trade selling merchandise brought into port by blockade runners. As a civilian residing in Charleston Charles lived through the highs and lows created by news from the front. Additionally, Charles and his family also experienced the clash of arms much closer to home in the form of Union incursions aimed at Charleston.

In the summer of 1863 a Union army attempting to take Charleston established batteries on islands near the city. For a period of months Charleston was periodically shelled by long-range federal artillery. Charles, and his family, were not immune to the fear and terror that such a circumstance could breed. In later years one of his relatives described how it was to live in a besieged city, "We were startled from our sleep on a summer's morn, just at dawn, by the explosion of a shell, and we awoke to the reality that the powerful mortars that had been placed on Morris Island had the city within range of their shell and in the city there was safety no longer. The panic produced by the knowledge that our heads might be blown off at any moment, each imagining they were to be the certain victim, brought about the wildest scenes of confusion." (79)

Charleston did not fall at that time to the surrounding Yankees but the experience of having his home under fire may have contributed to Charles Whilden's renewed efforts to join the army. In January of 1864 Charles was successful in joining the 1st South Carolina. At that time the Confederacy was beginning to scrape the bottom of the barrel so to speak for potential soldiers. In that environment of need a nearly forty-year-old man with epilepsy was more acceptable as an enlistment candidate than earlier in the fray. Therefore Charles boarded a railroad car along with other new enlistee and headed to Virginia to serve under the command of Robert E. Lee.

      Charles arrived in Virginia at a point when the Army of Northern Virginia, albeit a formidable force, was no longer the freewheeling and attacking group that it once had been. The battlefield losses of earlier campaigns linked to the ongoing superiority of Northern capacities to produce men, arms, and military machinery all weighed heavily against Lee's troops. However, Charles and his thousands of comrades in arms still wielded a fierce capacity for doggedness, dash, and valor. Charles was also entering the army at a time and place where some of the harshest and most prolonged fighting of the war was about to commence.

      The Civil War encompassed some horrible battles. However, no portion of that war was more ferocious and unremitting than the spring Overland Campaign that General Grant unleashed and to which General Lee's minions responded. Starting in May of 1864, the two opposing forces began an embrace of death that persisted for essentially the remainder of the war. As a part of the 1st South Carolina, Charles was to find himself in the epicenter of some of this terrible fighting. It was during this part of the war that Charles was to rise to the surface and become an unlikely but undeniable hero.

      Charles' first experience of combat came at the Wilderness. There, Grant and Lee's two hosts waged a brutal and unforgiving battle. The Wilderness was a brutal fight that featured confusion, uncertainty, mercilessness, and bloodshed enough to satisfy any ghoul. Charles was part of the Color Company of his regiment. He was not slated to be a likely flag bearer but the economics of the Wilderness Battle dictated otherwise. After losing numerous flag bearers it fell to Charles to pick up the regimental colors and bear them in a fight that was not among the proudest moments of his unit. Yet, Charles fulfilled his duty and held his unit's colors aloft in the midst of a fierce engagement.

Indeed, the Wilderness was a battle that one federal officer described in the following Biblical manner, "It seemed as though Christian men had turned to fiends, and hell itself had usurped the place of earth." (165)

If the Wilderness was Charles' baptism of fire, it was at Spotsylvania that his moment of truth came to fruition. In every person's life moments come that mark us in some way. These pivotal events can include the birth of a child, a wedding, the death of a loved one, or any of a host of life changing experiences. For Charles Whilden such a moment presented itself at the height of a battle that, even by Civil War standards, stood out due to its ferocity.

In the pre-dawn hours of a damp May day the Union forces attacked the Rebel lines at a salient in General Lee's entrenchments. This bulge in the Confederate defenses was referred to at the time and subsequently as The Muleshoe. Using the unconventional tactics of Emory Upon, the Yankees caught their Confederate foes off guard and successfully overwhelmed their first line of defense. Confederate defenders of the salient were crushed and a significant gap was torn in the Rebel defenses. Seeing disaster coming forward along with the morning's sunrise, General Lee threw whatever units he could into the emerging breech in his line. Fighting continued and rose to a crescendo of violence that may never have been equaled in American military history. Simply put, fighting at the Muleshoe and the Bloody Angle was, as one participant described it, "blood and death, an indescribable pandemonium." (193)

In later years those soldiers who fought in this battle and subsequently wrote about it struggled to find the words to describe an engagement that was fought at close quarters for over ten hours. One Confederate soldier remembered, "The breastworks were slippery with blood and rain, dead bodies underneath half trampled out of sight." (203) A Federal officer remembered looking on in horror as one of his fellow officers waved at him just as an artillery shell took off his head above the lower jaw. This stunned soldier late remembered that, "As I passed he fell backward, and in looking down at him the tongue was moving in its socket as if in the act of speaking—a horrible sight I can never forget." Another Yankee simply saw the battle as "a saturnalia of blood." (203)

It was into this maelstrom that the forty-year-old soldier with epilepsy that Charles Whilden had become came to the forefront. The 1st South Carolina was one of the shock units that General Lee threw into the battle at the last possible moment to secure enough time to construct a suitable defense line behind the location of the breached salient. If this effort were to succeed—if this line was to hold—Charles and his comrades would need to prevail in stymieing the Yankees.

As the 1st South Carolina advanced into battle Charles was in a weakened state. He had exhausted himself in the Wilderness Battle and was in a terrible state of health. He was forced to ask a close friend to bear the flag and its staff for him as the regiment approached the front. After the war this comrade described Charles at the cusp of battle in this way, "Feeble in health and totally unfitted for active serviced…In fact, he was stumbling at every step." (208)

As the unit neared the Bloody Angle Charles took possession of the regimental banner. Lines were dressed, commands given, and the 1st South Carolina went forward into the inferno of this terrible battle. Remarkably, despite a volume of fire that slew men and literally cut down trees near the fighting, Charles survived to reach the contested works. It was a moment of truth for both Charles and the army with which he fought. There, atop the head log of the works, Charles stood alongside his comrades, bearing the banner of his regiment. The effect was electric, there amid the carnage; the unit's flag flew. Bullets flew, artillery rounds passed, and still Charles held his flag aloft.

As the fighting raged Charles must have been preparing for his own imminent death. Flag bearers were a prime target in the Civil War and their life span in battle could be quite short. At the close quarters of The Bloody Angle only a miracle of sorts could keep a color bearer completely safe. Charles felt the hiss of passing minie balls and must have braced himself for the inevitable. Yankee bullets passed through his shell jacket. They struck the staff and broke the gilt top of it. A ball struck Charles in the shoulder and hurt but did not critically wound him. Eventually so many Union rounds struck the flagstaff he bore that Charles was forced to take the colors off of it. He wound the regimental banner around himself and became a living standard.

But, still he remained at the front among his comrades and their fearful & desperate work.

As the tide of battle shifted the Confederates were successful in stymieing the Union advance. This occurred in spite of a heavy toll. One Confederate later recorded his experience at this critical point in the fighting, "In stooping or squatting to load, the mud, blood, and brains mingled, would reach up to my waist, head and face were covered with the horrid paint." (217) Then, over time, they drove the Federals back and resumed their defensive posture.

In those efforts, the 1st South Carolina played a vital role in plugging a gap and buying enough time to contribute to a last gasp defense. After a terrible toll of suffering and human loss the battle was drawn. Even more amazing than this result & the ferocity of this fight may have been the fact that Charles Whilden survived. Despite bearing his colors and then literally draping himself in them, Charles emerged from the battle wounded but unbowed.

Charles Whilden, an oldish and disabled man, had served not only his country but also himself quite well. That evening Charles was sent to a brigade hospital for his wound to be tended. That night, as he lay among the many wounded comrades who must have surrounded him, Charles wrote a letter home to his brother. In this document Charles downplayed his day's efforts and wrote, "We have been in another fight more terrible than the last. We fought from the 12th at daybreak to yesterday morning daybreak in our trenches full of mud and water, and our brigade suffered much…The top of my flag was shot away and a bullet tore open my clothes and gave a slight wound to my left shoulder, but I am alright. We know very little about how matters are going, as we are moving from point to point all the time, and today is the first rest I have had since I wrote you last." (232)

In an effort to minimize to his brother the suffering and travail he had experienced Charles went on in his battlefield letter to note, "I have from my position as one of the regimental color bearers a very agreeable time in comparison to many of my comrades." (232) In a moment of transparent realization Charles concluded this letter with instructions to his brother in case of his death. These included the disposition of his personal papers, a favored meerschaum pipe, and his watch and chain. Charles closed his letter by asking his brother to be sure to divide his monetary assets between their two sisters, Charlotte and Ellen Ann as, "I promised our dear mother that they should never want if I could prevent it." (233)

After his initial medical attention it became self-evident that Charles' condition warranted further rest and respite. First, Charles was sent to a hospital in Richmond. Then, in August of 1864, he was sent home to Charleston to recuperate. Charles' epilepsy worsened and he was kept on the regimental rolls in September and October as "absent, sick in Charleston." Finally, on October 25, 1964 Charles was afforded a formal Certificate of Disability for Discharge listing "confirmed epilepsy" as the determining cause.

There, in Charleston, Charles remained until the conclusion of the war and the arrival of Southern defeat. In post-war Charleston making a living was difficult. The hard hand of defeat and attendant occupation left many Southerners, who had once been prosperous, facing hard times. Charles tried his hand at lawyering, a profession he had dabbled in prior to the war. While a number of folks knew of his military exploits Charles was rather tight-lipped about his experiences. It is very probable that many people had no knowledge of the deeds that Charles had done on a brutal May day in the blood and mud at Spotsylvania.

Charles' story closes in a somewhat bittersweet manner. While he had survived the tempest of battle he still waged a war with his own infirmities. On September 25, on a rainy Charleston day, Charles experienced a *gran mal* seizure while walking in the muddy streets. On a day in some ways similar to the one on which he had borne the battle flag of his regiment onto the works at the Bloody Angle, Charles fell, face down, into a puddle. There, while overcome by his illness, and unconscious, he drowned. His family buried his mortal remains at Magnolia Cemetery where his body rested under a spreading oak draped with Spanish moss.

The flag that Charles bore in battle remained with the family for a number of years following his death. Eventually, after several refusals, Charles' family agreed to entrust the banner to a former officer of his regiment. The flag was to be sent to the state capital in Columbia and there treated as an honored war relic. However, that officer died prior to sending the flag to state authorities. There is no record of its existence and, to date, no one has come forward as possessing it. In a very real sense, the banner that Charles bore and risked his life to support simply vanished.

The story of Charles Whilden has the ring of fiction—but it is true. This singular Confederate soldier's story remains one that could well have been completely forgotten if members of his family had not serendipitously attended a talk given by historian Gordon Rhea and then entrusted him with Charles' letters & papers. It is from these primary source documents that this compelling story has been constructed. Through this fortuitous set of events the raw material of Charles Whilden's life has been brought to life once again. It is a story of unlikely sacrifice and unpredictable heroism. It is also the story of a person who overcame his disability to accomplish remarkable things. As such it is worthy of attention, study, and remembrance.

Source

Gordon C. Rhea. *Carrying the Flag: The Story of Private Charles Whilden,*
The Confederacy's Most Unlikely Hero. NY, New York: Basic Books,
2004.

12

Lucius Barber's Civil War

Looking back on his experiences in Company D, 15th Illinois, Lucius W. Barber proudly noted, "In the War for the Preservation of the American Union, the principles which were involved in the struggle met with a glorious triumph in maintaining the integrity of the Union and the supremacy of constitutional law. Striking the shackles from four millions of human beings, it has purged our land from the foul stain of human slavery, thus placing it upon a firm foundation for the preservation of freedom by granting to all who come under its protection "life, liberty and the pursuit of happiness." (7)

For Lucius Barber, and perhaps many of the more than 250,000 other soldiers who came from Illinois to serve the Union, the Civil War may have been the defining moment of his life. During the course of his service Lucius Barber maintained a diary. In this record book Barber recounted his thoughts, dreams, fears, experiences, and opinions. In so doing Barber left behind a treasure trove of information about a wide range of subjects. Subsequent to the end of the war, Barber's diary was published and remains one of the best sources of information not only about its author but also regarding the common experiences of a Western Federal soldier. In tracing Lucius Barber's Civil War the reader encounters all the vicissitudes and pride that soldiering in the Civil War could produce.

Lucius Barber enlisted in the army on April 27, 1861. A scant two weeks had passed since the Rebel firing upon Charleston's Fort Sumter. Like so many northern men Barber looked at the uprising of the secessionists as a crime against his nation. Barber, seeing the break down of the Union as a disaster, chose to leave his quiet life in Marengo, Illinois and travel down what was to become the hard road of war.

Barber enlisted in a company of men that drew its membership from small northern Illinois towns such as Genoa, Hampshire, Seneca, and Marengo. Eventually this group of comrades in arms would be folded into the 15th Illinois Volunteers. Barber would remain in Company D of that regimental organization for the duration of the war. In the spring of 1861 little did Barber know that his journey as a soldier would last beyond the close of hostilities four years hence.

Barber's first experiences as a soldier were typical of the many other men who went off to war in search of quick victory and manly honor. For Barber, initial impressions of a military life swiftly faded into dust and sweat. Soldiering did not mean proud uniforms, pomp, and glory. Instead, Barber and his regimental comrades, spent countless and tiresome hours drilling under the sun & rain. Early on in his diary Barber recorded his impressions of drill, "Drilling soon became the order of the day. We were up taking the double-quick before breakfast, trotting around camp until sheer exhaustion would compel us to stop; but this practice was soon discontinued as it began to tell on the health of the men. Moderate exercise before breakfast promotes health, but undue exercise destroys it." (12)

Another aspect of a soldier's life that surprised Barber was the food. Like so many other Civil War soldiers Lucius Barber was amazed at the general poorness of the fare he was expected to eat. Within a few weeks Barber described his diet in this way, "We now began to get a foretaste of army fare. Our bacon was so maggoty that it could almost walk, and our hard-tack so hard that we could hardly break it." (20) Throughout his four years of service the quest for adequate food remained a primary search. Sadly, as Barber repeatedly noted in his writings, that quest was generally a futile one.

Aside from drilling another aspect of Barber's early war experiences that was unexpected to him was the sheer exhaustion that marching could create. Lucius Barber was a fit young man, but the harsh realities of the march soon struck him as practically overwhelming. When the 15th was moved to Missouri, Barber began to realize just how tough it was to be a soldier. In the heat of summer packing up your gear and heading down the dusty or muddy roads of the South could be unbearable. In August of 1861 Barber wrote the following, "The weather was extremely hot and I came near "bushing" the first day, but being too proud to show symptoms of distress, I struggled on, although I could scarcely put one foot before the other. It was ten o'clock that night before we went into camp, and I was about used up and I immediately retired, supperless and sick. We had marched twenty miles since noon." (22)

As the days, weeks, and months passed Barber became inured to many aspects of being a soldier. However, like many other veterans who left behind a diary or memoir, the harshness of the march remained a consistent theme throughout Barber's service. After more than one year's service Barber still described the grueling nature of some days on the march, "The 19th of July (1862) was the hottest day we had yet experienced. The army moved very slowly, resting ten minutes every half hour, in the shade, when we could find it, but notwithstanding, scores of men would drop down, some dying instantly, others so far gone as not to be able to move. It was a common sight that day to see dead soldiers by the roadside. I came very near going under, but by exerting every nerve I managed to get along, but it injured me." (73)

Marching was to remain a cross to bear for Lucius Barber and his fellow members of the 15th. Indeed, like many western units, the 15th put in an enormous number of miles on roads, riding trains, or ensconced in river transports. Barber's regiment traveled a grand total of 10,897 miles during its full term of service. That number is astounding to contemplate and bespeaks the hardships that both Barber and many of his Civil War colleagues endured during their terms of service.

Another theme that Lucius Barber emphasized in his recountings was that of soldierly comradeship. Barber knew several of the men he enlisted with. Once in camp, Barber grew very close to his comrades. As did many other Civil War veterans, Barber thought of his messmates, comrades in arms, and unit members as a group of men who he entrusted with his very life. Barber spent years with some of these men. During those days the men got to know each other in ways that friendship back home in the safety of peace could not quite equal. At one point Barber described his winter tent-mates this way, "Every night we would huddle around our little fire-place, our feet to the fire, and tell stories, crack jokes and debate. Sometimes our discussions were loud and warm, but very seldom were any ill feelings manifest. The subjects discussed were usually politics, religion or favorite generals. Every night before the entertainment began we would buy some apples, crackers or oysters to refresh the inner man, while we listened to the torrents of eloquence which fell from one another's lips, and altogether we passed a pleasant, jolly time, even though stern winter did hold us in his icy grip." (38-39)

Camp life was not always so pleasing. In fact, in camp the worst temptations caused some soldiers to adopt patterns of behavior that were self-destructive. Barber notes that drunkenness, brawling, and profanity were all aspects of camp life that troubled him. Lucius Barber was no goody-goody, but he did note that placing so many young men together was a surefire pathway to some riotous behavior. Peppered throughout Barber's pages are events such as drunken privates who were punished for accosting officers, winter snowball fights that got out of hand and drew in hundreds of men until the threat of shootings stopped them, and jealousies that ended up resulting in sometimes fatal outcomes.

One particular vice of camp life that Barber noted was gambling. Soldiers left with little to do and time on their hands would turn to games of chance to occupy their time. Barber was not a gambler but he observed the results of such penchants, "Many a soldier would venture all his hard earnings on the throw of a dice, and thus lose in a few hours what it had taken him months to earn. This species of gaming was carried on to such an extent that an order was issued prohibiting it. If anyone was caught at it, he was arrested and his money confiscated, but this did not stop the practice. So great had the passion of some become for gaming that they would even risk their lives for the sake of indulging in it. Gaming engendered other vices and too many of the boys gave free rein to their passions and indulged in all manner of excesses of the grossest nature." (40)

Of course, one of the prime directives of soldiering was combat. Armies were raised, sent forth, and trained with the goal in mind of defeating the enemy. For Lucius Barber and the 15th the reality of war took many forms. Barber's unit fought at places such as Shiloh, Vicksburg, Champion's Hill, and Kennesaw Mountain. In his days of service Barber saw terrible things happen. Those experiences marked him and remained part of his memories. When he joined the army Barber probably had the same naïve visions of war's realities that most young men of his day-and-age held. Barber's wartime experiences would drain the blood of those images and leave behind the hardhearted reality of war for Barber to ponder.

One of the first impressions Barber had of fighting was that, once the possibility of combat sunk in, men all behaved in different ways. Some of the loudest proclaimers of personal bravery would cringe when the enemy approached. Conversely, men who remained reticent about their courage often served very well. Early on in his service Barber and the men of his regiment were formed in line of battle in anticipation of a Confederate attack. Faced with the reality of fighting some men handled things badly. In Barber's words, "We were ordered to arm and fall into line as quickly as possible. Some were taken suddenly ill—one boy was chilly, another was lame, and one great overgrown booby wanted to be excused on account of having the "belly-ache." We could hear the chattering of teeth very audibly. We expected a fight. It was our first call. It is not to be wondered at that some would feel a little shaky." (24)

As Barber and his unit comrades became more seasoned there came a greater calm before battle. Men never became completely inured to the possibility of death or maiming but they became more realistic about their lot as soldiers. At Shiloh Barber experienced the worst sort of combat. In thinking about his feelings during that bloody battle Barber noted, "I knew that I was equal to the task of doing my whole duty without flinching, but to me, as well as to every other soldier just before entering the battle, an involuntary awe and dread crept over me; but if true and brave, these feelings gradually die away in the excitement of the fight until they become almost extinct, unless a sudden reverse throws everything in confusion, then all is terror and excitement." (52-53)

Barber was becoming veteranized by his experiences. However, even a stouthearted lad like Lucius Barber had limits. At Shiloh where "Terrible and complete was the surprise" even brave men floundered. (51) Barber's unit was among the many ill-prepared Union formations that were taken aback by the sudden and unexpected fury of battle. At Shiloh, Barber was fortunate enough to escape serious injury. Death and destruction surrounded Barber as the Confederate host surged forward. In Barber's words, "Our brave boys were dropping by scores. A ball struck the stock of my musket, shivering it and nearly knocking it from my grasp. Another ball passed through my canteen, while another cut the straps to my haversack. Thick as hailstones the bullets whistled through my hair and around my cheek, still I remained unhurt." (53)

Every man has his limits. Barber was more than willing to bear the terrors of battle so long as his unit held fast. However, at Shiloh on the first day of battle, many Union units failed to persevere. The 15th was one of those regiments and eventually it broke. At that point Barber, the perpetual realist, realized that it was time to move, "Something within said to me, "This is not a safe place for Lute Barber," and that if I wanted to live to fight another day, I must retreat out of that, and retreat I did, very rapidly too. I cannot say whether I did it in good order or not. To tell the truth, I became slightly confused." (54)

Barber survived Shiloh and lived to fight another day. However, some of the sights and sounds he absorbed in that battle, and subsequent ones, must have had an impact upon his dreams, memories, and emotions. Barber was a sensitive man as evidenced by his writings. In seeing the carnage of battle he was deeply affected by the suffering and loss he observed. There are times in Barber's diary where he shares anecdotes about the death of a woman caught in a crossfire or the useless deaths of soldiers who perished from disease or wounds that leave the distinct impression that Barber's wartime experiences struck him as both necessary and frightful. For example, Barber had the opportunity to survey the Fort Donelson battlefield only a few days after that struggle and recorded the impact of that setting in his journal.

In looking at the dreadful detritus of the Fort Donelson battle Barber reflected upon the faces of the dead men he saw, "Some of the countenances bore a peaceful, glad smile, while on others rested a fiendish look of hate. It looked as though each countenance was the exact counterpart of the thoughts that were passing through the mind when the messenger laid them low. Perhaps that noble looking youth, with his smiling up-turned face, with his glossy ringlets matted with his own blood, felt a mother's prayer stealing over his senses as his young life went out. Near him lay the young husband with a prayer for his wife and little one yet lingering on his lips. Youth and age, virtue and evil, were represented on those ghastly countenances. But oh, what is that? Before us laid the charred and blackened remains of some who had been burnt alive. They were wounded too badly to move and the fierce elements consumed them." (44-45)

      In the face of such sights and memories how could any decent person remain unchanged? War touched Lucius Barber, as it did literally millions of Americans during the 1860's. At times the loss of friends, the horrors of the battlefield, and the general destruction that was bred by conflict must have overcome Barber. Yet, there were moments when the terrible grandeur of men in battle struck home as well. At one point, during the siege of Vicksburg, Barber described a scene of battle that struck home with him, "Some evenings when not on duty, we would crawl to the top of the hill near camp and watch the gunboats shell the city. From the instant the shell left the gun, we could trace its progress through the air. The shell had a rapid rotary motion and the burning fuse with its red glare showed its course, describing a semi-circle in traveling four miles. When at its highest altitude, we could hear the report of the gun. When it neared the earth, we could see the flash as it exploded, and after several seconds, we could hear the report." (112)

      Those exploding shells rained destruction down upon the heads of men, women, and children not unlike Lucius Barber, himself. Barber was not insensitive to the fate of the residents of Vicksburg. Rather, he was a soldier doing a tough and terrible job that he viewed as in pursuit of a just cause. To spend an evening watching the shelling of Vicksburg was almost like a Fourth of July fireworks display. One can almost imagine Barber and his comrades resting on a hill after a grueling day in the fieldworks. The men watch the glowing shells fly upward and then down into the town. In this vein war becomes a spectator sport with all its immensity of time, energy, resources, and effort.

      Another experience that Barber was to encounter was that of imprisonment. In the fall of 1864 Barber's company was detailed as a train guard near Atlanta. In that capacity, and badly led by their captain, Barber and his fellow members of Company D were taken prisoner. Initially, while under the control of veteran Confederate combat troops, Barber was relatively well treated. Then, when placed under the guard of militia or home guard units, the Union prisoners were despoiled and treated like vermin. Eventually, Barber and his mates were sent to the most notorious of all Civil War prisons—Andersonville.

At Andersonville Lucius Barber saw "misery in its worst form." (168) In absorbing the nature of Andersonville Barber was struck by, "Such squalid, filthy wretchedness, hunger, disease, nakedness and cold, I never saw before." (168) In Andersonville, "All who gave way to their grief soon sunk into the arms of death." (167) Likewise, elements of human nature emerged at Andersonville that perplexed Barber. At one point Barber records a curious and sad aspect of behavior in Andersonville, "There was one curious phase of human nature exhibited here in regard to helping one another. One would naturally suppose that being thrown together, as we were, that banding together and helping one another would take place, and when a squad, company or regiment was captured together, this was generally the case, but if one was captured alone, put with strangers and became sick, it was ten chances to one that he would die unattended by any human being. His fellow sufferers would pass him with perhaps this remark, "Let his friends take care of him. I have no more than I can see to now," and so the poor sufferer expires uncared for and unknown." (169)

In Andersonville Barber was shocked by the amount of death that surrounded him. For a period of time Barber was assigned to the "deadhouse" where the disposal of corpses was facilitated. In that capacity Barber saw hundreds of dead prisoners and observed how their remains were handled, "It was very shocking to human feelings to see the way the dead are disposed of. They are piled up in a wagon like so much wood, taken to holes dug for them and piled in, with no respect for decency or humanity." (171) Fortunately, Barber was only in Confederate hands for forty-seven days. Then a fortuitous twist of fate enabled his exchange along with a batch of seriously ill Federal prisoners. In this instance Barber must have had a guardian angel looking after him as several of his closest friends remained behind and ultimately perished at Andersonville.

In the end, Lucius Barber survived camp, battlefield, prison, and the daily grind of the Civil War. His unit fought across the Southland and left behind a legacy of fine service. Barber took part in the Grand Review in Washington City where he encountered members of the Army of the Potomac for the first time. Meeting these eastern soldiers left Barber with an interesting impression that bespoke the rivalry between various sections of the North, "Our present camping ground is dotted as far as the eye can reach with spots where was camped the vast Army of the Potomac, the brave but unfortunate army which has fought so bravely, suffered so much and accomplished so little." To the end, Lucius Barber maintained a fierce pride in his regiment, army, and homeland of the Midwest.

Returning home to Marengo, Lucius Barber must have been overjoyed to be back in the embrace of his family. Yet, the hard hand of war had exacted a great cost from Barber. The constant exposure to weather, stress, poor food, and disease left Barber somewhat broken. Barber was twenty-one when he enlisted. In 1872, after only seven years of peace, Barber died of respiratory failure. In reality, the seeds of his demise were sown in camp and at Andersonville. Barber's constitution was strong but it was battered by the daily life that confronted and killed many of his past comrades. In his obituary Barber was described as "a very worthy, exemplary young man, much beloved by his friends and acquaintances." It was also noted that Lucius Barber was "one of the first to enroll his name amongst his country's defenders." Barber's remains were interred in the family burial plot on "the old homestead." There, Barber still rests after a short but eventful life. (223)

Like so many other Civil War soldiers Lucius "Lute" Barber chose to leave behind hearth and home to serve his country as he saw fit to do so. Barber fought in some of the bloodiest battles in American history. He watched friends perish by shell, shot, and disease. Barber also experienced the degradation that a Civil War prison could dish out. Throughout his service Barber gave evidence of common decency and thoughtfulness. Lucius Barber was not a famous Civil War participant. But, more importantly, he was typical of the type of men who marched off to fight a war that shaped their country's destiny. It is altogether fitting and proper that he should be remembered and revered as one of the multitude of men who sacrificed everything in order to fight for a cause they believed in.

Source

Lucius Barber, *Army Memoirs,* Chicago, IL: The J.M.W. Jones Stationary & Printing Co., 1894.

13

Albert Cashier: An Uncommon Civil War Soldier

By: Erin Elizabeth Romaneck

Albert Cashier was one of more than 250,000 Illinois soldiers who served in the Civil War. Cashier joined the 95th Illinois Volunteer Infantry at Camp Fuller in Rockford, Illinois, on August 6, 1862. Albert Cashier served until June of 1865 and took part in forty battles and skirmishes while earning the respect of comrades and officers alike. These fellow fighting men did not know that Cashier's real name was Jennie Hodgers, an Irish immigrant who came to the United States in the late 1840's and settled in Illinois.

During the four years of the Civil War, in which over 630,000 Americans lost their lives, women participated in many ways. Some women worked the farms let behind by their men folk. Others took jobs in shops, stores, and factories. Some females became nurses or conducted charitable work on behalf of the fighting men. In a few cases women took on the role of espionage and became spies. But some women chose to disguise themselves and become soldiers. Such women joined the respective armies for many reasons inclusive of a search for adventure, patriotism, or to be near husbands or sweethearts. One such adventurous female was Jennie Hodgers.

For male impersonators who chose to join the army the lax medical standards of the day helped them to hide their gender. Many army doctors had little medical training. During many pre-enlistment medical "exams" the men remained fully clothed. Such "exams" generally consisted of little more than two or three taps on the chest. A woman recruit was unlikely to face a medical exam much more rigorous than exhibiting a trigger finger and opening her mouth to show that she possessed enough teeth to rip open a cartridge.

Aside from the quality of medical examinations, women soldiers sometimes remained undiscovered because bathing and hygiene upkeep was far from comprehensive in Civil War armies. Additionally, standards of modesty associated with the mid-19th century often inhibited men from displaying nakedness even amidst fellow soldiers. Therefore, a woman such as Jennie Hodgers could conceal her sex and transmogrify into Albert Cashier.

Another factor that aided and abetted concealment were the baggy uniforms generally handed out to recruits. Such loosely hanging clothing served women fighters well as they could more readily conceal their body type. Further, the fact that many soldiers were quite youthful helped beardless women to pass as young men. Higher voices also could pass for the prosody of younger men. Finally, the fact that most officers were young volunteers with limited military experience who were generally overwhelmed with the task of learning the rudimentary facts of drill left them with little capacity for detective work among the ranks.

In Jennie Hodgers' case she had ample experience in hiding her identity. Prior to the war Jennie had worked as a farmer and sheppard who often wore men's clothing to secure employment by hiding her gender. Jennie was described in this pre-war period as having a light complexion, blue eyes, and auburn hair. There is no record as to why Jennie Hodgers chose to change her name to Albert Cashier or why she often had passed for a boy prior to the war, but it can be confirmed that at the outset of the conflict she chose to become a soldier.

Once Albert was enlisted in the 95th he was accepted by his fellow soldiers. Albert was described by a comrade in the regiment as "the smallest man in the company" but he was sturdy enough to serve out both his enlistment and the duration of the war. The 95th Illinois was in General Grant's Army of the Tennessee. Albert's first battle was at Holly Spring in northern Mississippi in late 1862. Albert and the 95th then took part in the

Vicksburg Campaign. In May of 1863 Albert fought at Jackson, Raymond, and Champions Hill. Cashier also took part in two assaults on the fortifications surrounding Vicksburg. In those dual attacks the 95th lost sixty-one soldiers killed or wounded. For two months Albert lived in the trenches surrounding the besieged city of Vicksburg. Finally, on July 4th in 1863, that southern citadel capitulated—and Albert was there.

    In the late summer and early fall of 1863 Albert Cashier participated in the siege of Natchez, Mississippi. The following spring Cashier served in the ill-fated Red River Campaign in Louisiana. Later that year Cashier was nearly captured at Brice's Crossroads in Mississippi when Nathan Bedford Forest's forces overwhelmed an advancing Union task force. The 95th also fought at Franklin and Nashville where Union troops shattered General John Bell Hood's Army of Tennessee. The 95th, with Albert in the ranks, pursued Hood's beaten force into Alabama and, in April of 1865, took part in the capture of Fort Blakely at Mobile. In June of 1865, Albert Cashier and the rest of the 95th Illinois were mustered out of the army and returned home. Albert had served well and accomplished the feat of surviving her tour of duty across many miles and great travail. Her officers reported her to be quiet, shy, and a fine soldier.

    After the war Albert kept her identity as a man. Cashier worked as a manual laborer, handyman, and farm worker for a number of years. In 1899, as Albert aged into elderliness she applied for a government pension. At that time Albert was examined by three army doctors, none of whom discovered her sex. Shortly thereafter Albert was granted a pension that she collected for slightly over twelve years. Throughout much of that time period Albert resided in a retirement home established for Illinois veterans of the Civil War. But, in 1911 fate took a hand in Albert's affairs.

    In that year Albert was involved in an automobile accident as she was run down by one of those early model cars. Cashier was hospitalized due to her injuries. While doctors treated her for a broken leg, and while she was unconscious, Albert's long hidden identify was found out. In short order the government issued an edict that required Albert to attend a hearing at the Bureau of Pensions to determine her worthiness to maintain her pension.

As part of Albert's defense she asked fellow members of her unit to testify as to her service. None of the veterans questioned in Albert's review hearing had any prior idea that she was a woman. Several of Albert's comrades from the 95th remembered that she had been "shy and hard to know." One Illinois soldier noted that, "Cashier was very quiet in her manner and she was not easy to get acquainted with." Another veteran from the 95th explained how it was possible for Albert to conceal her identity during the war, "When we were examined at induction we were not stripped. We were examined on the same day. All that we showed was our hands and feet. I never did see Cashier go to the toilet nor did I ever see any part of his person exposed by which I could determine the sex. He was a very retiring disposition and did not take part in any of the games. He would sit around and watch but would not take part. He had very small hands and feet." (Wiley, pp.338)

Every veteran who testified at her hearing was surprised to discover that she was a woman. When asked to identify Albert from pictures of her as a soldier and a male civilian Robert D. Hannah of the 95th expressed his surprise, "About two weeks ago I learned that Albert D.J. Cashier is a woman. I never suspected anything of that kind. I knew that Cashier was the shortest person in the Co. I think he did not have to shave. There has never been any doubt in my mind since it came out that Cashier was a woman but that it is so. I have not seen Cashier since a few years after the war. I am not able to identify the right hand figure in the double picture you show me. It has been too long ago, and fifty years make too many changes in a person for me to identify the right hand figure. I have no doubt about the left hand figure being the picture of Albert D.J. Cashier." (Pension Records Document, January 1915, pp. 5)

After hearing the testimony of many veterans, the Bureau of Pensions ruled that Albert Cashier was a veteran of the Civil War, and that he was Jennie Hodgers. As such Albert Cashier and his alter ego, Jennie Hodgers, were eligible for a continuance of the pension awarded years before. Albert's pension was reinstated and she continued to live in the veterans' retirement home. In 1915 Albert died and was buried in her Civil War uniform with full military honors.

Although Albert D.J. Cashier's wartime experiences were unique, she was not the only Civil War era woman to serve in the ranks. Mary Livermore of the U.S. Sanitary Commission wrote, "a larger number of women disguised themselves and enlisted in the service for one cause or another, than was dreamed of." Another such woman soldier was Sarah Rosetta Wakeman who served in the Red River Campaign along with Albert Cashier under the pseudonym of Lyons Wakeman. However, unlike Albert, Wakeman died in 1864 after becoming critically ill along the Red River. Lyons was one of sixty women reportedly killed or wounded as Civil War soldiers although no accurate accounting is truly possible.

Not every woman who attempted to become a soldier was so successful at disguising themselves as Albert Cashier was. Although several woman soldiers were promoted to the ranks of sergeant, lieutenant, or captain, many were discovered—most of them quickly. Generally women whose sex was discovered were summarily discharged and sent home. For many men such women were thought of as insane and certainly misplaced. The Rebels once sent a captured woman soldier back to the Union lines with a note that read, "as the Confederates did not use women in the war, this woman, wounded in battle, is returned to you." (Burns, pp. 149)

In the end, Albert Cashier faded into memory. Yet, Cashier's name remains inscribed on the Illinois Soldier's Monument in what is now the Vicksburg National Military Park. Albert's name stands there—carved and silent. That name rests there in stone along with those of thousands of other Illinois soldiers who were participants in one of the pivotal battles of the American Civil War. Though long gone Jennie Hodgers-Albert Cashier lives on as one of the more interesting Civil War soldiers. She served well and surreptitiously. She continues to intrigue modern readers as a fascinating and uncommon Illinois soldier of the Civil War.

Sources

Blanton, D., (Spring, 1993), "Women Soldiers of the Civil War." Prologue: Quarterly of
    the National Archives, Vol. 25, No. 1, available online at
    < http://www.nara.gov/publications/prologue/womenl.html. >

Burgess, L., *An Uncommon Soldier,* London, England: Oxford University Press, 1994.

Davis, W. & Wiley, B., *Photographic History of the Civil War: Fort Sumter to*
   Gettysburg, New York, NY: Black Dog & Leventhal Publishers, 1994.

Governor's Report: History of the 95th Illinois Volunteer Infantry Regiment, Illinois State
   Archives.

Hattaway, H., *Shades of Blue and Gray,* New York, NY: Harcourt, Brace & Co., 1997.

Hicken, V., *Illinois in the Civil War,* Urbana, IL: University of Illinois Press, 1991.

Illinois Women in the War. Infobahn Outfitters, Inc., available online at
   < http://www.rsa.lib.H.us/-ilwomen/war.htm >

Massey, M., *Women in the Civil War,* Lincoln, NE: University of Nebraska Press, 1994.

Military & Pension Records of Albert Cashier, National Archives.

Robertson, J., *Tenting Tonight: The Soldier's Life,* Alexandria, VA: Time-Life Books,
   1984.

Ward, G.; Burns, R.; and Burns, K. *The Civil War: An Illustrated History,* New York,
   NY: Alfred A. Knopf, 1990.

Wiley, B., *The Life of Billy Yank: The Common Soldier of the Union,* Baton Rouge, LA:
   Louisiana State University Press, 1991.

Women in the Civil War, Home pages, Inc., available online at
< http://www.geocites.com/Pentagon/Quarters/women.html. >

14

William Wiley's Civil War

At the age of twenty-four William Wiley decided that the time had come to join the Union army. Wiley had spent a quiet life working as a farmer near Peoria, Illinois. However, after closely following the events of the first year of war, William Wiley came to the conclusion that it was a true and honorable thing to volunteer and serve for the cause of union. At that time Wiley began to keep a diary and just prior to his enlistment he wrote, "Somehow from the day the war was declared I felt that I was to have a hand in the conflict, but not being disposed to rush into it heedlessly and in deference to the feelings of my parents that felt very keenly the dire necessity that might cause myself and my brothrs (sic) to have to take up arms in defense of our country. I put off enlisting until I felt it to be my imperative duty." (Winschel 2-3)

Wiley was to become a member of the 77th Illinois Volunteer Infantry within which he served with bravery and distinction. In August 1862 Wiley set off to be a soldier. He also continued to maintain his journal. That diary was eventually published in 2001 and remains a fine gift to those modern day students of the life of everyday Civil War soldiers.

In terms of Wiley's early experiences as a soldier they fit very well into the pattern that was shared by so many other men who left home and family behind to join both the Union and Confederate forces. Early on, Wiley was fairly naïve about what life in the army would entail. However, even at the outset of his soldiering experiences Wiley fully realized that food and nutrition would be a problem. In one of his first journal entries Wiley ruminates about the realities of cooking in the field that confronted both himself and his brother who served in the same company with him, "The first experience at cooking the army…sow meat was rather droll and we soon began to think that it would be a good thing to take mother along to do our cooking and make our bed if the regulations would only permit of it." (7)

Another factor that swiftly became and remained a harsh reality for William Wiley was the hard nature of living out-of-doors twenty-four hours a day for months on end. Civil War soldiers lived an exceedingly rough-hewn life and William Wiley was no exception to that rule. In a number of places in his diary Wiley recounts some of the hardships that he faced in camp. On one occasion while marching in Kentucky Wiley recalled how hard winter campaigning could be, "There had about six inches of snow now fell during the night. We were aroused at an early hour shook the snow from our tents and strated on another Sabbath day's march of 20 miles in the snow to Paris KY where we went into camp on a hillside just outside of town. After scraping the snow away we carried off a neighbors strawstack to bed ourselves with." (18)

Snowy weather was not the only hardship that wore on Wiley and his comrades in the 77th. Sanitary conditions in camp and on the march were generally primitive. On one occasion Wiley recalled marching all day without water only to finally see his comrades find some after camp was set up in the dark, "They found a pond in a little field (sic) where they got water to make coffee that night and the next morning before daylight and after daylight they went to the pond to fill their canteens before starting on the march again when they discovered a big rotten hog or two floating around in the water which made their coffee sit a little unsteady in their stomaches. But we did not allow such small matters to disturb us but we did fill our canteens later on." (17-18)

Rain was a constant threat to the comfort of Wiley and other Civil War soldiers on the march. In numerous places in his diary Wiley writes about how miserable camping out in the rain was. In December 1862 Wiley wrote about a wet night in the winter's cold, "The ground where we layed was very low and flat and it came on a terable (sic) heavy rain during the night and the water gathered in around us and then some of us awoke we were covered with water. Our little greenbacks and everything in our pockets was well soaked. So we got up and leaned against the trees until morning passing jokes…to keep up our spirits." (30)

This type of misery was not uncommon as Wiley noted in another entry in July 1863, "Passing through the little town of Bolton Miss. We marched on until night turned around and marched back aways and went into camp in a cornfield. We cut up the green corn to bed ourselves with, laid down on it and drew our ruber (sic) blankets over us. That night came a terable (sic) heavy rain and we got well socked (sic). We had to crawl up out of the furrows onto the ridges to keep from drowning." (64)

Little wonder that this sort of hard-handed life would wear down a man and lead to illness or even death. As was the case with so many other Civil War soldiers William Wiley succumbed to what would prove to be debilitating illnesses. During the Vicksburg Campaign Wiley fell prey to malaria a disease that was to dog him for the remainder of his life. For a period of nearly five months Wiley was either in hospital or reduced to limited duty with his company as a result of raging fevers, chills, and anemia. At one point Wiley was forced to spend a prolonged period of time on an army hospital ship while his comrades fought the then indecisive elements of Grant's Vicksburg strategy. While in hospital Wiley recounted how miserable that experience was, "I could not speak above a whisper for several days and from the effects of the feavor (sic) and enclosure I became so stiff and sore that I could hardly walk about and remained in that condition for the next three or four months until the weather got dry and pleasant the next spring and I got so poor I hardly would make a shadow as the saying is and I began to think that I would sell out my chances pretty cheap." (35)

For the remainder of his service Wiley was periodically plagued by the aftereffects of his nearly fatal bout with malaria. Yet, despite his broken health, Wiley remained with the 77th and soldiered on through some of the fiercest combat any American soldiers ever experienced.

During his service in the Union army Wiley fought at places such as Vicksburg, Mansfield, Pleasant Hill, and Mobile. In those engagements Wiley performed in a creditable fashion. Still, very little space in Wiley's diary is dedicated to the nature of combat. Like so may other veterans Wiley resisted the temptation to glorify or brag about what he had seen and done. In later years Wiley went back and reworked parts of his diary. Perhaps those rewordings edited out some of his wartime remembrances that were too painful to recall? At any rate, although Wiley spends little time recounting his combat experiences he does allow for enough mention to provide a vivid glimpse of the life of a combat infantryman in the Civil War.

Wiley's first experience in combat occurred at Vicksburg. Looking back at that event Wiley honestly recorded his initial impressions of seeing the elephant, "This being our first introduction to Johnny reb and the smoke and music of the battle. We felt strange sensations crawling up our backs and out to the ends of our hairs." (28) At Vicksburg Wiley was involved in siege warfare that provided daily dangers that even the most wary soldier could not count on avoiding. Like many Union regiments involved in that siege the 77th camped behind the trench lines in a relatively secluded hollow. But, despite this seeming safety Wiley remembered that "they would drop an occasional shell down amongst us and an occasional solid shot would rebound from the top of the hill and come tearing down through our camp. Samuel Sharkey of Co K had his head taken off by a solid shot just as he was rising from his bed in the morning." (55)

Combat experiences in Wiley's journal are far from glorious. Wiley reported on some of his more awkward comrades tripping during advances over broken country only to have their muskets discharge nearly killing other unit members. In other entries Wiley described the fear that gripped soldiers as they awaited a battle. At Mansfield, during the inglorious Red River Campaign, Wiley described his own less than heroic exit from the field of battle once the Union line crumbled, "The other boys were somewhat amused at myself as we retreating across that open field as I had on a pair of boots that had become badly run over at the heal (sic) and were not the best thing for fast running which we were practicing just at that time so I sat down in the middle of the field and pulled those crooked boots off and made the balance of the race barefoot." (103)

Interestingly enough one theme that runs throughout William Wiley's recollections is that of incompetence among the Union officer corps. While Wiley recorded great respect for generals such as Grant and A.J. Smith he held many other officers in contempt. In his years of service William Wiley was commanded by a number of men whom he saw as unfit. Perhaps typical of Wiley's scorn for his commanders was the following description of Lieutenant Silas Wagoner, "He was a very small man in a very large body. He was very over bearing and abusive. His little authority seemed to hurt him. He cursed and abused the men at a terrible rate until the colonel had to reprimand him. One would have thought from his talk and actions that he would tear the confederacy (sic) all to pieces in a little while but I noticed that he was one of the first to resign when we got where the rebel bullets begun to sing around in a careless manner." (26)

Late in his diary Wiley recalled a point when some of his unit members had reached their limit with a particular officer's foibles. In May 1865, after combat operations had ceased and peace was at hand, Wiley's brigade commander persisted in posting guards and drilling in a manner more appropriate for the middle of the war. Finally, members of the 77th had enough of these seemingly unnecessary and draconian measures. Wiley, without any criticism, described what those insubordinate veterans did, " Some of the more reckless of the boys broke up some cartridges and put the powder in an old canteen and sliped (sic) over to the general's tent when he was asleep and sliped it under the edge of his tent and fired the fuse and sliped away and let it go off and woke the Gen up sudden. He threatened pretty strong what he would do if he found out who done it but the boys exploded several more around his tent before morning. The general conceded that a camp guard had ceased a success and didn't order anymore." (166-67)

Despite a nagging disregard for many of his direct commanders William Wiley retained a great sense of pride for what he and his comrades-in-arms accomplished. For example, after the surrender of Vicksburg Wiley recalled the feeling of joy & accomplishment that surged through both he and his comrades, " To say that we rejoiced and felt very much releaved (sic) is putting it very mild as we felt that we had accomplished a great victory. One of great importance to the union cause as it opened up the Mississippi to the Gulf and cut the confederacy in two." (60)

Interestingly enough William Wiley also comes off of the pages of his journal as an advocate for abolition. This fact is somewhat surprising in that Wiley came form central Illinois a region that was a primarily a Democratic section of the state. However, in several places in his writing Wiley noted efforts made by members of his unit to hide fugitive slaves, assist in their escape, or support the use of African-American soldiers. Wiley also served in several campaigns wherein black soldiers were also present.

Up close and personally William Wiley saw the suffering and efforts that black troops made to rid the nation of the evil of slavery. At Fort Blakely, near Mobile, Wiley described the fervor of some of those black soldiers, "The colored troops so worked up by the time they got in the fort that their officers couldn't control them. They set up yell, Remember Fort Pillow and were determined to do as the rebels had done with the colored troops at Fort Pillow. Kill them, surrender or no surrender! They had to bring up a division of white troops to stop them."(150) Throughout his diary Wiley refrains form the use of common racial epithets that typify many other existing journals kept by Union soldiers. This is a fascinating element of Wiley's unknown personality and one that still earns him credit.

Even though William Wiley and the other members of his regiment experienced all the trauma and suffering that war can create they maintained a sense of humor about much of their lives in the military. In a number of places Wiley recorded mildly humorous episodes that must have served to buoy the spirits of men pushed to the limit of their endurance. At one point Wiley noted that, "Our boys had got to calling themselves Gen Smith's greyhounds on account of being run about so much and on this march whenever Gen Smith would come in sight they would set up the most unearthly howling like a pack of hounds." (69-70) At another point in his diary Wiley put a humorous slant on what would otherwise have been a miserable mud march, "It continued to rain until 10 AM. The ground was covered with water and every little while someone would plout into a hole where some artillery wagon had been dug out and would get wet all over. Then the boys would set up the yell. Grab a root, no bottom!" (143)

But in his traveling and campaigning William Wiley never lost sight of the human tragedy that the Civil War bred. In the pages of his diary Wiley wrote about the passing of friends, the destruction of towns, and the daily grinding that the war exerted upon the spirits of mankind. In one representative episode Wiley described a conversation he overheard involving an old woman in southern Alabama who displayed a Union flag as the troops marched by, " Some of the oficers (sic) rode up to the fence to speak to her and she pointed out a large house up the road aways where she said an old Dr lived who had been a rebel conscripting oficer and that he had come to their house sometime before to try to fource (sic) her son to go into the rebel army and that her son being a union man had refused to go and this Dr had shot him killing him before her eyes." (157-58) As a sidebar, after confirming the truth of these charges Wiley's regimental commander allowed his men to loot the old doctor's house as a form of just punishment for his past actions

In the end, William Wiley survived combat, illness, marching, terrible rations, and ill fortune to return home to Illinois in July of 1865. He had survived the war but as a broken man. The effects of his hard campaigning and illness never left William Wiley and reduced his ability to work. Until his death in 1902 Wiley was steadily more limited in terms of the physical labor he could undertake. Sadly, on three occasions Wiley petitioned for a veteran's disability pension. Twice Wiley's claim was rejected due to the obstinacy of bureaucrats who little understood the sacrifices of such men. Finally, in 1899, a $10.00 per month allotment was given to Wiley. However, this late dispensation did little to ease the poverty that Wiley's disability reduced him to.

In his postwar years William Wiley attempted to lead a productive life. In 1868 Wiley wed Leannah Patton of Elmwood, Illinois. The Wiley's raised one child, a son named Samuel. Throughout their life together they supported on another but lived an austere and impoverished existence. Yet, despite his poverty and the death of his wife in 1897, William Wiley never recanted the sense of pride he had in serving his country during the Civil War.

William Wiley took time near the end of his journal to describe the bittersweet mixture of emotions that the victorious end of the Civil War encompassed for himself and his comrades in the 77th, "We had nothing to be ashamed of. We had done well our part in atchieving (sic) a glorious victory in preserving and strengthening our institution and restoring peace to our land and felt hapy (sic) in the thought of soon returning to our homes and friends from whom we had been separated for 3 long weary years. But yet we could not keep a feeling of sadness at the thought of breaking up our organization and separating perhaps many of us never to meet again. As there is a strong bond of friendship ataches (sic) between soldiers after three years campaigning together cemented by mutual experiences hardships and deprivations which no one could fully appreciate but those that had experienced them." (175)

In these solemn words William Wiley described the band of brothers mindset that is so typical of combat veterans. Wiley shared a slice of life that only other soldiers with similar experiences could appreciate. In this way William Wiley returned to Illinois a changed man. No matter how much love and contentment he found in the embrace of his family and resurrected civilian life he could never leave behind the memories of the war that helped shape the remainder of his life. In this way William Wiley's Civil War was typical of the experiences of many Union and Confederate veterans of that bygone conflict. In that same way, William Wiley's Civil War was also unique and understood only by himself. This is the price of war in the 19th century and in our own age and beyond.

Source

Winschel, Terrence J. (editor). *The Civil War Diary of a Common Soldier: William*
   Wiley of the 77th Illinois Infantry. Baton Rouge, LA: Louisiana State
   University Press, 2001.

15

The Hawk Brothers

During the Civil War more than three million men served in the opposing armed forces. In four years over 630,000 American soldiers died in battle, of mortal wounds, via illness, or in prisons. The war broke families apart, widowed young brides, left orphans in its wake, and ended countless dreams. In the end, a Union victory led to the commencement of modern American history as we know it. While all of these facts are historically true they fail to convey the human side of the wartime experience. Each of the millions of men who served, were maimed, was imprisoned, or even perished left behind some loved ones who mourned his absence. To truly understand the human cost of America's Civil War it is sometimes best to take a close up view of the sacrifice that occurred in those tempestuous war years. The story of the Hawk brothers form north central Illinois serves as a good example of what the Civil War meant to everyday families.

Robert & Henry Hawk were young men working on their parent's farm when the war broke out. The Hawk's both came from solid farming stock who had migrated to Illinois from Pennsylvania years before. In 1861 when Confederate cannons fired on Fort Sumter the Hawk family resided in the vicinity of Sterling near Illinois's Rock River. The family was economically stable and made their living plowing, seeding, and cultivating the rich Illinois soil. But, the coming of the war was to greatly change the Hawk family's lot in life.

Though neither of the eldest Hawk brothers rushed off to volunteer for military service in the halcyon days of the war's first spring, a time would come for both of them to enter the blue clad Federal ranks. However, as the summer of 1862 approached Henry Hawk became the first member of his immediate family to answer the call of duty and join the infantry.

On August 9, 1862 Henry Hawk put aside his life as a civilian and instead became a member of Company F, 93rd Illinois Infantry. The 93rd was to be a hard fighting and tough marching unit that fought at places such as Vicksburg, Chattanooga, Atlanta, and the March to the Sea. For Henry, serving in the 93rd represented both an opportunity to defend the cause of Union and to do the manful duty that over 250,000 other Illinois men did during the Civil War. What he could not have realized when he signed onto his muster sheet and volunteered was the nature of the life he would lead as a soldier.

It is fortunate that a strange twist of fate has provided a glimpse into the world of Henry and Robert Hawk as they served in the Union army. Both Hawk brothers wrote a series of letter home to their parents or younger siblings. For years after the war those letters were stored in a family attic. Eventually, through a series of fortuitous events, the letters came into the possession of the great-great-nephew of these two Union veterans. That individual, Bradley James Hawk took the time to preserve and transcribe those family heirlooms. He also compiled a small unpublished booklet within which the original and transcribed versions of the remaining Hawk letters were cataloged. Also included in this booklet were several other documents and correspondences that enlighten some aspects of Henry and Robert's Civil War service. In reading these letters and documents a vivid picture of two men's Civil War experiences emerge.

For the first six months of his service Henry Hawk spent a great deal of time traveling across portions of Arkansas, Tennessee, Missouri, and Mississippi. Like so many Western Federal regiments, the 93rd Illinois was a hard marching unit. The men of the 93rd were called upon to endure all the hardships that campaigning, marching, and reconnaissance entailed in that era. In fact by war's end the toll of battle, marches, and disease was to claim the lives of 294 of the men of this unit. (Dyer 2)

By the early spring of 1863 the 93rd stood poised to become part of General Ulysses S. Grant's Vicksburg Campaign. That historic military movement involved tremendous effort and sacrifice on the part of thousands of Federal soldiers. Henry Hawk was destined to be one of those men. But, as of March 1863 when Henry's first letter was written, he had yet to experience combat or, as men of those days described that clash of arms, "see the elephant."

On March 22nd, 1863 Henry wrote home to his mother. In that initial letter Henry seemed certain that some military event was about to happen. He described the movements he thought might occur to his mother, "We expect to move from here today we will embark in small boats & go up or through the Yazoo pass, they say the rebels are avacuating (sic) Vicksburg and I suppose they want to get us in behind them & bag some of them if possible & I would not wonder if we should see some fun but I expect they will get away as usual I do not care much if they get them out of Vicksburg without the loss of too many lives I am satisfied we are bound to have Vicksburg this time fight or no fight." (Hawk Letters 3)

As Henry thought about the possibility of his first battle he took some time to reassure his beloved mother about his well being, "Mother you think this war is a very rough thing & you are right but the best way is to face the music—look on the bright side of the picture & keep up your spirits. This war is not going to last always & if our Country is saved we have been fully repaid for all our hardships." (Hawk Letter 3)

Henry then expressed his personal wishes that his younger brother, Robert, would be spared fighting in the war. A half-year of living out-of-doors, marching in the rain, eating poor rations, and living like a hog had taught Henry how difficult a soldier's life was. He had no wish to see his brother experience those hazards and he expressed those opinions when he wrote, "the conscription bill will fall rather heavy on some if it is necessary to bring it into force, which I hope it will not, and if it does I think Rob will be missed, I kind of feel it in my toenails that he will." (Hawk Letters 3)

In closing his missive to his mother Henry noted how fit he was. In fact, despite the hard traveling that he and his unit had already undertaken Henry could proudly state, "I have the best kind of health I have a belly on me like a squire so I think I can aspire to or for that office when I get home." (Hawk Letter 3)

From March until July Henry was part of the Federal force that went down the Mississippi River to lay siege to the strategically important Confederate city of Vicksburg. The 93rd was in the forefront of Grant's May advance around the Vicksburg fortifications as he attempted to invest the fortress city from the rear. From May 14-22 the 93rd marched and fought on a continuous basis. At places such as Jackson & Champion Hills, Henry and his comrades fought and defeated the desperate Rebel

troops of General Pemberton. Then, after forcing the Confederate troops back into their Vicksburg defenses, the 93rd was part of a general assault on the Rebel line that took place on May 22. General Grant felt that the defeated Rebels would be dispirited and might just be easily pushed off their seemingly strong fortifications with a minimal effort. Unfortunately for many a Union lad, General Grant was as wrong as a man can be about that assumption. On May 22nd Henry Hawk was part of a dramatic and futile assault. After only about twenty minutes of fighting the 93rd had lost 38 men killed, 113 wounded, and 11 missing. They were then part of a siege that was to continue until the final surrender of the Confederate garrison on July 4, 1863.
(Adjutant General's Report 1)

Subsequent to the capture of Vicksburg Henry next sat down to write home to his family on August 9. Once again Henry took time to reassure his family as to his well being, "I will drop you a line this morning that may inform you that I am quite well hoping this may find you and all the family enjoying the same rich blessing." (Hawk Letters 5) Henry then went on to mention that he had, in fact, been ill, for a while but was now recovering, "I had a little turn of fever and ague about a week ago but busted it with quinne (sic) and felt very well now." (Hawk Letter 5)

Malaria was a terrible fact of life for many Civil War soldiers. At that time there was no knowledge of the connection between mosquitoes, then commonly called gallinippers, and the disease. Quinine was used to good effect but medical science had not progressed to the point where adequate dosages of this ameliorative medication were consistently provided. As a result, men such as Henry Hawk would generally experience periodic reoccurrences of malaria not only during the war but also throughout their remaining life.

Henry touched on an interesting event in his life when he noted, "I got my likeness taken yesterday. I will send it to you. I suppose you will think I look rather rough. I had it taken just as I was in my every day & am very poor now to what I have been for the last six months." (Hawk Letters 5) In mentioning having his "likeness" taken Henry referred to the act of going to a photographer for a tintype, Carte de visite, or daguerreotype image of himself. For many soldiers, inclusive of Henry Hawk, the army years were the first opportunity they may well have had to have a picture taken. In the parlance of those bygone years, having your likeness taken was a "big thing" and worthy of mention in a letter home.

As the weeks passed Henry and his comrades in the 93rd languished as garrison troops in the intense southern heat. On August 26 Henry again wrote home and described how draining the southern summer weather was, "we have had the warmest weather for a week back we have had yet being more close and oppressive and I felt it more from the reason that I have had the diarhaea (sic) for some ten days, but am better now. I feel better today than I have for a week although I have done duty all the time. We come on guard evry (sic) other day. You would not think it very hard if you had to work only evry (sic) other day, but we loose (sic) so much sleep that it makes it rough on us, although I would rather do it than pretend to march in this weather." (Hawk Letters 7)

Henry went on to described a terrible accident that occurred in Vicksburg when a Federal transport carrying munitions exploded. Although Henry was not present at the time he was aware of the event and felt the concussion of the blast. Unbeknownst to Henry over 140 men were killed by that blast, the cause of which remains uncertain to this day. Additionally, Henry dedicated some space to his opinions about the growing Copperhead movement that was present in Illinois and other northern states.

As a fighting man at the front it was only natural that Henry Hawk held little affection for those homebodies who worked against the cause he was risking his life to defend. Henry reported to his mother that, "the war will be ended by this time next year & I think it will (if) there is enough loyal men yet to outride all disloyalty although they may retard our movements for a while, but thank God the army is universally loyal." (Hawk Letters 7)

By September 20, 1863 the hard hand of war had settled down on the life of Henry Hawk. Some of his closest friends had been stricken down not by enemy bullets but rather by the slow killer of the war—disease. Speaking of the Miller brothers, both of whom died of wounds or disease, Henry wrote about those sad events and expressed not only his feelings about the losses but also some of his personal religious beliefs, "This terrible war has carried a pang to many honest & loving hearts at home and doubtless the fatigue and anxiety to Morgan caused Joes (sic) being wounded & in the condition in which he was & his final death contracted the disease that cost him his life. But we can say after all our observations it is the Lord, let him alone, his ways are deep and fast finding out." (Hawk Letters 9)

Henry continued in this spiritual vein and revealed a great deal about his character and moral values, "I would not have you unhappy for anything in the world, my health physically is, at present & for the most of the time past, has been all I could desire, & morally God is my judge. I try to be as good a boy as I can and with the assistance of Almighty God & an interest in your prayers. I will meet you in another & brighter world if I never do in this, although I feel very confident that God will spare my life to return to you safe & sound. So make yourself perfectly easy & do not work too hard. I am afraid you will overdo yourself. There is no use in fretting, it only makes matters worse, although it seems sometimes as though one could not help it, but I have learned cheerfulness & kindness combined with morality give to mankind (yes & womankind too) solid comfort & enjoyment in this life, while an uneasy mind & ruffled temper bring happiness to none." (Hawk Letters 9)

In his closing comments Henry took time to lay out for his mother and other family members what being a soldier in the war has done and meant to him. In these lines Henry Hawk revealed not only a great deal about his own core values but also ethics that rang true for so many Civil War soldiers, " Mother although no pecuniary consideration could ever induce me to desert my country in her time of need, but I would be one of the happiest men on this continent if this war was closed, it would suit me tomorrow. There are two things in a soldier's life that I particularly dislike, for all the influences thrown about a man have a tendency to drag a man down rather than make him wiser and better. Second I don't (sic) like Uncle Sams (sic) grub, although I can get along very well with it when I know I have to, but you know I always was a great fellow for fruit and vegetables, of full supply of which it is impossible for me to get. But I tell you if I get home alright with leg and limb, I would not take a thousand dollars for my last years experience. I tell you it has brought me to my senses as regards of a great many things. It has taught me that we know nothing of ourselves until we see how the best of mankind lives and gets along. I often wished when I was a boy to see the South as it was, and now my heart is almost filled with sadness when I look over there." (Hawk Letters 9)

On November 23, 1863 Henry Hawk took pen in hand to craft a letter home. His unit had that day been involved in a skirmish with the Confederate troops who guarded a ford in the Tennessee River that the Federal soldiers forced their way across. The 93rd, as well as much of General Sherman's Army of the Tennessee had been dispatched to Chattanooga to assist the besieged Army of the Cumberland. General George "Pap" Thomas' Cumberland boys had been driven back into Chattanooga at the disastrous fight at Chickamauga approximately a month earlier. Since that bloody defeat the Cumberland lads had been eating short rations and stewing over the way they had been forced to skeedadle back to Chattanooga and lick their wounds. Now the moment had come when, under the overall command of General Grant, the Union boys could strike back at their Confederate foes.

As Henry scribed his final letter home he could have no idea what the next forty-eight hours would hold for him. Sitting in camp near Lookout Mountain and Missionary Ridge Henry knew that more fighting was in the near future. He wrote to his father and stated, "I think there will be a grand move on the whole line before long. Thomas men are reported to be moving forward now...Thomas will punch them up in front, which I hope will result in a skedadle on their part or else a capture of butternuts on our part." (Hawk Letters 13)

Interestingly enough, even though Henry must have known that he would be fighting fairly soon, he ended his letter with a long monologue regarding plans his parents had shared with him to build a new house on their farm property. At one point Henry enjoins his father to be careful about the scope of his proposed construction project, "This winter, as time is precious in your country at present, I would not advise you to build a great Barn of a house but one that would be large enough to be comfortable & no larger."
(Hawk Letters 13)

Two days latter Henry Hawk took part on the assault of the right wing of the Confederate Army of Tennessee's position along the top of Missionary Ridge. General Sherman's boys were supposed to roll up the Rebel right wing but as it turned out the Confederates on that part of the battlefield were just stubborn enough to slow down the Federal advance. Eventually it was the long suffering soldiers of General Thomas's Army of the Cumberland who were to successfully storm the seemingly impregnable Confederate position on Missionary Ridge and force a general and hasty Confederate retreat from the battlefield. However, by the time those events transpired Henry Hawk's Civil War was over. Henry had been struck by a Minie ball in his upper right thigh and his soldiering days were over.

Henry was carried from the battlefield by a comrade and taken to a military hospital in Chattanooga. There, army doctors examined Henry's wounds and found that it was impossible to amputate his shattered limb. Apparently the wound was too high in his thigh and might well have been close to Henry's femoral artery. Thus, all that could be done was to make Henry as comfortable as possible and wait for fate to complete the work begun by the Confederate soldier who shot him.

On December 12 Lieutenant William M. Herrod of Company F, 93rd Illinois, wrote to Mr. Daniel Hawk, Henry's father. There is no record of when the Hawk family received this letter but its contents were unmistakable. In that note Lieutenant Herrod sadly informed the Hawk's that, "Since the late battle at Chattanooga in which our regiment took part on mission ridge where your son Henry was wounded in the right thigh while nobly fighting for his country. It has become my pain full duty to inform you that on the fifth day of this month he died at the division hospital and was buried about 3 miles above Chattanooga on the banks of the Tennessee River. The wound was to (sic) high up for an amputation and I don't think the best of care at home would have saved his life." (Hawk Letters 19)

When he died Henry Hawk was twenty-five years old, 5 feet 7 ½ inches tall, with blue eyes and brown hair. His listed occupation was "farmer." Henry had no personal effects to send home. Henry was gone and one can only imagine the trauma his passing caused to the remaining members of his family. (Military & Pension Records)

While there is no record of how Henry Hawk's parents, siblings, and other relatives coped with his death what is known is that in March of 1865 his younger brother Robert joined the Union army. At the time of Robert's enlistment in Company G of the 156th Illinois Infantry, the Civil War was grinding to its conclusion. Union troops were only about a month away from finally defeating their dogged Rebel foemen. There is no record of why Robert Hawk chose to enlist at such a late stage in the war. What is known is that Robert would serve in the 156th until July of 1865.

Like his brother Henry, Robert wrote home to his parents and detailed some of his army experiences. Robert's first letter home was scribed from Camp Fry near Chicago on March 12th. In this first missive Robert comments on the poor health of many of his comrades, "There is a good may (sic) of the boys that is not very well, but not any of them that is bad enough to go to the hospital." (Hawk Letters 21)

As a new soldier Robert must have felt some pride when he was finally issued the blue coat, trousers, cap, and accoutrements that made him a true fighting man. In his first letter he commented, "we have drawn all our rig but our guns now, and think that we will leave here very soon...I think we will leave here in three days bound for I know not where." (Hawk Letters 21)

Sensing the worries that his bereaved parents must have still held due to the death of his brother, Robert closed his note by reassuring them about his well being, "I don't want you to worry about me for I am well and harty (sic) and one of the biggest (sic) eaters in the Co." (Hawk Letters 21)

The 156th Illinois was a high number regiment. That fact translated to its having arrived on the scene of war rather late in the game. As a result there was not too much call for their service as of March 1865. The 156th was sent south into Tennessee where it served essentially as guards for railroads that were periodically attacked by Confederate cavalry and guerrilla units. Sadly, Robert Hawk did not stand up as well as he thought he would to the rigors of soldiering.

By May of 1865 Robert's health had completely broken down. Sick with what was diagnosed by the medical staff at the army hospital in Memphis where Robert was sent as "typho-malarial fever" Robert wasted away. Throughout May and June Robert Hawk was listed in his military record as "Sick in Quarters." Eventually, on July 8th, Robert finally succumbed to the drawn out and merciless effects of the fever that he had contracted somewhere in Tennessee. When he died Robert was twenty-two years of age, 5 feet 9 inches tall, of fair complexion, blue eyed, brown haired, and one of 24 men in his unit to die of disease. He, like his late brother Henry, was recorded as being a farmer. (Military 7 Pension Records)

  The word of their second son's death in the army must have been a bitter blow for the Hawk's. First Henry who fell in battle and then the seemingly senseless death of Robert by the hand of disease months after the war was over. Although there is no way of knowing how the Hawk's went on with their lives after such twin blows all one can imagine is a life of limited possibilities bordered by the memories of two lads who were lost forever. All they could do was have friends write letters inquiring as to the possibility of having Robert's remains shipped home in a sealed, metal coffin. There is no written record as to their finally arranging this transfer of remains but one can only hope that it did happen and that a gravesite was chosen where the family could periodically come and pay homage to the lost child.

  In the end, each of us is mortal. Regardless of how much we attempt to conceal the fact from ourselves—we all will die. Some people are blessed with the good fortune to lead long and healthy lives. Others seem cursed by fate to suffer seemingly random pain & anguish. In the case of the Hawk brothers, their deaths at an early age stand out as tragic yet typical of the time they lived in. Wars kill people. There is no way to refine the reality of war's destructive nature. For Robert & Henry Hawk they chose to volunteer to fight in a cause they believed in. That same cause ended up consuming not only there well being but also their very lives. In taking the two Hawk brothers away from their loving family the war acted to limit the possibilities not only of the departed soldiers but also the entire network of friends and family members who knew them. And therein lies the greatest tragedy of the deaths of the Hawk brothers and every other soldier and civilian who perished in the Civil War. The death of any man, woman, or child diminishes all of us. When the Hawk brothers died so too did pieces of many other people. Therein rests the legacy of this story and of the wartime experiences and deaths of Henry & Robert Hawk.

Sources

Adjutant General's Report. *93rd Illinois Infantry Regiment History.*

Dyer, Frederick. *Dyer's's Regimental History of the 156th Regiment Infantry.*

Dyer, Frederick. *Dyer's Regimental History 93rd Regiment Infantry.*

Hawk, Bradley James, (ed.). *The Letters of Henry and Robert Hawk: A Civil War
    Account.* (Unpublished Booklet), 1990.

Hawk, Robert & Henry. *Military & Pension Records.*

Part II: Civilian Stories

1

Hannah Ropes: Civil War Nurse

During the Civil War approximately 2,000 women in total served as volunteer nurses for the North & South.[79] Among that brave cadre of women was Hannah Ropes, a native of New England. The story of Mrs. Ropes' wartime service is a fascinating one and also a tale that for the longest time went unnoticed. Indeed, until 1980, the diary and letters written by Hannah Ropes while she served as matron of Union Hotel Hospital in 1862-63 were unknown save to the descendants of this brave hearted woman. Subsequent to their publication it became apparent that Hannah Ropes had served her nation, and more specifically the lads who were her charges at Union Hotel Hospital, amazingly well. Thus, it is altogether fitting and proper to recount the service and life of Hannah Ropes as a prime example of the contributions that women nurses of the Civil War made to both their nation and the men & boys who came into their helping hands.

    Hannah Ropes was a woman who led a life filled with ideals and stouthearted deeds. Born in New Gloucester on June 13, 1809 as Hannah Anderson Chandler, Ropes was the seventh of ten children. Hannah Ropes' parents were both educated and capable people. Her father was a prominent Maine attorney. An older brother, Theophilus Parsons Chandler, was a leading attorney who practiced in Boston alongside John Andrew, a man who would eventually become governor of Massachusetts. A younger brother, Peleg Whitman Chandler, also served as an attorney in Boston and developed an outstanding reputation throughout New England as a litigator. Hannah's mother was a kind and religious woman who was committed to her children's education.[80]

cxxiii———————————————

[79] Isabel M. Stewart & Anne L. Austin, *A History of Nursing from Ancient to Modern Times, 5th ed.* New York, NY: Putnam's, 1962, 132.
[80] John R. Brumgardt, *Civil War Nurse: The Diary & Letters of Hannah Ropes.* Knoxville, TN: University of Tennessee Press, 1980, 7.

While there is no written record of the education that Hannah received her later accomplishments and writings would surely indicate that it was not wanting in depth and breadth. In addition, as was to be evidenced by the ease with which Hannah Ropes moved among the highest circles of civil and political society, her preparation and learning was sufficient to allow her access to powerful personages throughout her life.

In 1834 Hannah Chandler wed William Henry Ropes at Bangor, Maine. Hannah's spouse was college educated and served as a teacher and principal in a number of New England institutions of learning. In addition, William Ropes tried his hand at farming and writing. Over the first decade of her marriage Hannah wrote home and described her wedded state as "very happy and contented" and that everything between herself and her spouse was "comfortable and pleasant around us."[81] Yet, although the Ropes had four children, two of whom survived to adulthood, their time together ceased in 1847. In that year William Ropes moved to Florida where he remained until his death in 1864.

While there is no written record parlaying the reasons for this separation several possibilities exist. Hannah hints in her writings that her husband may have moved to Florida due to ongoing health issues that required a relocation she, herself, was unwilling to make. A second explanation rests in her husband's inability to secure lasting & fulfilling work in New England. Whatever the case may have been, from 1847 on Hannah lived the life of a single parent.[82]

Throughout her adulthood, Hannah Ropes presented herself as an advocate for equalitarian causes. In no area was this clearer than in her opinions related to the issue of slavery. During the Civil War Hannah once described the stakes that she saw at play behind the terrible suffering that accompanied the conflict, "Now is the judgment of this world. Each man and woman is taking his or her measure. As it is taken even so must it stand—it will be recorded. The activities of war quicken into life every evil propensity as well as every good principle."[83] For Hannah Ropes, both prior to the war and during its course, the struggle was one of universal evil in the form of human slavery versus the

cxxiv―――――――――――――――――

[81] Ibid., 8.
[82] Ibid., 9.
[83] Ibid., 48.

advancement of freedom & decency. That attitude predated the war and was evident in the life choices of Hannah and her family.

In the fall of 1855 Hannah & her daughter Alice set out for Kansas Territory. There, Hannah's son, Edward, had established a homestead near the free soil center of Lawrence. Once in Lawrence, Hannah Ropes came to experience firsthand the realities of "Bleeding Kansas." In her home Hannah kept, "loaded pistols and a bowie-knife upon my table at night, (and) three Sharp's rifles, loaded, standing in the room."[84] Soon Ropes saw the proslavery forces in Kansas as "mean and cowardly" foes who were "cruel, heartless, dishonorable men" to whom murdering a man was "not much more than to shoot a buck."[85]

By April of 1856 Hannah Ropes had seen enough of Kansas and decided to return with her daughter to New England. Once back in Maine, Hannah Ropes compiled her journal entries and letters into a book that she felt described the realities of internecine warfare in Kansas. Hannah's book was titled Six Months in Kansas: By a Lady and was published by a Boston firm in 1856. This was not to be the only book scribed by Hannah Ropes as, in 1859, she saw the publication of a novel titled Cranston House. In this fictional work Hannah Ropes touched upon themes of social egalitarianism set in the far west. Once again, Hannah used her talents to create a literary platform to express social views that were based upon her innate sense of justice and liberty.

The coming of the war in April 1861 roused a strong desire on the part of Hannah Ropes to serve in some vital way. Perhaps at that time Hannah felt the same internal strife that one of her female characters in Cranston House expressed, "O woman! Chafing against the walls of thy home, and crying out for a larger sphere of action and enterprise."[86] Such feelings could only have deepened after the May 1862 enlistment of Edward Chandler in the 2nd Massachusetts where he was to serve for the duration of the war in a regiment that saw some of the heaviest fighting of the entire conflict.[87] Whatever the case, by the summer of 1862, Hannah Ropes was determined to engage in the field of service

---
[84] Ibid., 17.
[85] Ibid., 17.
[86] Ibid., 2.
[87] Ibid., 28.

she felt most inclined toward and that had been a part of her family life throughout her years as a mother—nursing.

While there were several thousand women who served as Civil War nurses it was a relative handful that left any sort of detailed written record of their service.[88] For those women nurses who did leave a record of their experiences many of them saw their service as an extension of the maternal roles so typical of that era of femininity. Louisa May Alcott saw her patients as "my big babies" and relished her authority over them. For others, serving as a nurse was an opportunity to play a role in historical events that created a longing to serve equal to the feelings in the heart of a man who volunteered for the army. These sensations were aptly described by nurse Katherine Prescott Wormeley, "We all know in our hearts that it is thorough enjoyment to be here, it is life, in short; and we wouldn't be anywhere else for anything in the world!"[89] In June of 1862 Hannah Ropes went to Washington to engage in this same sort of "life."

After undergoing the scrutiny of Dorthea Dix, the great gatekeeper of the nursing field for northern women wishing to pursue this vocation, Hannah Ropes was permitted that honor. In June, Hannah was assigned as head matron to Union Hotel Hospital on the outskirts of Washington in Georgetown. As indicated in its name, the Union Hotel Hospital was previously a boarding house. As a result, the inner structure of the facility was inadequate to meet the needs of a medical building. In 1861, when it was initially opened as a hospital, medical inspectors described the establishment in this way:

> The Union Hotel Hospital, Georgetown, was occupied as its name implies,
> until recently hired for its present use. It is considered capable of accommodating
> 225 patients, and at present contains 189. It is well situated, but the building is
> old, out f repair, and cut up into a number of small rooms, with windows too

cxxvi————————————————
[88] Louisa May Alcott, *Hospital Sketches,* Boston, MA: Applewood Books, 1993, Katherine Prescott Wormeley, *The Other Side of the War with the Army of the Potomac,* Boston, MA: Ticknor, 1889.
[89] Wormeley, 44.

small and few in number to afford good ventilation. Its halls and passages, are
> narrow, torturous, and abrupt, and in many instances with carpets still unremoved
> from their floors, and walls covered with paper. There are no provisions for
> bathing, the water-closets and sinks are insufficient and defective, and there is no
> dead-house. The wards are many of them over-crowded and destitute of arrangements for artificial ventilation. The cellars and area are damp and undrained, and much of the woodwork is actively decaying.[90]

> It was to the maimed & ill inhabitants of this somewhat ramshackle facility that,

from June 1862 until January 1863, Hannah Ropes was to dedicate her mind, body, spirit, and life. Simultaneous to Hannah Ropes late June arrival at Union Hotel Hospital, Union General George B. McClellan was advancing toward Richmond in what was to become the Seven Days Campaign. That ultimately fruitless campaign was to provide Hannah Ropes and her staff their first real taste of the realities of both wartime nursing and the brutal effects of war.

Oddly, the first patient that Hannah Ropes served was not a common soldier boy, but rather, Massachusetts Senator Henry Wilson who was also an officer in his state's militia. Senator Wilson arrived at the Union Hotel Hospital on the morning of June 26 only to become ill. In Hannah Ropes' first letter to her daughter, Alice, from her new posting she described this strange turn of events, "Strange to say, the first work offered me was to nurse General Wilson, who, a few hours before my arrival, fell in a fainting fit in the entry. Tell Aunt Eliza I used the whole of her bottle of annice over his head and arm, for he was a good deal hurt by the fall and is unable to rise this morning."[91]

Interestingly enough, although the bulk of Hannah Ropes service was dedicated to everyday soldiers who entered her

---

[90] U.S. Sanitary Commission, *Documents of the U.S. Sanitary Commission, 3 vols.* New York, NY: U.S. Sanitary Commission, 1866-1871, 1, Document No. 23.

[91] Brumgardt, 49.

hospital, she did establish or maintain acquaintances with a number of powerful figures in Washington. During her six months service at Union Hotel Hospital, Hannah Ropes interacted with figures such as General Nathaniel Banks, Secretary of War Stanton, Senator Wilson, and Senator Charles Sumner. The ability to get in touch with such influential men directly affected not only Hannah Ropes capacities for producing results in her hospital duties, but also the way in which Union Hotel Hospital was run.

Like many other nurses Hannah Ropes was looked down upon by the chief surgeon of her hospital. Indeed, during her time in service, Hannah Ropes came to regard the doctors and stewards who were responsible for attending to many of the patients medical needs as an extremely mixed bag. At one point Hannah Ropes described her initial hospital chief surgeon in a very critical fashion, "He was ignorant of hospital routine; ignorant of life outside of the practice in a country town, in an interior state, a weak man with good intentions, but puffed up with the gilding on his shoulder straps."[92]

In regards to the hospital's stewards, Hannah Ropes saw this group of men as uniformly unfit for duty. At one point Mrs. Ropes described her frustrations with the hospital's stewards in a letter to her daughter, "The wars on the James (are) nothing with the fights I have with the stewards. We now have our fourth, as big a villain as ever walked unhung. I have entered a complaint with the Surgeon General but I don't suppose it will do any good at all. But at any rate I shall have nothing to do with him. I ordered him out of my room and I don't speak to him now."[93]

In the end Hannah Ropes did use her political influence to unseat both the chief surgeon of Union Hotel Hospital and its stewards. After seeing the administration of what she saw as arbitrary and capricious discipline upon several patients, Hannah Ropes went directly to the office of Secretary Stanton. There she revealed her complaints and was able to directly access this powerful wellspring of influence. In the end, it was Hannah Ropes who remained at Union Hotel Hospital while the unfortunate but culpable doctor and steward were removed from

---
[92] Ibid., 73.
[93] Ibid., 70.

office, temporarily jailed, and then reassigned to "frontline duty."[94]

While serving as matron of her hospital Hannah Ropes saw all the suffering that war can breed. Her life at Union Hotel Hospital was filled with endless work and travail. Yet, throughout her writings Hannah Ropes continuously defined her service as one she was happy to fulfill and proud of. At one point in her diary Hannah Ropes took some time to describe her sense of service, "I am here to do my Master's work; the poor privates are my special children for the present; I never wash their hard, worn, and sore feet without a special memory of Him who gave us the example; I never see them wronged, or neglected, or in want, without the feeling that every drop of my blood would be well spent if it could make up to them a tithe of the loss they have experienced in health, in spirits, in weakened faith in man, as well as shattered hope in themselves."[95]

In her direct service with her ill and wounded patients Hannah Ropes demonstrated a total commitment to their well-being. To Ropes, the lads who crossed her path at Union Hotel Hospital were like her surrogate children. In a letter to her mother Hannah depicted the nature of both this service and her feelings about it via but one tragic incident in her work, "The young man who was shot through the lungs, to our surprise and, as the surgeons say, contrary to all "science," lived till last night, or rather this morning. We considered him the greatest sufferer in the house, as every breath was a pang. I laid down last night and got asleep, when I was roused by hearing him cry, very loud, "Mother! Mother! Mother!" I was out of bed and into my dressing gown very quickly, and by his side. The pressure of blood from the uneven circulation had affected the brain slightly, and, as they all are, he was on the battlefield, struggling to get away from the enemy. I promised him that nobody should touch him, and that in a few moments he would be free from all pain. He believed me and, fixing his beautiful eyes upon my face, never turned them away; resistance, the resistance of a strong natural will, yielded; his breathing grew more gentle, ending softly as an infant's He was a brave soldier and a truthful boy."[96]

---
[94] Ibid., 83-84.
[95] Ibid., 74.
[96] Ibid., 67-68.

Such emotional events cannot help but leave a mark upon both the psyche and body of a sensitive person. However, although the male medical personnel Hannah Ropes worked with were suspect, she was fortunate to have a generally very capable nursing staff. While several skilled nurses were mentioned in Hannah Ropes' writings it is of particular interest to read a portion of her diary entry dated December 13, 1862, "We are cheered by the arrival of Miss Alcott from Concord—the prospect of a really good nurse, a gentlewoman who can do more than merely to keep the patients from falling out of bed, as some of them seem to consider the whole duty of a nurse."[97]

It is interesting to note that the justly famous Louisa May Alcott spent her time as a Civil War nurse working under the supervision of Hannah Ropes. In Alcott's first widely accepted work, Hospital Sketches, the great 19th century writer described her time at Union Hotel Hospital. While Alcott left the place where she worked unnamed, and refrained from identifying key figures at the hospital by name, she did occasionally mention her matron and the fine attitude & service she provided. At one point in Hospital Sketches Louisa May Alcott chronicled both her fears for the nutritional well-being of her patients and the benign demeanor of her matron, Hannah Ropes, "when I suggested the probability of famine hereafter, to the matron, that motherly lady cried out: "Bless their hearts, why shouldn't they eat? It's their only amusement; so fill every one,
and, if there's not enough ready to-night, I'll lend my share to the Lord by giving it to the boys." And, whipping up her coffee-pot and plate of toast, she gladdened the eyes and stomachs of two or three dissatisfied heroes, by serving them with a liberal hand."[98]

However, despite the assistance of such stalwarts as Louisa May Alcott, the wear and tear of being matron of such a house of suffering did take its toll upon Hannah Ropes. In November Mrs. Ropes was struck by a bout of neuralgia that was "such torture as one cannot well smile on graciously."[99] That illness brought on pain that Hannah Ropes described in her diary as "the mean imp of evil" which "stabbed her in both eyes."[100]

---

[97] Ibid., 112.
[98] Alcott, 88-89.
[99] Brumgardt, 100.
[100] Ibid., 100.

Despite her illness, Hannah Ropes persisted in her duties as hospital matron. She continued to work tirelessly at duties that were breaking her down. On January 11, in her final letter to her daughter, Alice, Hannah Ropes described the overwhelming pressure of her hospital work, her attempts at resting, and the calling she felt about her work at Union Hotel Hospital, "I have had the devoted attention of the whole house, and all the surgeons say even if I can't do anything at all, I must stay or the house will go down! Stuff. I think the rest will do me good. Mercy! What do the women at home know of work? We never stopped until the whole house were pronounced doing well."[101]

Tragically, the cost of working for six months under great pressure and among terminally ill patients resulted in a dire state of personal health for Hannah Ropes. Only days after penning the lines above, Hannah Ropes' condition took a serious turn for the worse. Ropes was diagnosed with typhoid fever and accompanying pneumonia. Although nursed by both the hospital staff and her daughter, Ropes' condition continued to worsen. On January 20th 1863 Senator Henry Wilson sent a telegraph to the commanding officer of Hannah's son, Edward, serving at the front with the 2nd Massachusetts Infantry. In that communication Senator Wilson wrote, "Mrs. Ropes, Matron of Union Hotel Hospital Georgetown is dying please have her son Edward E. Ropes of Co. D come immediately,"[102] Unfortunately, that message arrived too late for Edward Chandler to attend to his mother. On January 20th Hannah Ropes succumbed to her illness and died.

In death one of Hannah Ropes' closest friends and nursing colleagues wrote, "I shall always feel that she has given up her life to her country, as freely as anyone who died on the field."[103] This close friend went on to describe Hannah Ropes as a "True soldier of the Lord."[104] The body of this "True soldier" was carried back to New Gloucester where it was interred near her grandfather's old house.

In death Hannah Ropes left behind a legacy of service and commitment that was noble indeed. Following Mrs. Ropes' death

cxxxi—————————————————

[101] Ibid., 122.
[102] Ibid., 124.
[103] Ibid., 127.
[104] Ibid., 127.

that legacy was most closely defined via the work of her children. Edward Chandler continued to serve in his regiment and fought at places such as Chancellorsville, Gettysburg, Atlanta, and Savannah. Alice Chandler, urged on by Senator Sumner and his family, sojourned to New Bern, North Carolina, where she served as a teacher of newly emancipated African-American slaves. Although gone in death, if spirits can gaze down upon the world and see the work of others, the efforts of her two surviving children could well have filled Hannah Ropes with pride. After all, Hannah once compared the perpetual changes that life brings to us by comparing it to a kaleidoscope, "Every turning of the glass brings out a new and ever more surprising combination of colors."[105] In Hannah Ropes case, the colors of her life were vibrant and selfless. For that reason it is good to recall them and the efforts of a thoughtful woman who served as a mother, nurse, and lifesaver for her family and many others.

---

cxxxii

[105] Ibid., 87.

2

Illnesses of the Civil War Era: A Brief Compendium

On January 5, 1863, Emeline Ritner sat down to write to her husband, Jacob, who was far off at Vicksburg serving as a captain in the 25th Iowa Volunteer Infantry. While word had spread back home of some of the bloody repulses suffered by the Federal troops Emeline was more concerned with other matters, albeit ones that bespoke life and death matters, "You said I must go to Jefferson and stay two or three weeks. I should have gone two weeks ago, but couldn't get there at all. There has been no chance for some time and now I will not go, for the smallpox has spread so, that I know the people there wouldn't thank me for coming. I understand that they are very much frightened about it. I don't think I have been exposed to it at all, but I know they will be afraid to have me come right in the midst of it." (Larimer, p. 96)

Disease was a fact of life that shaped human behavior far more during the Civil War than it does now in the United States. In an age when medical technology had not progressed far enough to allow for protections we now take for granted, many diseases, once contracted, led to debilitation or death. In Emeline Ritner's case a vaccination procedure did exist against smallpox. However as Mrs. Ritner pointed out later in that same letter, even that was no guarantee of pure immunity, "Some have had it who were vaccinated and didn't go to bed. But I will tell you, it has spread from one end of town to the other." (Larimer, p. 96)

In order to more fully understand the thinking of 19th century people it is important to have a working knowledge of keynote social factors and language. Letters from that time period are often peppered with references to medical needs, nursing, home remedies, and doctor visits. At a time when almost 1.3

million Federal soldiers were treated for acute diarrhea and over 42% of Union troops were ultimately discharged due to chronic illness it is understandable that civilian discourse would focus so heavily upon disease. (Adams, p. 241).

What follows is a concise and dictionary-like compendium of commonly used medical terms of the Civil War era. While some terms are very standard in our own age, others are unfamiliar. It is hoped that this simple reference tool will afford some assistance in better understanding both the writings and thought patterns of our 19th century predecessors. This information has been primarily drawn from fascinating genealogical and medical websites that those readers wishing a more comprehensive look at this language issue should visit.

Ascendancy or Acescency: A tendency toward sourness of the stomach or slight acidity
Achor: A scalp eruption featuring great itchiness.
Ague: Common term for malaria
Apoplexy: Stroke resulting from a sudden stoppage of blood flow to the brain resulting in loss of movement, speech, muscle control or respiration.
Atavism: Term used to refer to hereditary traits or "breeding".
Barber's Itch or Rash: Infection of the hair follicles in the beard area thought to be transmitted by dirty shaving brushes – possibly impetigo.
Bilious Fever: General term for illnesses resulting in fever, vomiting, diarrhea, and oft times jaundice such as typhus, typhoid, or hepatitis.
Black Dog: Common term for depression.
Blackwater Fever: Severe form of ague in which blood was passed in the urine hence looking "black".
Bloody Flux: Dysentery.
Boneshaw: Sciatica or back pain.
Brain Fever: Severe and debilitating fever that was often mortal – possibly meningitis or Typhus.
Bricklayer's Itch: Eczema of the hands often resulting from skin exposure to mortar.
Bronchial Catarrh: Acute bronchitis with significant mucous discharge.
Camp Diarrhea: Typhoid fever.

Camp Fever: Typhus.
Caul: Birth membrane that protects infants in utero – thought to be a sign of good fortune if the infant was born with it still intact around the head.
Chilblain: Swelling with attendant itching and burning sensation of the extremities due to exposure to the cold.
Child Bed Fever: Infection in the mother following childbirth. High mortality rate and caused by unhygienic practices or examination.
Cholera: An acute and often fatal disease featuring profuse diarrhea, cramps, and vomiting. Caused by ingestion of contaminated water or food due to fecal matter contact.
Consumption: Tuberculosis or pulmonary tuberculosis and the associated wasting away of the body and spirit.
Corruption: Infection or degeneration of tissue.
Croup: Horse coughing associated with the swelling of the larynx, trachea, and bronchi in infants and young children.
Diphtheria: An acute infection of the throat, nose, and upper respiratory
 track – sometimes confused with scarlet fever and croup.
Dropsy: Fluid retention often due to heart or kidney disease.
Dropsy of the Brain: Encephalitis.
Dysentery: A number of disorders marked by intestinal inflammation and the evacuation of blood and pus.
Dyspepsia: Acid indigestion possibly chronic.
Efflux ion: Refers to "flowing out" but generally to bleeding
Emesis: Vomiting.
Empyema: A collection of pus in any body cavity but generally the pleural lining of the lungs.
Erysipelas: A contagious skin disease due to streptococcal infection of surface and subcutaneous tissues – often fatal due to corruption.
Excrescence: An unnatural or disfiguring skin growth or protrusion.
Falling Sickness: Epilepsy or seizure disorder.
Fatuity: Senility or dementia.
Fever & Ague: Common term for malaria.
Fit: Sudden attack of anything (e.g. coughing) – if unspecified a seizure.

Flux: An excessive flow or discharge of bodily secretion or excretions – often related to dysentery.
French Pox: Syphilis.
Furuncle: Boil.
Gallinipper: Common term for mosquitoes.
Galloping Consumption: Pulmonary tuberculosis.
Galloping Paralysis: Polio.
Gangrene: Death, decay, or necrosis of bodily tissue, usually in a limb, due to injury or disease resulting in a stoppage of blood supply to the affected region.
Gathering: A collection of pus.
General Yellow Jack: Common term for Yellow Fever.
Goiter: Enlargement of the thyroid gland resulting in moderate to severe neck swelling.
Gout: An inflammation of joints or extremities caused by dietary patterns resulting in a buildup of uric acid at the affected site.
Grip/Gripe/Grippe: Influenza.
Grocer's Itch: Skin disease caused by mites in sugar or flour bins.
Heart Dropsy: Heart disease.
Hydrophoby: Rabies.
Incubus: A night terror or illness that materializes or comes at night.
Infantile Paralysis: Poliomyelitis.
Intermittent Fever: Illness featuring periodic febrile patterns – probably malaria.
Itch: Scabies.
Jaundice: Yellowish discoloration of skin, whites of the eyes, and mucous membranes due to an increase of bile in the bloodstream.
Kinkcough or Kruchkusten: Common term for Pertusis or Whooping Cough.
Lockjaw: Tetanus.
Long Sickness: Tuberculosis.
Lumbago: Back pain.
Lung Fever: Tuberculosis or Pneumonia.
Lying In: Time of delivery of a baby – childbirth and labor.
Mad Hatter Disease: Psychosis often found in hatters who were exposed to large amounts of mercury used as part of the process of stiffening felt hats.
Malaria: A widespread and chronic disease caused by the bite of anopheles mosquitoes infected with parasites that then transfer to

the human bloodstream. Periodic hatches of these parasites then result in the symptoms most significantly marked by high fever and chills.
Melancholia: Severe depression.
Miasma: Poisonous vapors thought to spread through the air and cause disease.
Milk Sickness: Poisoning resulting from drinking milk from cows that have consumed white snakeroot – often mortal it is best known for causing the death of Nancy Hanks Lincoln, President Lincoln's mother.
Mope-Eyed: Short sighted or blind in one eye.
Mortification: When used in a medical sense it refers to gangrene, necrosis, or severe infection.
Nervous or Nerve Fever: Typhus.
Palsy: Sometimes refers to stroke or, in other instances, some muscle paralysis.
Paroxysm: Usually refers to a convulsion or fit – anything that happens suddenly, violently, and unexpectedly.
Pulmonary Apoplexy: Severe coughing – possibly an asthma attack.
Quinsy or Quinsey: Pus-filled swelling of the tonsils that could be fatal due to fever, infection, or obstruction of the breathing passages.
Rag: As in "on the rag" – refers to menstruation.
Rickets: Disease of the skeletal system now known to be caused by a Vitamin D deficiency in childhood.
Scrumpox: Impetigo or severe skin rash.
Scurvy: Thought of as a seaman's disease it results in weakness, fatigue, spongy gums, tooth loss, and hemorrhages under the skin – caused by a lack of Vitamin C it was treated appropriately via fresh fruit and vegetable consumption.
Septicemia: Term used to refer to general blood poisoning.
Smallpox: Contagious viral disease featuring fever and blisters – vaccination was available with mixed results.
Suppuration: The production of pus – often seen as a precursor to healing.
Syphilis: Sexually transmitted or transmitted at birth via the mother to the newborn this disease featured a long and multi-staged emergence – incurable until the discovery of penicillin in 1928.

Tetanus: An infectious and often fatal disease resulting from bacterial intrusion of the body via wounds. Symptoms include severe muscle spasms, especially of the jaw, hence "Lockjaw". Transmission is now known to primarily result from exposure to bacteria in soil infected through horse or bovine feces.
The Drip: Gonorrhea.
Typhoid Fever: An infectious fever caused by ingesting food or water contaminated by sewage or contacted by infected flies or a human carrier. Results in severe diarrhea and is frequently fatal.
Typhus: Communicable fever characterized by very high temperatures, headache, constipation, bronchitis, and a rash. Mouse or lice born this disease featured a high mortality rate.
Wet Nurse: A lactating woman employed to nurse another mother's infant.
Yellow Fever: An acute and often deadly infectious disease of warm climates transmitted by mosquitoes – also known as Yellow Jack, Yellow Jacket, & American Fever.

Sources

Adams, George Worthington, *Doctors In Blue*, LSU Press, Baton Rouge, LA, 1996.

Larimer, Charles F. (ed.), *Love and Valor: Intimate Civil War Letters Between Captain
    Jacob and Emeline Ritner*, Sigourney Press, Western Spring, IL, 2000.

http://www.paul_smith.doctors.org.uk/links.htm.

http://entomology.unl.edu/history_bug/civilwar/gallnippers.htm

3

Simple Remedies of the Civil War Era

It is a well known fact that medical practices of the mid 19th century, as compared to those of our own age, were indeed primitive. Along with the prescriptions of the physicians of that time period there were numerous common or "folk" remedies that were widely used. These remedies sometimes were passed from mother to child and became part of family medical practices. In more literate families the purchase of an almanac or housewife's guidebook often provided some compilation of generally accepted home interventions for common illnesses. What follows is a brief summation of some of these prototypical home remedies. These homilies are drawn from a fascinating little book entitled *The American Frugal Housewife*.

Written by a woman who was simply recorded as Mrs. Child, *The American Frugal Housewife* was marketed as a compilation of suggestions for homemakers. Published in 1833 this guidebook was in circulation during the time leading up to the Civil War. *The Frugal Housewife* was "dedicated to those who are not ashamed of economy" and could be used as a recipe for any number of household activities. Among the many topics covered by Mrs. Child was the subject of illnesses and their treatments. Listed below are some bullet statements drawn from Mrs. Child's nostrums.

- Cotton wool, wet with sweet oil and paregoric, relieves the earache very soon.

- A good quantity of old cheese is the best thing to eat when distressed by eating too much fruit, or oppressed with any kind of food.
- Honey and milk is very good for worms.
- For a sudden attack of quincy or croup, bathe the neck with bear's grease, and pour it down the throat.
- Equal parts of camphor, spirits of wine, and hatshorn, well mixed, and rubbed upon the throat, is said to be good for the croup.
- Cotton wool and oil are the best things for a burn.
- A poultice of wheat bran, or rye bran, and vinegar, very soon takes down the inflammation occasioned by a sprain.
- In case of any scratch, or wound, from which the lock-jaw is apprehended, bathe the injured part freely with lye or pearl-ash and water.
- A rind of pork bound upon a wound occasioned by a needle, pin, or nail, prevents lock-jaw.
- Spirits of turpentine is good to prevent lock-jaw.
- If you happen to cut yourself while cooking, bind on some fine salt: molasses is also good.
- Flour boiled thoroughly in milk, so as to make quite a thick porridge, is good in cases of dysentery.
- Black or green tea, steeped in boiling milk, seasoned with nutmeg, and best of loaf sugar, is excellent for dysentery.
- Flannel wet with brandy, powdered with Cayenne pepper, and laid upon the bowels, affords great relief in cases of extreme dysentery distress.
- Whortleberries, commonly called huckleberries, dried, are a useful medicine for children. Made into tea, and sweetened with molasses, they are very beneficial, when the digestive system is in a restricted state, and the digestive powers out of order.
- Blackberries are extremely useful in cases of dysentery. To eat the berries is very healthy; tea made of the leaves

and roots is very beneficial; and syrup made of the berries is still better. Blackberries have sometimes effected a cure when physicians despaired.
- Loaf sugar and brandy relieves a sore throat; when very bad, it is good to inhale the steam of scalding hot vinegar through the tube of a tunnel.
- A stocking bound on warm from the foot, at night, is good for a sore throat.
- An ointment made from the common ground-worms, which boys dig to bait fishes, rubbed on the hand, is said to be excellent, when the sinews are drawn up by any disease or accident.
- If a wound bleeds very fast, and there is no physician at hand, cover it with the scrapings of sole-leather, scraped like coarse lint.
- Balm-of-Gilead buds bottled up in N. E. rum, make the best cure in the world for fresh cuts and wounds. Every family should have a bottle of it.
- Half a spoonful of citric acid, (which may always be bought of the apothecaries) stirred in half a tumbler of water, is for the head-ache.
- Boiled potatoes are said to cleanse the hands as well as common soap.
- Water-gruel, with three or four onions simmered in it, prepared with a lump of butter, pepper, and salt, eaten just before one goes to bed, is said to be a cure for a hoarse cold.
- Nothing is so good to take down swellings, as a soft poultice of stewed white beans, put on a thin muslin bag, and renewed every hour or two.
- The thin white skin, which comes from suet, is excellent to bind upon the feet for chilblains.
- Always apply diluted laudanum to fresh wounds.
- Burnt alum held in the mouth is good for the canker.
- The common dark-blue violet makes a slimy tea, which is excellent for the canker.

- Tea made from slippery elm is good for the piles, and for humors in the blood.
- An ointment of lard, sulpher, and cream-of-tarter, simmered together, is good for the piles.
- The constant use of malt beer, or malt in any way, is said to be a preservative against fevers.
- Black cherry-root bark, barberry bark, mustard-seed, petty morrel-root, and horseradish, well steeped in cider, are excellent for the jaundice.
- A poultice made of ginger or common chickweed, that grows about one's door in the country, has given great relief to the tooth-ache, when applied frequently to the cheek.
- A spoonful of ashes stirred in cider is good to prevent sickness of the stomach.
- When a blister from a burn breaks it is said to be a good plan to put wheat flour upon the naked flesh.
- Vinegar curds, made by pouring vinegar into warm milk, put on warm and changed pretty frequently, are excellent to subdue inflammation.
- Chalk, wet with hartshorn is a remedy for the sting of a bee.
- Boil castor-oil with an equal quantity of milk, sweeten it with a little sugar, stir it well, and, when cold, give it to children for drink. They will never suspect it is medicine; and will even love the taste of it.
- Whiskey that has had Spanish-flies soaking in it is said to be good for ring-worms.
- It is worthwhile to mention what is best to be done for the bite of a rattlesnake—Cut the flesh out, around the bite, *instantly*; that the poison may not have time to circulate in the blood. If caustic is at hand, put it upon the raw flesh; if not, the next best thing is to fill the wound with salt—renewing it occasionally. Take a dose of sweet oil and spirits of turpentine, to defend the stomach. If the whole limb swells, bathe it in salt and vinegar

freely. It is well to physic the system thoroughly before returning to usual diet.

In looking back at these household remedies one can come away with a clearer understanding of what common folk thought worked as medicinal cures. Each of these prescriptions was applied with some regularity when people were confronted with illness or injury. How well they worked is open to debate but the fact remains that *The American Frugal Housewife* was a publication that had some longevity. Published through twelve editions by 1833 it remained on bookshelves for generations as a well-worn and tattered resource book. The ideas it contained about simple first aid must have had a broad application. Therefore, by looking back at some of these common sense or odd remedies we better grasp what every day people of the Civil War era did when confronted by health concerns.

Source

Mrs. Child, *The American Frugal Housewife*, Chapman Billies, Inc., Sandwich, MA
    1833, ISBN: 0-939218-2

4

Civilians and the Antietam Campaign

In many ways Americans have been fortunate in terms of their exposure to war. Although American history is liberally sprinkled with conflict it has avoided the horrors inflicted on the people of some other lands. While Americans have died on far off Pacific Islands, on European farmland, in Middle Eastern deserts, and all across this vast nation we have been much more blessed than quite a few nations. For example, an American born in the 1920's may well have lived through the Depression, World War Two, the Korean Conflict, the Vietnam & Persian Gulf Wars, and the Cold War. However, there is a high probability that factors of distance, geography, geopolitics, and chance made it improbable that he or she was a military casualty. In contrast, a person living in Moscow would have had to survive the bloody Russian Civil War, Stalin's purges, massive land expropriation, enforced famine, the Nazi onslaught of World War Two, more purges, the Gulag system, general social and economic disorder, and ultimately the impoverishment of modern Russia. In this equation of potential and actual suffering there is simply no comparison. America, despite the tragedy of 9/11, has been generally shielded from the direst effects of total warfare.

It is because American history is somewhat sheltered from the scourges that have affected places like Russia, China, Germany, Serbia, and Vietnam that the American Civil War stands out as such an amazing event. Americans are puzzled by the notion of their nation divided, brother against brother, and armies sweeping across the national landscape. Yet, even people who have read about the Civil War in depth sometimes forget that there were real people involved who experienced actual loss, pain, and anguish because of the conflict. The armies that camped, slept, marched, and fought during those four years of discord were not functioning in a vacuum. The farms they foraged in, the fences they burned, the families they dispossessed, and the homes they despoiled were American ones. While the Civil War was not fought in a manner remotely similar to the ideological conflicts of the twentieth century it did contain elements of brutality operating on a grand scale. Civilians were not generally brutalized or destroyed as in, for example, the Nazi-Soviet War. Still, there were occasions wherein the coming of the armies changes things forever. One prime example of such an alteration of life was Robert E. Lee's Maryland Campaign of 1862 that culminated in the bloodiest single day in American history at the small, and previously sleepy, hamlet of Sharpsburg.

In looking at the Maryland Campaign a great deal of attention has been paid to the lost orders, the capture of Harper's Ferry, the Battle of South Mountain, and the climactic struggle at Antietam. Yet, one element of that series of marches, battles, and eventual Confederate withdrawal which is often overlooked is the impact of those events upon the lives of civilians living in that sector of Maryland. War does not occur isolated from the people who participate in it. It is all too easy to lose track of the simplistic fact that when fighting occurs it is real people who pay the price. During the Maryland Campaign it was the lot of local residents to host events that now can all too simply leach away into the faded pages of history books. Hopefully, by taking a closer look at the feelings, behaviors, and reflections of Maryland civilians we can garner a deeper understanding of what the Civil War meant to those common and uncommon people.

BEFORE THE ARMIES CAME

Western Maryland is still a land of great beauty. Rolling hills, well tended farmer's fields, charming villages, and contrasting landscapes afford the visitor a visual feast. In many ways that part of Maryland remains very similar to how it was in the fall of 1862. In those days General Lee was able to convince his superiors that the time was right to move the Army of Northern Virginia into Union territory. Ample crops and bounteous possibilities for foraging tempted the Confederates. Even more interesting was the widely held notion that Maryland was indeed a state held in the Union against its will. Many Confederate leaders, and even common soldiers, thought that a Confederate invasion would be greeted by the citizenry of Maryland as a liberation. These thoughts often turned to the early war song *Maryland My Maryland* that invited southern troops to free Marylanders from a tyrant's grasp. However, once Confederate troops began to move north in August it quickly became apparent that things were not as anticipated.

The portions of Maryland that became the centerpiece for international attention that fall were marked by sharply divided beliefs. For example, one resident of Sharpsburg later remembered that, "My grandfather Urner believed the sun rose and set in Abraham Lincoln, and my grandmother Floyd just as stoutly maintained that same astronomical tribute applied to Jefferson Davis." (Ernst, 34) In another home tenants on different floors favored opposing sides. These "secessionists" and unionists" maintained a tenuous peace by avoiding any political discussion while womenfolk in the respective families spent their nights anxiously worrying about their sons in uniform in opposing armies. (Ernst, 34)

Tensions among Maryland residents were evident in many of the towns that were to host both Union and Confederate forces that fateful September. One local historian looked back upon that time period and recounted, "No trust could be placed in a friend, no confidence in a guide, and it was well for a man to keep the doors of his mouth from her that lay on his bosom, for the son rose against the father, the daughter-in-law against the mother-in-law, and a man's enemies were often the men of his own house." (Ernst, 22) Such division mirrored the national schism but did so within a much narrower spectrum. It truly must have been a difficult time for many families as long-term neighbors turned away from one another thus reflecting the national divide.

Maryland was a divided land and one that was as ripe for resistance to the Confederate hosts as to welcoming them. Lee seemed to realize this fact better than his superiors. In a September 7th letter to Jefferson Davis Lee noted, " I do not anticipate any general rising of the people on our behalf." Lee hoped that some recruits could be added to his force but he did not expect more than 200 or so men to take up arms and "free" Maryland. (Sears, 93) In this case, as in many others, Lee was a realist. Maryland was not a land that would rise up on its hind legs and shed rivers of blood in a way that places like Missouri did. While there was division it did not result in extremes of behavior that led to the terror of partisan warfare.

GREETINGS

Once the wheels of incursion were set in motion and the forces of Lee's and McClellan's armies were on the march it became an obvious inevitability that the lives of civilians would be affected by that set of realities. Everywhere that the troops went they eventually came across outlying homes, small towns, and crossroad communities. At each of these domiciles or towns residents had to make some fundamental decisions. Would they stay at home despite the fact that armies were coming through? If they abandoned their homes were they taking a greater risk than staying? How should they greet the respective forces that were descending upon their homes? Each of these basic questions was important at an elemental level. Sometimes very little time was available to address each of these interrogatories and lives changed because of the way they were answered.

When Confederate forces entered places such as Frederick, Middletown, Funkstown, and Sharpsburg they received a decidedly mixed reaction. Anticipating a joyous welcome many Rebel soldiers were to be disappointed. Aside from political divisions, fear of Federal retribution, and strong Unionist sentiments one factor that seemed to work against the Confederates was the particularly nasty appearance their men presented. Lee's veterans had already put in a tough campaign season and they were rough around the edges. One Marylander described the southerners in this way:

They were the dirtiest, lousiest, filthiest, piratical-looking cut-throat men
I ever saw. A most ragged, lean, and hungry set of wolves. Yet there was
a dash about them that the Northern men lacked. They rode like circus riders

Many of them were from the far south and spoke a dialect I could scarcely
understand. They were profane beyond belief and talked incessantly.
(Murfin, 92)

Dr. Lewis Steiner, a Frederick native, looked at Stonewall Jackson's men with distaste and recorded this pithy view of that legendary force, "A dirtier, filthier, more unsavory set of human beings never strolled through a town—marching it could not be called without doing violence to the word." (Ernst, 42) A Union woman living in Frederick as well saw the Rebels in this light:

I felt humiliated at the thought that this horde of ragamuffins set our grand army
of the Union at defense. Why, it seems as if a single regiment of our gallant boys
in blue could drive that crew in the river without any trouble. And then, too, I wish
you could see how they behaved—a crowd of boys on a holiday don't seem
happier…Oh! They are so dirty! I don't think the Potomac River could wash them
clean; and ragged!—there is not a scarecrow in the corn-fields that would not scorn
to exchange clothes with them. (Ernst, 42)

Lee's troops took this type of reaction in stride. A drummer boy with the Fifth North Carolina retorted to a detractor who took offense at his shabbiness by calmly stating, "We have a dirty job to do—whipping you Yankees, and you reckon we're going to put on our clean clothes to do it in?" (Ernst, 42) When asked why he was so ragged one witty Rebel replied, "Our mamas always taught us to put on our worst clothes when we go to kill hogs." Another bystander then asked why so many of the men were barefoot and the soldier's reply was "We wore out our shoes running after the Yankees." (Ernst, 75)

The neglected appearance of Rebel soldiers probably was somewhat disconcerting to southern sympathizers. One reporter indicated that the sometimes icy response the Confederates received from potential allies stemmed from the "coldness and even terror with which the Maryland secessionists regarded their ragged and needy liberators." (Commager, 206) However, Marylanders did not uniformly shun the Confederates. William Owen, an officer in the Washington Artillery, wrote, "Every one we meet says he is a 'rebel' and we are most hospitably received wherever we go." Troops in Stonewall Jackson's contingent were greeted by a farmer who responded to a request for permission to burn a few fence rails by saying, "Burn away! That's what fence rails are for when there's no other wood about." (Murfin, 100). In another case a Confederate surgeon reported, "The ladies would have buckets of water at their doors to give to the thirst soldiers as they marched by…One said 'remember a Union lady is giving you water'" This amicable physician went on to declaim that "Maryland is the finest state I have been in." (Sears, 106)

In general, southern soldiers were not impressed with the willingness of the Maryland men to come out and join their force. One Virginian wrote, "This part of Maryland does not welcome us warmly…I have long thought the State is a humbug." (Ernst, 56)
John Stevens of the Fifth Texas put it more pragmatically when he concluded, "The romance had all vanished from their patriotic sentiments, war was now a reality; they had learned that war meant fight and fight meant kill and kill meant to be dead." (Ernst, 58)

Despite the variable greeting the Confederates received they behaved themselves well throughout the campaign. It was the norm for Confederates to pay for everything taken and display courteousness toward the locals. (Bailey, 17) In some cases the payment was in Confederate script that was less than acceptable to businessmen. One example of this was the fate of Mr. A. J. Delashman a leading secessionist in Frederick who fervently welcomed Lee's troops. However, after the Rebels requisitioned his store's full inventory of shoes and boots in exchange for Confederate money he had to "fairly grit his teeth in silence when some of his Union friends congratulated him on the fine business he was doing." (McGrath, 9-10)

For Yankees used to a foul welcome during their campaigning in Virginia traversing the dusty roads in Maryland was a welcome relief. While there was mixed loyalty in Maryland the greatest concentration of secessionist sympathy rested in the Eastern Shore. The Frederick vicinity was strongly pro-Union as was much of the surrounding area. Major John M. Gould captured his joy at being in a northern state again when he wrote in his diary, "The women and young ladies opened their doors and windows to give us bread and butter, meat, apples, peaches, and preserves...I tell you it was cheering to see their pleasant faces, clean, white, and beautiful, after we had been so long in the Virginia wilderness, where the few women have ruined their faces by looking sour." (Sears, 118)

Many Union soldiers were treated to buckets of ice cold water at farmer's gates as well as lemonade. The Fifth Connecticut made a heavenly find when they found one such bucket to be filled with whiskey rather than water. Such generosity moved another Federal officer, Major Thomas W. Hyde of the 7th Maine, to exclaim, "Like the Israelites of old, we looked upon the land, and it was good." (Sears, 118)

In one instance the gratitude of the local women created a situation where second thoughts were called for. A private in the 12th Ohio recalled a time when his regiment was demonstratively greeted:

...the task of driving the rebels was extremely laborious, yet the gallant troops who
accomplished the duty, felt themselves to be more than recompensed in the grateful
demeanor of the citizens, particularly among the females, who were delighted even
to wildness. They caught up and kissed hundreds of dusty, travel-begrimed soldiers,
hugging them as if they were endeared by ties more binding than simple gratitude...
one young lady in the intoxication of joy, jumped up and declared that she could kiss
the whole army. A grizzly old sergeant who overheard her remark, at once proposed
that she start on him. On second thought, however, she declined the proceeding.
(McGrath, 6-7)

When passing through Frederick most Federal units were welcomed with open arms. "There is no question of the loyalty of this part of Maryland," wrote Brigadier General John Gibbon. (Ernst, 59) When General Burnside's troops entered the city they were met with, in the words of one soldier, "Such huzzaing (sic) you never did hear." (Ernst, 62)
American flags were displayed everywhere and people shouted, "We thought you were never coming!" and "This is the happiest hour of our lives!" (Ernst, 62) One Pennsylvania soldier described his unit's greeting in this way:

> Our reception by the people of Frederick City was an ovation.
> They illuminated their houses, the Stars and Stripes were thrown
> to the breeze, patriotic songs were sung, and refreshments were urged
> upon officers and men. General Burnside's passage was blocked up by
> citizens, eager to thank and bless him as their deliverer; ladies crowded
> about and insisted upon kissing his hands, and from the balconies of
> private residences bouquets rained upon him. (Ernst 63)

Still, despite the adulation that was rained upon the boys in blue Maryland remained an alien state to many of them. Some Federal soldiers distrusted the positive greetings and even feared that the mugs of water they were being given might be poisoned. (Ernst, 59) New England troops in particular seem to have viewed the civilians they encountered as backward and untrustworthy. Abner Small of the 16th Maine Volunteers wrote that "There was a lack of womanly delicacy in the feminine chivalry of Maryland…There was a coarseness, an absence of the nicety of manners that we had expected to find…As for the young men, they looked and bore themselves like the greenest rustics, and exhibited a reckless indifference to dress and deportment." (Ernst, 59) A Midwesterner serving with the First Minnesota acknowledged the agricultural results of the area but chided the locals by stating, "The people lacked that thrift and ambition that

Northerners possess to make the most of their resources." (Ernst, 59)

As the Federal soldiers marched along warmly welcomed yet maintaining that brand of bigotry that seems to make people see the superiority of their own home territory when compared to anywhere else they moved toward a historic nexus. These blue clad men were destined to come to grips with their old foes in Lee's army. What lay ahead of them as they trod along was to be the most terrible day of combat American soldiers were ever to endure. They were unaware of this as they drank lemonade and flirted with pretty young girls. Somewhere up ahead lay South Mountain and Sharpsburg. For many of these young veterans those locales also held an appointment with destiny that, ultimately, none of us can escape.

BATTLE

Maryland Civilians living along the pathway of battle in September 1862 could not anticipate what was in store for them. This was an area that had been spared much of war's cruelty. Unlike their relatively nearby neighbors in Virginia there had been no Generals Hunter or Pope to burn their barns. Confederate raiders like John Singleton Mosby or Nathan Bedford Forest did not ride through their farms in lightening war. Instead, these were quiet towns and hamlets that seemed out of the way. One such quaint and seemingly remote town was Sharpsburg.

A rural community that happened to be a hub for several roads, in 1862 Sharpsburg was a single year short of one hundred years old. Founded a dozen years prior to the Revolution the town was named in honor of Maryland's colonial governor, Horatio Sharpe. With approximately 1,300 residents living in brick and frame houses Sharpsburg presented itself as a typical Western Maryland town. Many residents were of German extraction hence names such as Mumma, Otto, Poffenberg, Rohrbach, and Middlekauf. Living on prosperous farms these thrifty "Dutchmen" cared for their property. Fields were evenly tilled, rail fences snaked their way along property lines, and fruit hung heavy in the trees. With both Antietam Creek and the Chesapeake & Ohio Canal nearby one can almost imagine young boys taking a cane pole and some worms to go down to the water to bob for bluegills. Clustered around Main Street this small town gave no evidence of the fact that on September 17 it was to be the stage for an amazing day of death and destruction. (Sears, 185)

Nothing could prepare the citizens of Sharpsburg for what was to come. Those people who heard anything about the earlier battle at South Mountain realized that the armies were massing for a really big fight. Several days before the climactic battle Lee had brought the portions of his army traveling with him into Sharpsburg. This settling in gave the residents an inkling that a confrontation was in the offing. Armed with this knowledge quite a number of locals elected to leave town until the dust settled. Many of these people chose to travel to the nearby caves along the Potomac as well as tunnels near the canal. (Bailey, 66-67) Other residents took to some of the hills in the vicinity and prepared to watch what seemed to be a "big thing". If any of these folks had a true understanding of what war could mean for their neighbors left in town, their homes, or property they might have been more upset. The experience of Henry Wise, whose farm happened to be where part of the South Mountain Battle had occurred would have served as a vibrant lesson.

For Mr. Wise, his return to his farm on September 15 must have been akin to a walk into the "infernal regions". His once peaceful fields were covered with death and devastation. Soldiers, wagons, and ambulances constantly surged along the road that passed by his home. His house and barn had been taken over and put to use as a surgical hospital. Amidst the screaming of men in extreme pain Wise observed burial details digging up parts of his property to inter the dead. A Massachusetts soldier found a dead Rebel and Yankee in Wise's barn who must have killed one another in a hand-to hand fight. (Ernst, 103) Another deceased Confederate straddled a fence on the property, seemingly frozen in the act of scrabbling over the obstacle. Some grim wag had placed a biscuit in the dead man's mouth in an odd twist to the never-ending search of Rebel soldiers for enough to eat. (Ernst, 103) Other Federal soldiers, too tired or too lazy to dig graves tossed Confederate dead into Wise's well. Wise moved to halt the Ohio soldiers who were doing this but eventually relented. Ultimately Wise was paid one dollar per Confederate corpse to allow for this type of burial service. Feeling that his well would never be useable again Wise consented and earned $58.00 for this grisly service. Any resident of Sharpsburg knowing about this tale would have thought twice about any dreams of war's glory. (McGrath, 24-25)

There were a number of families that elected to batten down the hatches and ride out the storm of battle. One such brave hearted clan was the Kretzer family. They owned a large stone house on East Main Street and they felt that their abode could withstand the shock of battle. When artillery shelling started on September 17 the family retreated to the basement where they were joined by some neighbors and their children. The Kretzers had five children and they attempted to make their guests as comfortable as possible. One daughter, Theresa, later remembered, "We carried down some seats, and we made them board benches around, and quite a number of us got up on the potato bunks and the apple scaffolds. We were as comfortable as we could possibly be in a cellar, but it's a wonder we didn't all take our deaths of colds in that damp place." (Ernst, 136) The dampness was particularly hard on Mrs. Henry Ward who had just delivered a baby girl one week previous to the battle. She and her newborn were carried up to the kitchen to give them some relief from the cold and dankness below. However, shortly thereafter a shell struck the home and immersed the kitchen in dust and smoke. Quickly, Mrs. Ward and her infant girl were hustled back to the basement where she declared, "I'd rather take my chances with taking cold and dying, than to be killed with a shell or a canon ball." (Ernst, 136) Later, as the battle raged outside several Confederate soldiers joined the denizens of the basement and rode out the battle there.

Other families taking refuge in their downtown homes also felt the wrath of war. Shells brought trees crashing down and struck many of the town's buildings. One shell struck the linen chest of Aaron Pry and left a hole clean through all of his sheets. Henry Webb, another local resident, felt compelled to watch the shelling through his front door. He stepped away from the spot momentarily and as he started back to his observation post a canon ball from a Napoleon passed directly through the doorway. Another family seeking safety in their cellar had a shell land in an upstairs featherbed setting it ablaze and requiring the family to quickly become a bucket brigade. (Ernst, 136)

Confederate soldiers moving through the town came across one elderly gentleman sitting on his back porch with his wife. This senior couple seemed eminently calm and rebuffed any suggestions from the Rebels that they take refuge. The old man responded to these warnings by saying "that they had no place to go, that this had been their home all their lives…and that they would rather die here than to leave it; he had not done the Rebels any harm…that they should not come and drive him out of his house; no they would not go; they intended to stay. 'Do we not?' he added appealing to his aged spouse, who only answered by an emphatic nod." (Ernst, 139-140) As there were no aged casualties reported after the battle one could only assume that these determined people made it through the battle all right.

A large group of women and children sought refuge in a stone farmhouse on the Nicodemus property. Unfortunately, this house was under heavy bombardment that sent some of the pilgrims into motion attempting to flee it. Confederate cavalryman William Blackford saw the door of the house fly open and terrified women rush out "like a flock of birds…hair streaming in the wind and children of all ages stretched out behind." (Sears, 202) The women and children stumbled across the field toward the Confederate lines and occasionally one of them would fall. When this happened "the rest thought it was the result of a canon shot and ran the faster." (Sears, 202) Blackford and several other Rebel horsemen rode out to assist the poor women and children while Federal gunners decently held their fire during the rescue. No one was hurt in this episode but the memories of all parities involved must have been engraved with those events.

In another instance the Roulette family also remained on their farm as the clash of battle swirled all around them. At one point the elder Roulette stepped out of his cellar in order to see what was happening. When he noticed the blue clad soldiers of the 14th Connecticut escorting some Confederate prisoners away from his springhouse he could contain his emotions no longer. Roulette went wild with apparent joy and screamed "Give it to 'em!" He then told the Connecticut lads to "Drive 'em! Take anything on my place only drive 'em!" Roulette then ran rearwards overcome by emotion. (Priest, 141)

Back at the Kretzer home the family, neighbors, and Rebels housed in the basement continued to experience the bombardment. The house was built in such a way that a spring flowed through the basement thus alleviating any need to go out for water. However, whenever a shell struck the sturdy home a cacophony of sounds would break out. One woman ensconced in the basement later recalled, "Everytime (sic) the firing began extra hard, the babies would cry and the dogs would bark, and some of the aged old men would break out in prayer." (Bailey, 135) Although the home was struck a number of times its residents took no casualties.

Some residents chose to bring refreshments to the men on the battlefield. Many years after the battle Martin L. Moats told his daughter that he had "waded through blood up to his shoetops" to bring water and food to the wounded. (Ernst, 145) In another example of a local resident acting out the role of Good Samaritan canoneers of Captain William Graham's First US Battery were stunned to see a civilian ride up to their position in a carriage. The artillerists had suffered with heavy losses in their position near the Sunken Road and they were surprised to see a non-combatant in that hot spot. The man, who never identified himself, stepped out of his two-horse carriage and began to hand out ham and biscuits to the gunners. Having fed the men he helped load several wounded Federals into his rig. As he did so he leaned down and examined a slight wound to one of his horses. Satisfying himself that his horse was all right, the man saw to the wounded and departed. (Catton, 297-198)

In earlier histories of the Antietam Battle this good-hearted man was unidentified.
However, we now know he was Martin Eakle, a miller from nearby Keedysville.
Eakle apparently made a second visit to Captain Graham's battery as well as several more mercy trips to different spots on the battlefield. Although one of his horses was wounded, Martin Eakle made it through his missions of mercy unscathed. (Ernst, 145-146)

As the men in blue and gray continued to struggle throughout that long day the residents of Sharpsburg who remained in town held their collective breath. It is interesting to try to imagine the thoughts that passed through the minds of those besieged people as the hours slowly passed. Occasionally one of them would pop up or outside to ascertain the course the battle

was taking. Catching a glimpse of the conflagration could not have provided much clarity but it may have assuaged their fears to some extent. One young girl, a unionist at heart, went up to her home's attic to take a look at the events at hand. Her memory of that glimpse of history stirred enough emotion to allow her to later set it down on paper, "On all the distant hills around were the blue uniforms and shining bayonets of our men, and I thought it was the prettiest sight I ever saw in my life."
(Sears, 311) Interestingly, what was the prettiest sight in the eyes of one young girl may well have been the last moment of many a man's life.

      Long though September 17 must have seemed to the people in or around Sharpsburg it did eventually draw to a close. As combat sputtered out and the Battle of Antietam drew to a close each person left hail and hearty despite the carnage of the day must have heaved a sigh of relief. To have made it through that epic battle might seem amazing to us sitting in comfort as we read. At that time, with death and destruction all around, it may have seemed miraculous to the people who actually lived through it. Still, the end of combat brought a new set of challenges to the civilians of this region. In some ways, what followed the battle was even more terrible and disturbing than the armed aggression itself. As a precursor of this grim reality one family emerged from their home and journeyed out onto the battlefield that had once been their farm. They brought food, baskets of supplies, and quilts for the wounded. One of the daughters in the family later recounted:

There was a red haze on the sunset…the brick of the church was red, and as far as
  I could see were suffering crying, or dead men…red, red, red. It was a red stew.
  I can remember my mother laboring with three baskets and I holding her pettiskirts…
    pulling a large bundle along the ground…and all of us, my brothers and sisters,
      too afraid to cry. (Ernst, 154)

AFTERMATH

As the morning of September 18 dawned and the hours of the "day after" lengthened the citizens of Sharpsburg came out of their homes to gaze upon what the two armies had wrought. Seemingly everywhere they looked they were confronted with terrible scenes of carnage and destruction. Smashed artillery pieces, abandoned muskets, dead horses, wounded men, and thousands of corpses greeted these stunned people. One young girl returning with her family from their hiding place in the nearby Killiansburg Cave years later told her own grandchildren of having to step over corpses as they walked back to their home. (Ernst157) As the Grice family came home they too were confronted by bodies with hordes of flies hovering around them. A young girl in that family carefully led her pony, Logan, back to his homestead. She described her experience in this way, "the dead lay so thick that old Logan would be very careful not to step on any of the dead." While the young Grice girl's father appeared to be nearly overcome by these sights her mother "a thoroughbred Irish woman of pluck, would shake father and cause him to recover, and make fun of him and tell him to go back on the horse and continue the trip" (Ernst 157)

There were 17,000 wounded men after the battle. While the rapidly departing Confederates took many of them with them Sharpsburg became, in the words of one reporter, "one vast hospital." (Bailey, 109) Veteran soldiers who looked at the battle's wreckage were taken aback. One Union Lieutenant stated, "I hope that I may never see such a sight again. The dead were thicker here than I had seen them anywhere else." (Bedwell, 92) Henry Kyd Douglas, A Marylander and a member of Stonewall Jackson's staff, described the Antietam Battlefield thusly:

It was a dreadful scene. The dead and dying lay thick on the field like harvest
sheaths. The pitiable cries for water and pleas for help were much more
horrible to listen to than the deadliest sounds of battle. Silent were the dead
and motionless, but here and there were raised stiff arms. Heads made a last
effort to raise themselves from the ground. Prayers were mingled with oaths,

and midnight hid all distinction between blue and gray. (Bedwell, 92)

If trained and hardened soldiers viewed Antietam in this way what could possibly have prepared the civilian population to cope with this monumental level of suffering? When Henry Piper guided his family home they found wounded soldiers lying on the floor of every room in the house. The Reilly family came home to find their house ransacked, two dead soldiers in their yard, and three more in the house. The Mummas returned to a home that had been burned down to prevent its use as a site for snipers or observation. While it was the only house deliberately destroyed during the battle this fact most have given little solace to the homeless family. Emory Smith, residing downtown on Main Street, came home to a truly gruesome sight. One Confederate by the family well and two inside in the kitchen had apparently been killed when an artillery shell struck the home. While the dead man in the yard was reasonably intact the men inside had been torn to pieces. Oddly, one shattered man still gripped a bunch of onions in his bloody hand. (Ernst, 157-159)

Everywhere the story seemed to be the same. Soldiers after the battle had swept through the homes and farms looking for something to eat or drink. Devastation both due to battle and looting was widespread. Places like the Dunker Church, Nicodemus farm, and the Poffenberg homestead became hospitals overcrowded by a sea of wounded men. In these places one southern journalist reported, "There was a smell of death in the air, and the laboring surgeons are literally covered from head to foot with the blood of the sufferers." (Ernst, 161) Ada Mumma, a young girl, returned to her home where she found her grandparents attempting to assist the medical staff at work in their residence. She later recalled, "I could not sleep. I could hear those poor men calling for 'water…for God's sake, give me a drop of water.'" Brigadier General Isaac Rodman remained in the Mumma home until his death in November. A hired man working for the family remembered that Rodman's infected wounds "became so offensive…we were obliged to set the dining table on the porch, as it was impossible to partake of food in the house." (Ernst, 161)

The Miller family came back to a farm that, prior to the battle, was ripe for the fall harvest. Afterwards, as General

Hooker stated, in the Miller's cornfield, "Every stalk of corn in the northern and greater part of the field was cut as closely as could have been done with a knife, and the slain lay in rows precisely as they stood in their ranks a few moments before." (Bedwell, 93) On Margaret and William Roulette's farm 700 men lay dead in the Bloody Lane each of whom was destined to be buried on their property. (Ernst, 163)

On the Mumma place not only were there human bodies to deal with but numerous horses as well. Mr. Mumma dragged fifty-five horses from his farm to the East Woods where he burned them. One witness remembered the smell of burning horseflesh that seemed to linger forever, "The stench was sickening...We couldn't eat a good meal, and we had to shut the house as tight as we could of a night to keep out the odor. We couldn't stand it, and the first thing in the morning when I rolled out of bed I'd have to take a drink of whiskey. If I didn't I'd throw up before I got all my clothes on." (Ernst, 165)

Strangely, there were people who voluntarily chose to come to see the "sights" at Antietam. Shortly after the final shots were fired and Lee's retreat tourists of a sort came out to Sharpsburg. Scores of sightseers found a way to get out to the battlefield. John Koogle recorded his curiosity trip to Antietam in his diary where he wrote, "Was to the Battle Field of Antietam to-day...The road was so full of men and wagons that we could hardly travel. We saw plenty of wounded and dead, a most lamentable sight, the worst I ever beheld." (Ernst, 167) Expressing his incredulity in a letter home one Federal officer described these seemingly ghoulish visitors in this way, "Hundreds of tourists were scattered over the field, eagerly searching for souvenirs in the shape of cannon, balls, guns, bayonets, sword, canteens, etc." (Ernst, 167) People, to this day, seek out the macabre. Perhaps that was what was operating in September of 1862?

For every strange tourist to the battlefield there were any number of local people who did everything to succor the maimed. One family that was visiting a hospital to offer comfort to the men was deeply moved by their experience. During their visit, which included the family's small son and their host, a physician, the family encountered one particular soldier, "As we were going through the wards a man with an amputated leg called the little boy to him and took him by the hand. A flood of tears rolled down his sunburnt face... I was then vividly impressed with the fact that every soldier in this vast army however humble has an invisible but strong cord reaching away back to his loved ones at home." (Ernst, 173-174)

The cords that those sensitive folks spoke of did exist and drew another group of visitors to the region. For each man in hospital there was a family waiting for word of his fate. Families hosting these injured men often felt compelled to assist in getting word back to their charge's loved ones. Additionally, many family members came to Sharpsburg, Frederick, and other near at hand towns that were hosting the wounded. Sometimes these visitors came looking for a missing loved one. Mr. Allen Sparrow of Sharpsburg remembered one family from Massachusetts who came in search of their beloved son. These people paid Sparrow ten dollars to hire him to guide them across the Antietam field in search of the lad. Eventually the son was found in a battlefield grave, "partly buried, one foot sticking out". Sparrow remembered that he "did not want to witness such a seen (sic) again." (Ernst, 174)

The concept of MIA's is not a new one. In an age when battlefield identification was cursory at best there were literally thousands of families who had no idea what had happened to their child, husband, father, or brother at Antietam. Some families placed advertisements in local papers while others used posted handbills in an effort to gain information about their missing loved one. One such handbill that was nailed up in Sharpsburg contained the following information (Bailey, 151):

<u>INFORMATION WANTED</u>
<u>Of Orderly Sergeant</u>
RICHARD A. SANDERS
Co. F., 106th PENNSYLVANIA VOLUNTEERS
He was seriously wounded in the battle of Sharps-
Burg, and was last seen in an Ambulance. Should any
Person discover a Grave marked as above he will con-
fer a favor by writing to
Wm. Frontz,
<u>**Hughesville, Lycoming Co., Pa.**</u>

**Printed by F. H. Irwin, Odd Fellow Office Boonsboro, where all kinds
of Printing is done**

There is no real way to know how effective such postings were. What can be counted upon is that those families who came to Maryland in search of a missing person often met with sadness. One host remembered a widow who "threw herself prostrate upon her husband's grave and wept bitter tears o agony." (Ernst, 176) In another instance a woman shared a tragic story:

>Among the many who came to visit the Battlefield was a young wife whose
frantic grief I can never forget. She came hurriedly as soon as she knew her
husband was in the battle only to find him dead and buried two days before her
arrival. Unwilling to believe the facts that strangers told her—how in the early
morning they had laid him beside his comrades in the orchard—she still insisted
upon seeing him. Accompanying some friends to the spot she could not wait the
slow process of removing the body but in her agonizing grief, clutched the earth
by handfuls where it lay upon the quiet sleeper's form. And when at length the
slight covering was removed and the blanket thrown from off the face, she needed
but one glance to assure her that it was all too true. Then passive and quiet beneath
the stern reality of this crushing sorrow she came back to the room in our house.
(Ernst, 176)

Pain and suffering appeared to be everywhere. Where once a quiet country lane passed along through the fields women and children could now behold, "the wagons bringing the wounded to Frederick for us to look after…There was so much blood dripping out of the back of the wagons and falling on the dirt road that eventually the mud became red as the wagon wheels ploughed through the streets." (Ernst, 177) Fields that for years had been carefully tilled became places where it "was common to see human bones lying loose in gutters and fence corners for several years." (Ernst, 185)

One resident wrote, "frequently hogs would be seen with limbs in their mouths." (Ernst, 185)

      These physical engravings of the battle must have plagued the memories of adults and children alike for years if not the rest of their lives. In 1934 a historian visited the Poffenberger family. As part of the researcher's tour of that historic site "The lady…took me into the parlor, raised the curtains, and turning up the corner of the large rug which covered the floor, showed me a big blood stain which told the story of some poor sufferer who lay there after the battle. 'I have washed and scrubbed that spot again and again until I have thought I had got it all out' she said, 'but as soon as the floor dried the spot would appear as plane as ever'" (Ernst, 235) In a sense that single blood stain is representative of many physical and mental scars that plagued Marylanders for decades.

      Along with the horrific vestiges of the battle Sharpsburg residents had to beware of other dangers. Shells that had failed to explode littered the landscape. Each of these projectiles represented an unknown package of lethal possibilities. An article in a local paper understated this dangerous situation by reporting, "Many unexploded shells have also buried themselves beneath the surface, and if these should come in violent contact with the plow cutter they would certainly explode, and render plowing a very unsafe work in such soil." (McGrath, 72) For children these relics of the battlefield were often too tempting to pass over.

      Young William McDermot found a shell, took it home, placed it on the stove, and was blinded and lost an arm in the resulting explosion. George Reilly found a shell and set fire to it only to have it explode and nearly kill two passersby. Another youngtser, Alvah Shuford was killed by a shell he has handling. Sadly, his parents, Reverend Shuford and his wife, had already lost three younger children to diphtheria. All in all, in a way akin to the many landmines left scattered about in modern warfare, the unexploded shells continued to increase the casualty toll of the Antietam Battle for months afterwards. (Ernst, 186)

After the battle even nature itself seemed different to the civilian population. The crash of battle was followed by an odd silence. After a while residents began to realize that wildlife commonly seen before the battle were strangely absent after it. It is easy to understand why many animals would avoid a location that had been so disturbed and devastated. Yet, it was another factor of change that startled the people. A hired man working on the Nicodemus farm remembered this change in the following way:

> Another queer thing was the silence after the battle. You couldn't hear a dog
> bark nowhere, you couldn't hear no birds whistle or no crows caw. There wa'n't
> no birds around till the next spring. We didn't even see a buzzard with all that
> stench. The rabbits had run off, but there was a few around that winter—not many.
> The farmers didn't have no chickens to crow. Our'n didn't commence for six months.
> When night come I was so lonesome that I didn't know what lonesome was before.
> It was a curious silent world. (McGrath, 71)

CONCLUSION

In the years after Antietam the Confederacy was slowly and painfully ground into the dust. Soldiers who survived the war began to trickle back to their homes across the land. In the areas of Maryland impacted by Lee's campaign men also came back to their families. Often these veterans were strikingly altered by the war. Daniel Mowen of the Seventh Maryland returned to his loved ones, "not the hale, hearty young man of three years previous, knowing nothing of pains and aches...but with hollow cheeks, sunken eyes, a weak, gaunt creature, like the flickering of a candle, ready to go out." (Ernst, 232) Women and children who greeted these spiritually and physically wounded soldiers also had been changed. They had seen war close up and they knew the images of pain and anguish that leered at you during and after a battle.

      Civilians living in the parts of Maryland touched by the 1862 campaign held a virtually unique place among Union residents. Save for Gettysburg, no other people in the northern states could compare their first-hand experience of suffering to the people of Sharpsburg. When all the dust of battle had settled some people pondered about the war years and wondered what it all had really been about. Jacob McGraw looked back at that tumultuous time and said, "I favored the South early in the war, but later I didn't care which side won if only they put a stop to the fighting." (Ernst, 241) In a very real sense Mr. McGraw's admission that once people gained a realistic understanding of war's great human cost they could only wish for its cessation is a vital one. In that statement and belief lies a lesson as yet to be learned by mankind. We can learn a great deal about heroism, fortitude, and strength by studying the experiences of civilians who survived the events of the Antietam Campaign. We can also gain a deeper understanding of the true nature of man's cruelty to one another. Herein lies a lesson not to be forgotten for war means killing and you cannot refine it.

SOURCES

Bailey, Ronald H. (1985) *The Bloodiest Day: The Battle of Antietam*. Alexandria,
   Time-Life Books.

Bedwell, Randall (ed.) (1999) *Brink Of Destruction: A Quotable History Of*
   The Civil War. Nashville, Cumberland House Publishing, Inc.

Catton, Bruce (1962) *Glory Road*. New York, Doubleday.

Commager, Henry Steele (ed.) (!973) *The Blue And The Gray: Volume One.*
   Indianapolis, Bobbs & Merrill Company, Inc.

Ernst, Kathleen A. (1999) *Too Afraid to Cry: Maryland Civilians In The*
   Antietam Campaign. Mechanicsburg, Stackpole Books.

McGrath, Thomas A. (1997) *Maryland September: True Stories from the*
   Antietam Campaign. Gettysburg, Thomas Publications.

Priest, John Michael (1989) *Antietam: The Soldier's Battle.*
   London, Oxford University Press.

Murfin, James W. (1965) *The Gleam Of Bayonets.* New York, Curtis.

Sears, Stephen (1983) *Landscape Turned Red.* New York, Warner Books.

5

Agnes Lee: A Child of Good Fortune

In our own age, as well as that of our Civil War predecessors, the reading of another person's diary would be considered a gross violation of privacy. Diaries are designed as avenues of expression for individuals who wish to consign their innermost thoughts, hopes, and dreams to a trusted and secret "friend." That "friend" takes the form of their diary. The act of sitting down to open up your very soul to the printed page is an act of expression that sometimes allows a cautious or shy person to put down in print what they could, perhaps, never say aloud. To intrude into such a vehicle of purgation is in bad taste. Yet, from a historical perspective, the perusing of diaries and other forms of personal correspondence is one of the best ways to gain insights into the lives of people of distant eras.

In *Growing Up in the 1850's* readers are afforded a unique opportunity to learn about the personality of Agnes Lee. The fifth-borne child of Mary and Robert E. Lee, Agnes was only eleven years old when she took pen in hand and began to maintain a diary. The entries edited and compiled in this publication encompass years that took Agnes from girlhood to the cusp of young womanhood. Edited with care by Agnes' own niece, this book allows readers to take a look behind the scenes into not only the aspirations of one southern girl but also the inner workings of the Lee family. Also included are a series of family letters written by Agnes and her family. Through these diary entries and familial correspondences readers will be better able to grasp the way in which one prominent southern family operated. In addition, the humble writings of young Agnes Lee reveal a world of growth and development that bespeaks the eternal questioning that make up part and parcel of growing up in any age.

Agnes' diary begins with the rather mundane world of a young schoolgirl. Agnes notes early on in her writing that, "I must keep a journal it will improve my "style." At any rate it will be amusing in after years to know what I did and felt when I was young." (4) However, in even her early journal entries readers will come across certain themes that are particularly relevant to enhancing an understanding of mid-19th century life. Topics such as religion, death, and illness make up a large part of what Agnes writes about. This may seem unusual to the contemporary reader but it must be remembered that each of those subjects were often contemplated in an age where fatal disease, childhood mortality, and strength of religiosity were common.

     At the age of twelve Agnes was to write about the death of her beloved maternal grandmother at Arlington. That memory was a stark one for her and she expressed it in the pages of her diary, "O that funeral, it seemed as if we could not let her be shut up in the dark earth. Though I know it was only her body, her angel spirit may have been hovering above us, wanting to comfort her poor children. It is so beautiful to look through the green trees at the blue sky above & think she may be there." (13-14) Death, for Agnes and people of her time period, was a source of grief but also a pathway to salvation. Religious faith was much more a part of everyday life and had to be used as a tool for coping with grief at a time of loss. In Agnes' diary this theme comes up time and again and affords us a glimpse of the way in which Americans of that age saw life and death.

     The theme of religion permeates Agnes' writings. At one point young Agnes recounts a sermon she heard and notes, "I remember almost every word of it! It was an invitation to come to Christ. I solemnly determined to dedicate myself to God & I have tried, but Oh! I don't think I have improved in the least there is so much to try me. I do wish I was a Christian! But it is hard to be one." (18) This combination of religious faith and self-doubt runs throughout Agnes' diary and letters. It appears that, for Agnes, the goal of being a good Christian was one she both yearned to achieve but doubted her capacity. At sixteen Agnes continued to ruminate on this battle for salvation:

     I have often determined to try to be a Christian, I have thought I had asked for
     Aid from Above, but in a day everything good has vanished. Sometimes the
     awful thought comes to me, I am one of those who are never to be good—one

of the doomed. (79)

Eventually, Agnes Lee became confident both in her faith and her ability to be deserving of it. Yet, it is striking that a girl ensconced in a loving family and free from any material want could question so deeply her personal worth and salvation. Perhaps the pondering of such theological questions may seem alien to modern readers but they are representative of the spiritual age in which Agnes grew up.

Another interesting aspect of Agnes Lee's writings is the way in which the Lee family functioned. Agnes' father appears in the diary as the Superintendent of West Point or, more commonly, away from home on other assignments. Agnes' mother, Mary, is loving but wrapped up in her own physical pain due to nagging illness. Thus, Agnes spends much of her time communing with her siblings or, more commonly, alone. As a result, Agnes comes across as an introspective and diffident youngster who yearns for deeper meaning to life that that which can superficially be appreciated. Often self-critical to a fault, Agnes Lee seemed to lack confidence in her own value as a contributing member of society.

On New Year's Eve, 1854, young Agnes wrote the following self-criticism, "The last day of 1854! What reflections it brings with it. How much of it I employed well—how much wasted? I am afraid if I answer truly far *far* the greater portion has been misspent or wasted." (43) While the self-doubt of teenagers is a truism one comes away from Agnes' reflections wondering what type of family life or personality could have created so little confidence and resilience in a child?

Agnes was also a very shy person who preferred spending time with her family to the active social life expected of one of the first families of Virginia. On several occasions in her diary Agnes Lee bemoans the necessities of social life. When her father was transferred to West Point as commandant the Lee's were called upon to entertain a wide array of people. At one point Agnes records her insecurities in those social settings, "I have met a great many cadets, but it frightens me so, I am so dreadfully diffident." (27-28) Later on in her entries Agnes also describes some of the pressure she felt in the social gatherings hosted by her family and their acquaintances, "I feel differently too; young as I am I must sit & talk & walk as a young lady and be constantly greeted with ladies do this & that & think so all as if I was twenty but enough of this." (31)

While residing in Staunton Agnes noted, "If anyone hereafter should see what I have here written, they must not judge me too harshly, if they could only feel as I feel sometimes--& now they would pity me." (79) Are these the meanderings of an emotional schoolgirl or, rather, was Agnes Lee part of a family that, despite its spiritual and loving façade, was unable to understand her? Sadly, that question cannot be answered by reading the journal entries of Agnes as a child and teen. Additionally, Agnes was not destined to live a long life. She died in 1873 at the age of thirty-two. Unwed and childless, Agnes Lee was unable to pass on her legacy to future generations in any way short of her published journal. Yet, readers who wish to understand more about the Lee family, growing up in the pre-war years, and Agnes Lee, herself, would do well to peruse these entries. This is not a dramatic book but it is one that amplifies the experiences of one young girl who happened to be related to a family that was destined to accrue both great fame and great responsibility.

Source

Mary Custis Lee deButts (Ed.). *Growing Up in the 1850's: The Journal of Agnes Lee.*
 Chapel Hill, NC: The University of North Carolina Press, 1998.

6

Tillie Pierce: A Union Girl at Gettysburg

Twenty-five years after the Battle of Gettysburg had been fought in and around that Pennsylvania college town one woman reflected back upon her experiences on those July day, "The horrors of war are fully known only to those who have seen and heard them. It was my lot to see and hear only part, but it was sufficient." (Alleman 13) By that time in 1888, at age forty, Tillie Pierce Alleman could clearly remember the clash of battle that changed not only her life but also the course of national history. Her story of those wartime experiences stands out as one of the more enlightening of the eighty or so civilian accounts of that battle. As such, it provides some valuable insights not only into Tillie Pierce's saga, but the lot of noncombatants caught in the maelstrom of the Civil War.

In 1863 Tillie Pierce was fifteen years old. She was part of a family that included her parents, four siblings, and herself. Two of Tillie's brothers were serving in the Union army. One of those two brothers was in the 1st Pennsylvania Reserve and would take part in fighting in his hometown. Tillie was attending the Young Ladies Seminary, a private school located at the corner of High & Washington Streets. Tillie's life prior to the battle seemed to have been one of pleasant kinship and study. Looking back over her memories of her home and surrounding countryside Tillie recalled, "Little did I think that those lovely valleys, teeming with verdure and the rich harvest, would soon be strewn with the distorted and mangled bodies of American brothers; making a rich ingathering for the grim monster Death; that across that peaceful lane would charge the brave and daring "Louisiana Tigers", thirsting for their brother's blood, but soon to be hurled back filling the space over which they advanced with their shattered and dead bodies." (12-13)

PRELUDE TO BATTLE

Prior to July first, 1863, Tillie and her Gettysburg neighbors had been caught up in the fearful business of preparing for a potential Rebel onslaught. In the weeks leading up to the battle Tillie heard frequent accounts, rumors, and warnings about possible Confederate advances into Gettysburg. Faced with such an invasion the citizens of Gettysburg were called upon to form a citizen's guard to protect the town. Tillie remembered these men as "armed to the teeth" with instruments the likes of "rusty guns and swords, pitchforks, shovels, and pickaxes." (18)

Although this home guard was, fortunately, not called upon to serve the implication to other residents that a Rebel force might descend upon their town was a particularly unpleasant notion. One group of Gettysburg citizenry that Tillie remembers as having a special fear of a Confederate incursion was the sizeable population of Blacks who resided in town. Living at that time primarily in southwestern part of town, Black families had a fairly long history of having an established community within Gettysburg proper. The thought of a Southern army coming to Gettysburg had an especially terrifying connotation for African-Americans. During the Gettysburg Campaign, General Lee's men did press into servitude African-Americans they encountered. Thus, Blacks in Gettysburg had a very real reason to fear for their freedom. Therefore, most African-American residents of Gettysburg chose to refugee out of the town prior to the battle.

Tillie described the exodus from town of her "colored" neighbors in the following manner, "I can see them yet; men and women with bundles as large as old-fashioned feather ticks slung across their backs, almost bearing them to the ground. Children also, carrying their bundles, and striving in vain to keep up with their seniors. The greatest consternation was depicted on all of their countenances as they hurried along; crowding, and running against each other in their confusion; children stumbling, falling, and crying." (19-20)

The departure of the majority of the African-American population was a wise move on those poor people's part as Rebel raiders did enter Gettysburg several days prior to the battle. Tillie's first impression of these Confederate soldiers left

something to be desired, "What a horrible sight! There they were, human beings! Clad almost in rags, covered with dust, riding wildly, pell-mell down the hill toward our home! Shouting, yelling most unearthly, cursing, brandishing their revolvers, and firing right and left."
(22) The Confederates "wanted horses, clothing, anything and almost everything they could conveniently carry away." (22) Ultimately, the Rebels levied a "tax" upon the town that included a vast array of supplies and clothing as well as a fee of $5,000. When the town fathers indicated that their ability to meet these demands was limited the Confederates satisfied themselves with merely foraging for whatever they could find. (22-23)

      The Rebels visited Tillie's home as well. Once there, the invaders took foodstuffs as well as Tillie's father's horse. When Mr. and Mrs. Pierce pleaded their case they were dismissed by the Confederates. Mr. Pierce was described by one Rebel as a "black abolitionist" and the fact that the two Pierce boys were in Federal service was not appreciated by the Rebels. Interestingly, Tillie blamed one of her neighbors for sharing
these damming facts about her family with the Rebels. A young woman, who lived in town, unnamed in the book but described via her relations, was felt by Tillie to have spilled the beans to the Confederates. That person, Jenny Wade, was eventually to be the sole civilian killed during the battle. (26)

      Finally, after a fair share of foraging, the Confederates abandoned Gettysburg. As a final act of war the Confederates attempted to disable the railroad that ran through the town:

> That evening when these raiders were leaving, they ran all the cars that
> were about, out to the railroad bridge east of town, set the bridge and cars
> on fire and destroyed the track. (28)

      The departure of the Confederate cavalrymen was followed by the arrival of Union troops on Tuesday, June 30th. At that time the men of General Buford's force rode into Gettysburg. Tillie felt a great sense of relief to see the boys in blue. She later wrote, "I had never seen so many soldiers at one time. They were

Union soldiers and that was enough for me, for I then knew we had protection, and I felt they were our dearest friends..." (28)

Tillie and a crowd of "us girls" stood on the corner of High and Washington Streets and attempted to serenade the troops with patriotic songs inclusive of *Rally Round the Flag*. Unfortunately, since some of the girls did not know all the words to this popular tune they were left to primarily repeating the chorus. Although limited in their repertoire the efforts of the girls were apparently appreciated by the men as, "Their countenances brightened and we received their thanks and cheers." (29)

With the coming of Buford's men the day prior to the battle passed. For each of these Union soldiers, as well as their gray and butternut clad foemen, this may have been their last day of life. The future was unclear for these men as it was for the people of Gettysburg. On that night Tillie pondered the uncertainties of life and recorded these thoughts, "Thus in the midst of great excitement and solicitude the day passed. As we lay down for the night, little did we think what the morrow would bring." (30)

FIRST DAY

On July first Tillie rose early as, "It was impossible to become drowsy with the events of the previous day uppermost in our minds. We were prompt enough at breakfast that morning." (33) Tillie and her sister chose to dedicate themselves to preparing bouquets of flowers for the Union soldiers. Their intention was to throw them to passing troops as tokens of their support and regard. Shortly after breakfast Tillie and her sister went downtown to greet the Federal men.

Once downtown Tillie saw the advancing men of the Union force. In Tillie's minds eye those men stood out as the defenders not only of her home but her nation as well. Later she wrote, "First came a long line of cavalry, then wagon after wagon passed for quite awhile. Again we sang patriotic songs as they moved along. Some of these wagons were filled with stretchers and other articles; in others we noticed soldiers reclining, who were doubtless in some way disabled." (33-34)

Shortly after nine o'clock Tillie first heard the sounds of battle. Her first impressions of what was to become the largest battle of the war are worth recounting:

> At first the sound was faint, and then it grew louder. Soon the booming
> of cannon was heard, then great clouds of smoke were seen rising above
> the ridge. The sound became louder and louder, and was now incessant.
> The troops passing us moved faster, the men had now become excited and
> urged on their horses. The battle was waging. (34)

As Union soldiers heard that discordant call to battle they commented aloud about their chances. Overhearing this dialog Tillie little understood what was to unfold. In her words, "I remember hearing some of the soldiers remarking that there was no telling how soon some of them would be brought back in those ambulances, or carried on the stretchers. I hardly knew what it meant, but I learned afterward, even before the day had passed." (34)

Upon returning home Tillie found that one of the family's neighbors, Mrs. Schriver, was visiting. With her husband away in the Union army and her home out near the Weikert farm, Mrs. Schriver asked if Tillie could accompany her to her home. Tillie's mother acquiesced to this request and thus began Tillie's great adventure during the battle.

As Tillie and her neighbor headed out to the Schriver home she caught her first glimpse of the battle at hand:

> As I looked toward the Seminary Ridge I could see and hear the confusion
> of the battle. Troops moving hither and thither; the smoke of the conflict
> arising from the fields; shells bursting in the air, together with the din, rising
> and falling in mighty undulations. These things beheld for the first time filled
> my soul with the greatest apprehensions. (39)

After reaching the Taneytown road Tillie beheld an ambulance that contained the body of a single stricken officer. Some of the accompanying soldiers told Tillie that the man was General Reynolds, and "that he had been killed during the forenoon in the battle." (39) This encounter was the first of several that Tillie had with leading figures of this enormous battle.

As the condition of the fields and roads were somewhat muddy the progress of Tillie and Mrs. Schriver was briefly halted at a small house that was ultimately to become General Meade's headquarters. There the two travelers were given a ride in a Union wagon that took them to the Weikert farm. After that bumpy ride Tillie was to witness the buildup of Federal troops that marked that part of the first day's engagement:

It was not long after our arrival, until Union artillery came hurrying by.
It was indeed a thrilling sight. How the men impelled their horses!
How the officers impelled the men as they all flew past toward the
sound of the battle! Now the road is getting all cut up; they take to
the fields, and all is an anxious, eager hurry! Shouting, lashing the
horses, cheering the men, they all rush madly on. (41)

As these artillerymen sped by Tillie was to have her first personal experience with the human cost of actual battle. Looking out at the Union artillerymen's progression toward the front, "Suddenly we behold an explosion; it is that of a caisson. We see a man thrown high in the air and come down in a wheat field close by. He is picked up and carried into the house. As they pass by I see his eyes are blown out and his whole person seems to be one black mass. The first words I hear him say is: ' Oh dear! I forgot to read my Bible to-day! What will my poor wife and children say'" (41-42)

Scenes such as this one were to become common for Tillie as the three days of battle unfolded. Attempting to be productive in the face of such suffering Tillie went to the farm's well and began to draw buckets of cool water. She then stood by the road and offered up this refreshment to the Union soldiers as they sped past. In this manner Tillie passed the day.

That night, as Federal soldiers poured into farm delivering their wounded comrades to be tended in the barn and home on the Weikert property Tillie was to see other elements of war. As evening descended Tillie felt compelled to go out to the Weikert barn and help as she might. What she saw stunned her and left an impression that twenty-five years could not dull:

That evening, Becky Weikert, the daughter at home, and I went out to
the barn to see what was transpiring there. Nothing before in my
experience had ever paralleled the sight we then and there beheld.
There were the groaning and crying, the struggling and dying, crowded
side by side, while attendants sought to aide and relieve them as best
they could…We were so overcome by the sad and awful spectacle that
we hastened back to the house weeping bitterly. (44)

Back in the house the two girls were still somewhat overcome by what they had witnessed. Soldiers who were in the home looking for refreshments tried to cheer them up as best they could. A chaplain who was also in attendance looked at Tillie and said, "Little girl, do all you can for the poor soldiers and the Lord will reward you." Tillie was to take this advice to heart and apply it. The first day had passed and Tillie retired to bed "with the strange and appalling events, and many new visions passing rapidly" through her memory. (45)

SECOND DAY

On the morning of the second day Tillie once again saw streams of Federal soldiers passing in front of her. Artillery pieces, wagons, marching infantry and all the impediments of war passed before Tillie's eyes as she looked out on the Weikert farm.

Tillie hurriedly returned to her vocation of the previous day and stood by the roadside offering cooling water to the soldiers. As Tillie did so her thoughts turned back to her own family, "Were they well? Were they alive? Did I still have a home? These and many other silent inquiries, sprang to my mind without any hope of answer." (46)

As Tillie looked out at the passing troops she overheard one of the soldiers postulating what his fate that day might be. The fact that rough-hewn coffins had been stacked near the road for future dismal usage did not make the men jocular in their expressions. These men knew that their future was unclear. When asked if he thought he might end up in one of the coffins by day's end one soldier near Tillie responded thusly, "I will consider myself very lucky if I *get* one." (49)

Shortly after these men passed three officers rode up to the gate where Tillie was standing. One of these men came up to Tillie and asked for a drink. When Tillie responded by asking if he would mind using a tin cup that other troops had shared he indicated "Certainly; that is all right." After drinking from the rude cup the officer turned away, thanked Tillie nicely, bowed, and rode off. When Tillie inquired of some of the nearby soldiers as to the identity of this seemingly gracious man they responded with a well known name—General Meade. (50-51)

Another group of officers then arrived and asked if they might make some observations from the roof of the Weikert place. By and by the men asked if Tillie would like to come up onto the roof and take a look through their binoculars. Tillie agreed to and noted her observations:

The country for miles around seemed to be filled with troop; artillery moving
here and there as fast as they could go; long lines of infantry forming into
position; officers on horseback galloping hither and thither! It was a grand
and awful spectacle, and impressed me as being some great review.
(51-52)

After Tillie descended from the roof she realized that her very life had been endangered by this action. She "observed soldiers lying on the ground just back of the house, dead. They had fallen just where they had been standing when shot. I was told that they had been picked off by Rebel sharpshooters, who were up in Big Round Top." (52)

Faced with this type of fire the officers in the Weikert house felt it was no longer safe for the civilians to remain. They had the family quickly prepare to leave. A wagon was provided to the family and Tillie and they set out for a farmhouse about a half-mile to the east. However, after reaching that destination they were told by other Union soldiers that they were in graver danger there and should return to the Weikert home. A swift about face resulted in Tillie and her companions being right back where they started.

As the day drew to a close once again the broken bodies of men wounded in the fighting were brought to the Weikert place. Again, Tillie's young eyes observed the grim effects of battle upon its participants, "On this evening the number of wounded brought to the place was indeed appalling. They were laid in different parts of the house. The orchard and space around the buildings were covered with the shattered and dying, and the barn became more and more crowded. The scene had become terrible beyond description." (58)

Tillie was to establish a particular relationship with one wounded soldier. Asked to tend to a man while his friend went to get something to eat Tillie had a brief but touching conversation. The man felt he was gravely wounded. When Tillie asked if his wounds troubled him he said, "Yes pretty badly." Tillie told the soldier that she would do anything for him that she could. The man looked at the young girl and asked for a simple thing, "Will you promise me to come back in the morning to see me." Tillie agreed to this gentle request and started to go up to bed. Seeing her depart, the man reminded Tillie of her agreement, "Now you don't forget your promise." Tillie responded "No indeed." And went to her guestroom hoping for the soldier's recovery. (61-63)

THIRD DAY

At the crack of dawn Tillie awakened and hurried downstairs to fulfill her promise and check on the status of her wounded acquaintance. As she hastened down to see how the man was doing the sight of his friend sitting beside his dead body confronted her. Tillie was struck by the fact that "I had kept my promise but he was not there to greet me. I hope he greeted nearer and dearer faces than that of the unknown little girl on the battle-field of Gettysburg." (Alleman p. 64) When she was asked if she knew whom the soldier was Tillie demurred only to discover that he was General Weed, a New York man. Mortally wounded on Little Round Top, General Weed survived long enough to meet Tillie Pierce a little girl who may have reminded him of loved ones near and dear to his heart.

After facing this sad turn of events Tillie and the rest of the residents of the Weikert farm were once again shuttled out of harms way. Federal troops once again informed the civilians that they would have to relocate. While loading up the carriages a shell passed directly overhead. Tillie shrieked and ran to the barn. Some nearby soldiers laughed and chided her by saying "My child, if that had hit you, you would not have had time to jump." A tad chagrined, Tillie returned to the carriage and the refugees were once again on the road. (69-70) This brief reference is all that Tillie must have experienced of the massive bombardment that served as a prelude to Picket's advance

As Tillie and her neighbors journeyed along they passed the massed might of the 6th Corps. A little further along the road they came upon an interesting sight. Between the Taneytown and Baltimore pike Tillie "first saw Rebel prisoners; there was a whole field filled with them. Their appearance was extremely rough, and they seemed completely tired out." (70)

As Tillie gazed at the exhausted Rebels one of the Union guards took up a conversation with her. Tillie later described their exchange in this way:

While we were talking with our soldiers, I noticed one eating a "hard tack".
I, having had nothing to eat as of yet that day, and being quite hungry, must
have looked very wistfully at him, for he reached into his haversack and

presented me with one of those army delicacies. I accepted it with thanks,
and nothing that I can recall was ever more relished, or tasted sweeter, than
that Union soldier's biscuit, eaten on July 3, 1863. (70-71)

Finally, the travelers reached the farmhouse that was their destination. Toward the close of the afternoon the displaced residents felt that the din of battle was subsiding. Once again they determined that it was safe to return home. Along the way Tillie looked around at the surrounding countryside, once so prosperous and peaceful, and described it in this fashion, "As we drove along in the cool of the evening, we noticed that everywhere confusion prevailed. Fences were thrown down near and far; knapsacks, blankets and many other articles, lay scattered here and there. The whole country seemed filled with desolation. (71)

Once back at the Weikert farm Tillie as again confronted with the realities of battle. The farm remained a hospital with wounded seemingly pouring in from all sides. In Tillie's words:

Upon reaching the place I fairly shrank back aghast at the awful sight presented.
The approaches were crowded with wounded, dying, and dead. The air was
filled with moanings and groanings. As we passed on toward the house, we
were compelled to pick our steps in order that we might not tread on prostrate
bodies. (71-72)

Once settled back at the Weikert's home Tillie set about to once again make herself helpful. All the muslin and linen that could be spared was torn into bandages and applied to the poor and suffering soldiers. Tillie observed some sights that no person, let alone a child, should see:

By this time, amputating benches had been placed about the house. I must

have become inured to seeing the terrors of battle, else I could hardly have
gazed upon the scenes now presented. I was looking out one of the windows
facing the front yard. Near the basement door, and directly underneath the
window I was at, stood one of these benches. I saw them lifting the poor men
upon it, then the surgeons sawing and cutting off arms and legs, then again
probing and picking out bullets from the flesh…I saw the wounded throwing
themselves wildly about, and shrieking with pain while the operation was going
on. To the south of the house, and just outside of the yard, I noticed a pile of
limbs higher than the fence. It was a ghastly sight! Gazing upon these, too often
the trophies of the amputating bench, I could have no other feeling, than that the
whole scene was one of cruel butchery. (73-74)

AFTER THE BATTLE

By July 7th Tillie was finally able to return to her family. As she traveled back to her parents and sister Tillie looked at a landscape that was radically different than what she remembered. Near Little Round Top Tillie saw, "Dead soldiers, bloated horses, shattered cannon and caissons, thousands of small arms. In fact everything belonging to army equipments, was there in one confused and indescribable mass." (Alleman p. 81) Unable to use the roads due to mud and military traffic Tillie, Mrs. Schriver, and her two children took to the fields. There they saw even more of the destruction wrought by the battle:

Dead horses, swollen to almost twice their natural size, lay in all directions,
stains of blood frequently met our gaze, and all kinds of army accoutrements

covered the ground. Fences had disappeared, some buildings were gone, others
ruined. The whole landscape had been changed, and I felt as though we were in
a strange and blighted land. (82-83)

Once home, Tillie was warmly embraced by her family. Luckily the Pierce clan had suffered no great losses during the battle. Back home, Tillie and her family set about the ongoing process of nursing Federal casualties in their house. Among the men who were tended to in the Pierce home was Colonel William Colvill of the First Minnesota, a regiment that was virtually destroyed on the second day of fighting. As the days and weeks passed numerous family members of the wounded men cared for by the Pierces journeyed to Gettysburg to visit and nurse their loved ones. In this care-taking situation Tillie saw a new aspect of war's costs:

Many sad and touching scenes were here witnessed. Many a kind and affectionate
father; many a fond and loving mother; many a devoted wife faithful unto death;
many a tender and gentle sister, wiped the moisture of death from the blanched
forehead of the dying hero, as they eagerly leaned forward to catch the last message
of love, or to hear the announcement of a victory greater than death. (109-110)

Tillie Pierce could not have helped but to have been altered by these experiences. The Civil War swept across thousands of miles and hundreds of towns. Gettysburg was but one of those places. Likewise, Tillie Pierce was but one of the millions of Americans affected by the war. However, both Tillie and her hometown have come to be a part of historical events that retain their memorableness.

As the years passed Tillie went on with an apparently very normal life. She wed Horace P. Alleman in 1871 and they raised three children. Tillie was to live until 1914 a year when her nation stood on the brink of another war. At that time, as she approached her own death, perhaps she reflected back upon her experiences one week in early July when she was a mere strip of a girl. If so it can only be hoped that she was able to recall the kindness of a soldier who shared his food with her, the sacrifice of people who tended the wounded, or the good humor of veterans whom she encountered. Hopefully, the grim sights, sounds, and smells of battle that must have stayed with her throughout her life were left behind as she passed on to the great unknown that lies ahead for all of us. Tillie Pierce—one girl who stood in the pathway of history and took the time to write down her memories for all of us to remember.

Source

Alleman, Tillie Pierce, *At Gettysburg, Or What A Girl Saw And Heard Of The Battle,*
    Butternut & Blue, Baltimore, MD, 1994.

7

Harriett Dada: The Story of a Union Army Nurse

"The doctors...said I could not live and I was indifferent whether I lived or died, and she...bid me live. To her, more than to all else, I owe the life and strength and happiness which I now enjoy...What she did for me she did for hundreds of others as helpless and hopeless...She did for us all what a sister, wife, or mother could do." (10) Thus did William Bright of Company C, 22nd Wisconsin Infantry describe Harriet A. Dada one of the thousands of women nurses who chose to go off to war. Her story is one that comes off the pages of *Ministering Angel* a new release from Thomas Publications.

In *Ministering Angel* writer Edmund J. Raus presents readers with a compilation of ten articles that Harriet Dada wrote after the war. These articles were based upon the letters that Harriet Dada wrote during her four-year service as a nurse. Portions of Harriet's letters were originally published in 1867 as part of a compendium of Civil War biographies in a book entitled *Woman's Work in the Civil War*. Later, in 1884, Harriet Dada reconstructed her articles from these wartime letters and published them in the *National Tribune* under the "Ministering Angel" heading.

In this contemporary rendering of *Ministering Angel* readers will encounter a woman whose strength of character and desire to serve are self-evident. Editor Edmund Raus provides readers with a capably written introduction to Harriet Dada and this represents a fine effort at putting *Ministering Angel* and its author in context. Harriet Dada was reared in upstate New York. When war broke out she immediately applied for permission to work as an army nurse. Eventually, Harriet would not only receive permission to do so but also would come to be one of the approximately 2500 women to gain a military pension for her efforts. Yet, Harriet's service, like that of so many men and women who chose to leave hearth and home in 1861 was not what she had originally envisioned it to be.

When Harriet first arrived in New York City to begin her apprenticeship as a nurse in the surgical wards of several city hospitals little did she realize that this sort of work would encompass her life for four years. Like so many Americans, Harriet Dada expected the war to be a short-lived affair. Looking back over the years Harriet wrote about her original, and vastly misguided, expectations:

>Many remember the battle-cry, "On to Richmond," which filled the
>daily papers of July, 1861. The programme was: "One decisive battle,"
>then Richmond would be ours, and the Confederate congress captured.
>Sharing the general feeling, I was anxious to do my part in the "short
>struggle" in the way of caring for the sick and the wounded. Little did
>I then think that my services would be needed till the last of September,
>1865 (12)

When Harriet began her nursing service she swiftly came to realize that the coming of the war was indeed a dreadful event. The first sick and wounded soldiers she encountered reminded her that war equals pain and suffering. In one of her earliest articles she notes, "The pain felt was the realization of the long-dreaded fact that the sword had been unsheathed, the war had actually begun, and that fathers, husbands, and brothers were already dead, dying, and wounded on the battlefield, whom mothers, wives, and sisters could not reach…" (12)Yet, despite the reality of this suffering, Harriet felt pride in her service. The ability to take a hand in helping these wounded men offered Harriet Dada the only silver lining in the unfolding war. As she anticipated her service Harriet pondered upon her feelings of pride and wrote, "pleasure was the prospect of soon being amid those busy scenes, binding up the wounds and doing with my might all that could be done for the comfort of our country's brave defenders." (13)

Once Harriet arrived in her first military hospital in Alexandria, Virginia she quickly realized how overwhelming the work she had chosen was. The daily routine of backbreaking labor, linked to the all encompassing suffering she witnessed was a double blow to many apprentice nurses. Looking back, Harriet recounted her initial impressions of hospital work:

> Those who entered hospitals at a later day have no idea of the unsettled state of things that we found. At this time no soldiers were detailed for nurses, and were not until November, so we had wounds to dress with water every hour, faces, hands, and feet to wash, beds to arrange, food and water to distribute, medicines to give, and, in fact, everything to do for the sick and wounded, with no help except that of a contraband, who assisted about the various wards, and who, becoming weary of steady employment, would leave; when another one would be found, who in turn would take his departure. Thus for weeks, day and night, we were kept constantly busy. (14)

In addition to Harriet's steady and potentially crushing workload, another factor that ground down her spirit was the quality and quantity of her food. Army nurses, like their patients, did not always receive the best of supplies. In fact, writing years later, Harriet Dada remembered her rations with less than fondness, "our diet during those years in the hospitals was of the plainest and simplest character and included no delicacies. Many a time all that I had to eat was toasted bread with salt sprinkled on it, wet with water, and a cup of coffee; and sometimes only a dish of gruel. There were times, too, when I hardly had time to eat." (56)

Harriet, like the other women who joined her as nurses, was not always accorded respect for her service. The mid-nineteenth century was hardly what we would now refer to as an age of enlightened attitudes toward women workers. Thus, for some doctors, Harriet and her nursing comrades were subjected to a scornful demeanor and the notion that, "A lady ceases to be a lady when she becomes a nurse." (16) However, despite this bigotry Harriet Dada came to see her medical service as a calling in the truest sense of the word. Thinking back upon her service and the ill will of some of the male surgeons she encountered Harriet recounted, "Such unpleasant expressions fell with but little weight upon our ears; for we knew that our days and nights of care, watching and anxiety over the sick and wounded were appreciated by thousands of their friends at home. The many letters we received from the friends of those for whom we cared, so full of thanks, more than compensated for the unkind words and sneers." (16)

One of the saddest elements of this fine book relates to the many deaths that Harriet Dada witnessed. In the numerous hospitals within which Harriet labored literally thousands of men died. In her writings Harriet occasionally notes how many men per month expired while in wards she patrolled. In some instances over a hundred men might die in a given month while she was on duty. The mental and emotional cost of observing so much suffering must have borne down heavily upon Harriet and her comrades. In 1864, while serving in Chattanooga, Harriet wrote about this dance of death and how she felt about it:

> There were one hundred and fifty-three deaths in the month of
> November in this hospital. People in their comfortable homes
> can form no idea of the suffering there was in that hospital in
> this time. The patients, weary, exhausted, suffering from sickness
> and wounds, all night long would lie there in those dreary wards,
> thinking of loved ones far away at home, while they, the victims of
> that cruel war, were suffering and many of them dying there. No one
> but God knows the anguish—the death pangs—they suffered who

sealed their patriotism with their blood. (52)

After all was said and done—after the final bugle call was made, the drums were stilled, and the battle flags furled—Harriet Dada returned home from the front. She, like the thousands of other women who followed a nurse's calling during the war, had done well. Her work was both actual and inspirational. A brave hearted soul, Harriet Dada had saved lives in many ways. Such behavior arguably requires at least as much courage as is needed to go into combat. During the time of her service Harriet came to realize that, "If a patient gave up all hope he was almost sure to die; therefore, it was necessary to inspire courage." (50) The inspiration of courage can only flow from courage itself. This certainly appears to be a quality that Harriet Dada possessed.

A formal woman who, reportedly, only allowed one soldier to ever use her nickname, "Hattie", during her service, Harriet comes down across the ages to us via her writings. (8) In these pages we meet a woman who was commended by the men she served. H.G. Potter of the 74th Indiana Infantry described Harriet Dada in this way, "I knew Miss Dada as the good nurse and soldier's friend…with sleeves rolled up and towel in hand she would meet the wounded comrade fresh from the battle field, take charge of loving messages from the dying, and assist in Christian services for those desiring them." (9) Reflecting back on her wartime work Harriet Dada must have remembered many things that engendered pain and sorrow in her life. Still, despite the suffering she saw and ministered to, when all was said and done, Harriet felt her work was purposeful. In her own words, "Surely, I did receive my reward…it had been my privilege to minister to the sick and wounded soldiers—one of the greatest privileges given to an American woman." (6)

In bringing the words, thoughts, and accomplishments of Harriet Dada back into the consciousness of Americans Edmund J. Raus, Jr. does a service as well. This is a fine little book and one that allows its readers to better understand both the medical world of the Civil War and one particular human being who followed her lights and served her nation. *Ministering Angel* is a compact and primary source of information about nursing life at a time when hundreds of thousands of Americans suffered and died. The story of Harriet Dada is one that readers will want to get to know and remember.

Source

Edmund J. Raus, Jr. (editor), *Ministering Angel: The Reminiscences of Harriet A. Dada,*
 a Union Army Nurse in the Civil War, Gettysburg, PA: Thomas Publications. 2004.

8

Views of Childhood During the Civil War

    Like every military conflict, the Civil War exerted a tremendous effect upon the world of the millions of children whose lives it touched. For children, the causes of war are seldom clear. What is apparent is that fathers, brothers, uncles, and the men in their young lives are gone. In all too many cases, those departed male role models either never return or come home physically or emotionally altered by their experiences in battle. At home, mothers, sisters, aunts, and other female caretakers are overwhelmed by grief, fear, anxiety, and work. In our own day-and-age women may even take part in combat, thus leaving children with fears for mothers and fathers.

    During the Civil War over three million men served in the opposing armies. Many of those soldiers left behind children who cared about their fate. In other instances children themselves were swept up in the pathway of war. One need only think of the "March to the Sea" and the terrible battles that were fought primarily in the South to reconstruct the events that directly involved American children during the Civil War.

    Over the past few years several thoughtful books have been written about the combination of childhood and the American Civil War. What follows are summaries of some of the finest scholarship concerning this touching and relevant subject. Our children are the most beloved and important resource that exists. In looking back to see how children of the Civil War era were affected by that conflict we gain insights that can be applied to the present and future. We live in an age when warfare is a reality in many places across the globe. In learning about the effects of conflict on Civil War children we are better prepared to assuage the fears and losses attendant to it in our own age.

The Trauma & Effects of War

"They waved at passing troops, ran from canon fire, and hid in caves and cellars. Some longed to fight; others dreamed of peace as they huddled in the shadows of death. They were sons and daughters of a nation in agony—the children of the American Civil War." (Cohn XI) Thus does author Scotti Cohn introduce his moving book *Beyond Their Years: Stories of Sixteen Civil War Children*, a biographical study of children who lived through the war and reflected that rite of passage in later life. The sixteen children selected by Cohn each share a common trait. They survived America's bloodiest war and later looked back on those wartime experiences with pen in hand. The girls and boys chronicled in this concise yet valuable book took time in adulthood to write about their Civil War experiences. Hence, through these sixteen children we catch a glimpse of what war can do to the lives of its youngest victims.

In *Beyond Their Years* the author pieces together elements from the lives of eight northern and eight southern children. The litany of subjects in this well written work encompasses diverse experiences. Some of the presented children were civilians residing fairly far away from the maelstrom of battle. In other instances, the youngsters become underage soldiers and experienced war's lessons close up. In yet other cases the children saw war at first hand through the coming of the armies and attendant destruction. In each case, the events that they witnessed changed the course of their lives in a way that those of us who have not experienced warfare cannot imagine.

For Edwin Fitzgerald Foy the war began with a sea of pageantry. Edwin was five years old when Fort Sumter was fired upon and the coming of war was little understood by him. A resident of New York City, Eddie and his family were initially caught up by the excitement of the declaration of war. In a memoir he was to write many years later he recalled, "I have a dim recollection of being held up by Father and Mother at the curb to see long lines of soldiers marching down the streets—probably Broadway and Fifth Avenue—with flags waving and bands playing and crowds cheering, and it all seemed very fine." (Cohn 23) However, this initial colorful element of memory was swiftly replaced by grimmer stuff.

In 1862 Eddie's father joined the Union army. After being under arms for two months Mr. Fitzgerald was badly wounded. Eventually, Eddie Fitzgerald's father broke down mentally and was placed in the asylum on Blackwell's Island. A few months after admission Eddie's father committed suicide. Facing reduced financial means Eddie and his family relocated to a cheaper apartment on Eighth Avenue. There, in July of 1863, the Fitzgerald family witnessed one of the worst examples of civil violence in American history. The New York City Draft Riot swept through Eddie Fitzgerald's life and left permanent memories.

Eddie saw fights, stonings, arson, looting, and lynching. At one point Eddie came across the body of a black man hanging from a lamppost lynched by Irish mobs. Later he described his reaction in this way, "The sight almost turned me sick, and yet it had a terrible fascination for me. I loitered about, staring at it...Then a sudden revulsion overcame me and I ran home at top speed, scared, and breathless." (Cohn 26) Years later, after he had become a well-known entertainer Eddie Fitzgerald Foy remembered what he had seen, heard, and felt during his Civil War experiences.

For Eliza Lord Vicksburg, Mississippi had always been a peaceful place to romp and play. She and her family had known a life of security and prosperity. However, in 1863 the coming of the Federal forces changed all that. At that time the eleven-year-old Eliza Lord was to enter into a dark phase of her life and one that stayed with her for the remainder of her years.

As was the case with many residents of Vicksburg, the Lord family was to become all too familiar with bombardment, fear, and exile. Eliza, who later wrote an account of her wartime experiences, remembered the first exposure to northern artillery. As the family gathered for supper "the roar and crash came...A bombshell burst in the very center of that pretty dining-room, blowing out the roof and one side, crushing the well-spread tea-table like an eggshell, and making a great yawning hole in the floor, into which disappeared supper, china, furniture, and the safe containing our entire stock of butter and eggs." (Cohn 95)

In order to avoid the steadily increasing shelling the Lord family retreated to a cave where they shared space with a number of other citizens of Vicksburg. This underground life was odd and still filled with danger. Living accommodations were, to say the least, primitive. Eliza recalled the lot of one neighbor family with young children, "A big store-box lined with blankets held several babies, and upon a mattress on the damp floor lay a lady accustomed to the extremest luxury, with an infant beside her only eight days old." (Cohn 97)

    Despite their subterranean abode the Lords faced grave danger. On several occasions shells burst near Eliza and her family. Looking back at her childhood an older Eliza Lord could still dredge up these incidents and describe them thusly, "The air was filled with flying splinters, clods, fragments of iron, and branches of trees. The earth seemed fairly to belch out smoke and flame and sulpher, and the roar and shock were indescribable." (Cohn 100) Eliza could also recall an occasion when her younger brother, Willie, who was particularly adept at identifying the type of shell that was about to hit, instinctively ducked down only to have a Parrott shell pass over his back at a distance so close that it scorched his jacket.

    In the end, the sacrifices of the Lords and the thousands of other residents and defenders of Vicksburg went for naught. The city surrendered and southern hopes were dimmed. Years later, after she had married and raised six children, Eliza Lord took pen in hand and recorded her wartime memories. Those memories remained vivid for her even through the passage of time.

    Eddie Fitzgerald Foy and Eliza Lord are but two of the sixteen children addressed in this fine work. In other instances Scotti Cohn recounts the deeds of escaped slaves, teenaged infantrymen, the daughter of a Confederate spy, and a young girl fleeing the forces of General Sherman. In each of the sixteen thumbnail sketches presented by author Cohn the basic resilience of the person in question shines through. We, the readers, come to better understand what war does to the children who are placed in its pathway. In an age when conflict appears to be a way of life in many parts of the world it does us good to recall what history can teach us about violence and children. Perhaps, by reading about the experiences of Civil War children we too can come to the conclusion reached by the author when he recorded the following words, "What inspires us most, however, is the resilience of these children during times that devastated many of their adult contemporaries. They provided cheer in the midst of hardship, love in the midst of hostility, and faith in the midst of despair. In doing so, they displayed courage and wisdom beyond their years." (Cohn XI)

Children of the North

In the lexicon of the English language there may well be no greater abyss of contradictory meaning than stands between the words "children" and "war."
Commonly held images of childhood do not generally include wanton destruction, pain, loss, trauma, and deprivation. Yet, throughout history, mankind has inflicted war upon its youngest members. Whether the setting was Germany, Rwanda, Palestine, Vietnam, or Iraq, children, on a daily basis, have, and continue to have, the opportunity to view the horrific effects of war on a personal basis. In James Martens' recently published work entitled, *Children for the Union,* readers are afforded a great opportunity to learn more about how the Civil War affected the lives of children who lived in the North during those tumultuous years. In presenting the story of these children of war author Martens accomplishes a great deal and does so in ways that will both inform and move his readers.

In *Children for the Union* James Marten paints a historical portrait of a group of American children who had the unique experience of seeing their nation torn asunder and at war with itself. While, as Marten points out in this compelling book Northern children did not generally have the experience of invasion and desolation that all too many Southern youngsters had, they did live and grow up with enormous uncertainty, loss, and confusion. Living in the Northern states during the four bloody years of the Civil War may not have been a time of constant occupation or disruption by an alien military host but it was an era wherein children saw their lives and families turned topsy-turvy. Marten demonstrates this age of uncertainty and the attendant results of the wartime experience on Northern children in a variety of ways but none are more effective than his detailed exposition of the writings of children both during the war and in later years. Through the words of boys and girls who watched, waited, and worked while family members fought readers come away with a much clearer understanding of the way in which the Civil War altered the existence of oh so many children.

In Cincinnati young Dan Beard who, in later years, was to head up the Boy Scouts movement, scavenged discarded pistols and created miniature canons to blast away at toy soldiers and ersatz fortifications. As time passed, Beard observed the wounded soldiers who returned to his hometown and realized that warfare was far more than the fun and glory of demolished toy soldiers on a sunny day. These acknowledgements shaped Beard's ideas and subsequent orientation toward a combination of service and the purifying power of nature.

A Michigan girl named Anna Howard Shaw was a young teen when the war came. Living in rural Michigan Anna quickly saw her father and two brothers volunteer for military service and disappear for the duration of the conflict. Swiftly, Anna began to see the "relentless limitations of pioneer life…on every side, and at every hour of the day." (Marten 179) By age fifteen Anna was the primary support for her family and her life became "a strenuous and tragic affair" that "grew harder with every day." (Marten 179) At a time when Anna should have been enjoying the fruits of her childhood she was responsible for "an incessant struggle to keep our land, to pay our taxes, and to live." (Marten 179) For Anna Shaw the outbreak of the Civil War was a time when "life had degenerated into a treadmill whose monotony was broken only by the grim messages from the front." (Marten 179) In 1865, when the war ended, Anna Shaw exited from Michigan, went to college, and left that life of bitter work and want behind her. As she noted years later in her memoir, "The end of the Civil War brought freedom to me too." (Marten 179) In the case of Anna Shaw, war was not a glorious event but rather "simply another burden in already difficult lives." (Marten 179)

Hamlin Garland grew up on a farm in rural Wisconsin. As an adult Garland was to become a writer of great capability. His short stories, perhaps best epitomized in his anthology entitled *Main Traveled Roads,* focused upon what life was like on Midwestern farms during and after the Civil War. In his own life, Hamlin Garland watched as his kind-hearted father joined a Wisconsin infantry regiment and left his family behind. In Garland's world perhaps the most vivid impact the war had upon him was the way in which it both removed and irrevocably altered his beloved father. Richard Garland lived to return home but the things he had seen and done left him a different person.

As Garland noted in his post-war autobiography, "all was not the same as before." (Marten 153) Hamlin Garland's father brought back not only the physical reminders of wounds but also spiritual injuries that left him a different man. A strangely harsh side to Richard Garland's nature now existed as, in Hamlin Garland's words, "for my father brought back from his two years' campaigning...the temper and habit of a soldier...We soon learned...that the soldier's promise of punishment was swift and precise in its fulfillment...We knew he loved us, for he took us to his knees of an evening and told stories of marches and battles, or chanted war songs to us...but the moments of his tenderness were few." (Marten 154) For Hamlin Garland, the departure of his father meant the loss of the man he had once known and all which that entailed.

During the Civil War fully one third of America's population was made up of children. Warfare breeds separation, loss, and fear. These factors surely weighed heavily in the lives of Northern children as they saw their lives indisputably changed by the absence of fathers, the sometimes crushing demands of increased work responsibilities, the uncertainty of circumstances, and the daily concern over the possibility that a beloved family member might not return home. But life during the war years was also a time to simply live. In this area of what was childhood broadly like in the Civil War era James Marten also does an outstanding job. Marten details the toys children commonly played with, games typical of the era, literature that was produced, the way in which wartime patriotism impacted school books, and the creation of children's' publications in a manner that is striking. Amidst even the saddest of times children need to play, romp, and escape into fantasies. Sadly, in the Civil War as in other wars, the reality of wartime life intruded into those developmental needs in ways that ranged from distracting to devastating.

In *Children for the Union* James Marten describes an age within which children saw their lives shifted by forces upon which they had no control and only sporadic understanding. The Civil War was an age when, as one Northern woman later recalled, the war "made itself felt from the words and looks of those about us; there was some struggle going on in the world which touched all life, brooded in faces, came out in phrases and exclamations and pitiful sights." Such childhood memories do not fade away but rather help to shape the adult lives of their owners.

Like children in all too many war torn lands, American youngsters during the Civil War "could not avoid the war and could not be avoided by those who make war." As James Marten chronicles in this outstanding book, the children who grew up during and after the Civil War caught the "war spirit" of their elders in a way that "made their childhoods unlike any that came before or after." Simply put, the Civil War stamped itself upon the psyche of many children in ways that were unalterably different than other conflicts in this nation's history. That stamping process, while sadly not unique in world history, does stand alone as the singular moment in American history where children in this land had to cope with the existence of warfare as a neighbor of incredible power, scope, and proximity.

By telling the story of this generation of children James Marten both catalogs a touching aspect of Civil War history while also reminding his readers that when the decision is made to engage in warfare one of the longest lived consequences is the way in which that decision will shape, mold, and haunt the lives of its youngest victims. Children of war may survive but they will likely do so with the memories and scars that go along with mankind's saddest endeavor—the act of war. Thus readers of this fine book receive a double reward. First, they gain great insights into the way in which Northern children were affected by the Civil War. Second, they have the opportunity to ponder the questions of when, why, and how decisions should be made regarding the unleashing of the remorseless dogs of war upon not only soldiers but also children. In this manner James Marten has produced a book of great value, depth, and dignity and which readers will benefit from studying.

Reluctant Witnesses

On April 2, 1861, as war fever gripped the land, fifteen-year-old Elizabeth Horton of Mobile, Alabama wrote to her seventeen-year-old cousin, Emma, in Massachusetts, "Times are indeed troublous, when our city is so flooded with soldiers, thirsting for the blood of those whom they consider their enemies.

My fervent prayer is that not a drop of blood may be shed on either side." (Werner 7) Ten days later the bombardment of Fort Sumter signaled the start of the bloodiest years in American history. Both of these cousins sent kinfolk into the opposing armies. They also never resumed either their correspondence or relationships. The human cost of this simple severance of family ties bespeaks the impact that the Civil War had on the day-to-day life of so many youngsters and children across the nation.

War affects everyone who is party to it. In the case of children, the effect of war can be so overwhelming as to change the course of their lifelong development. The wars of the modern age generally target civilians far more than the opposing military forces themselves. Terrorism specifically aims at affecting the livelihood of non-combatants inclusive of children. Wars in places such as Bosnia, Chechnya, Palestine, and Rwanda, were carried in such a way that children were lumped into the mass of "enemies" and treated as such. During the American Civil War this level of brutality had not yet colored the nature of warfare to such a degree. However, hundreds of thousands of American children saw their lives permanently altered by the coming of war.

In *Reluctant Witnesses* psychologist Emmy E. Werner turns her attention to the impact the Civil War had on the nation's children. While there was no attempt to use tactics such as ethnic cleansing or total warfare against civilians as the twentieth century understands those concepts, there was loss, destruction, and death. Children were witnesses to some of the darkest days in American history at places such as Gettysburg, Antietam, and Atlanta. Thousands of children lost their fathers or other beloved relatives in a war that claimed over 630,000 lives. The passing of armies often resulted in devastation that included looting, burning, and pillaging. Children who saw dead and dying soldiers would never forget those sights. War struck in many places and, as the author of this fine book indicates, its effects continued to influence the nation's children into their adulthood.

Among the many ways in which war traumatizes children is the fear that it spreads. Children, both north and south, could not know when their fathers would return from the army. In all too many instances those men never did come home to hearth and families. On August 13, 1861 sixteen-year-old Maria Lewis of Ebensburg, Pennsylvania wrote to her father serving with the

Federal forces, "As I think for my first beginning I can't find one more worthy than my one dear Papa I will attempt to scribble a few lines to you to let you know that we are all well at least as far as health is concerned. But our minds are never easy on your account and never will be until your safe return. Dear Papa it is so lonesome here without you." (Werner 19) For young Maria, the thought of her father's service on a distant front was a source of daily stress. Sadly, Captain Andrew Lewis was wounded and captured in Virginia. Captain Lewis underwent an amputation that removed one of his legs. He succumbed to the effects of his wounds and died in July 1862. His daughter's reactions to the loss of her father can only be surmised.

For other children the effects of warfare were experienced on a first-hand basis. Union and Confederate forces waged war in locations that were generally either populated or near cities or towns. Twelve-year-old Celine Fremaux lived in Baton Rouge, Louisiana. There, in the summer of 1862, Union gunboats bombarded the town and reduced about one third of it to rubble. Celine was responsible for helping care for her six younger siblings inclusive of a newborn baby. She recalled her wartime experience that summer in this way:

At the time of the bombardment many persons had dug pits, from three to four
feet deep, and from seven to ten feet long, and about as wide. In these they
crouched in moments of danger and during the battle of August 16th. These pits
were now filled with dead men in various states of decomposition. When a pit
is filled up, and army blanket was stretched atop, the corners held down with
bricks, and these ended the disposition of the dead…People were often taken
with nausea on the streets. I saw most of these horrors on my way from school
to our house as I had to cross the heart of the city. (Werner 26-28)

For young Sue Chancellor the war literally came to her front door. Her family home was used by Union General Joe Hooker as a command post during his ill-fated confrontation with General Robert E. Lee at Chancellorsville. Sue, and the rest of her family, took refuge in their basement as artillery rounds landed all about the property. When they emerged the next morning they could see chairs riddled with bullets, piles of arms and legs outside their sitting room, and rows of dead bodies in their yard. Their house caught fire, presumably due to artillery rounds, and Sue and her family were forced to take flight. Years later she described this experience in the following way, "Slowly we picked our way over the bleeding bodies of the dead and wounded—Union General Dickinson riding ahead, mother with her hand on his knee, I clinging close to her, and the others following behind. At our last look, our old home was completely enveloped in flames. Mother, a widow with six dependent daughters, and her all was destroyed." (Werner 57)

Carrie Berry was ten years old when the forces of General Sherman arrived at the outskirts of her hometown of Atlanta, Georgia. Almost immediately, the coming of the Union soldiers changed Carrie's young life. Federal artillery began to bombard Atlanta and Carrie realized that new dangers had entered her daily routines, "We can hear canons and muskets very plane, but the shells we dread. One has busted under the dining room which frightened us very much. One passed through the smokehouse and a piece hit the top of the house and fell through...We stay very close to the cellar when they are shelling." (Werner 105) Eventually Atlanta fell and a determination was made by Sherman, prior to his commencement of the March to the Sea, to burn those portions of the city that had "military value." Surrounded by the ruins of her city Carrie Berry described this event in this following manner:

Oh what a night we had. They came burning the storehouse and about night
    it looked like the whole town was on fire. We all set up all night. If we had not
    sat up our house would have burnt up for the fire was very near and the soldiers

were going around setting houses on fire where they were not watched. They

behaved very badly. They all left town about one o'clock this evening and we

were glad when they left for no body knows what we have suffered since

they came. (Werner 114)

In our own age physicians and mental health professionals have identified some of the symptoms that children often manifest when they have survived the traumas attendant to war. In many ways these symptoms are not dissimilar to those reported by veterans of combat. As Emmy Werner notes within the body of this penetrating book, the keynote effects of war on the children who survive it can be subtle and all encompassing. At one point the author describes the types of thoughts that remain with the childhood survivors of warfare, "Memories of the traumatic events remain with them, causing nightmares, flashbacks, and hypersensitivity to sights, smells, and sounds that remind them of their wartime experiences: the sound of an exploding shell; the whistling of a bomb, the sparks of fire; the smell of burning wood; the unexpected knock at the door or a uniform that may evoke the memory of an enemy who might seize one's parents or one's earthly possessions." (Werner 151) One can only wonder what thoughts went through Carrie Berry's mind when she watched a fire, the dreams that Sue Chancellor might have had, or how Celine Fremaux handled the grim memories of burial trenches and death.

In many ways historians, reenactors, and Civil War buffs like to think of the War Between the States as a grim but somehow decent conflict. This thought is a flawed one as war is always an example of how brutal our species can be. In the case of children, the effects of the Civil War were deeply disturbing to hundreds of thousands of American youngsters. Those children who lost parents in the war saw their lives as inalterably changed. Other children witnessed carnage and destruction of the grossest nature. In all too many instances, soldiers who were no more than children themselves served in the armies as combatants and non-combatants. Their eyes observed warfare firsthand and in a way that remained with them throughout their mortal lives. In all cases, those children who were forced by circumstance to understand the nature of war were fundamentally transformed.

Years after her encounters with war at Baton Rouge, and later during the siege at Port Hudson, Celine Fremaux described the interweaving of her childhood and the war in this way, "In these few months my childhood had slipped away from me...Necessity, human obligations, family pride, and patriotism had taken entire possession of my little emaciated body." (Werner 154) The loss of Celine Fremaux's childhood stands as a testament to the impact the Civil War had upon youngsters all over America. That impact is an aspect of the Civil War that is generally ignored. We live in an age where the lives of children are once again devalued in the face of ongoing global warfare and the threat of seemingly random violence. It behooves us to look not only forward but backwards as well as we try to find ways to build a society within which the lives of children are not only valued but also protected. *Reluctant Witnesses* by Emmy Werner is a valuable literary tool in that process of historical understanding, moral education, and, hopefully, reflection on the terrible toll that war inflicts upon its youngest victims.

Boy Soldiers

Between 1861 and 1865 approximately three million Americans, north and south, joined their respective nation's armies. Among this multitude were tens of thousands of youngsters under the age of eighteen. These young soldiers served in a variety of capacities including musicians, hospital aides, naval powder monkeys, and combat soldiers. The story of these boy soldiers has most recently been re-told In G. Clifton Wisler's *When Johnny Went Marching Home: Young Americans Fight the Civil War.*

G. Clifton Wisler has written several memorable Civil War novels inclusive of *Red Cap* and *Mr. Lincoln's Drummer Boy.* He also has the honor of having several great-great grandfathers who served in Union regiments during the Civil War. Here, in this outstanding work readers will learn about the travails, accomplishments, and service of a select group of young soldiers. In a way, in an age when boy soldiers are once again a fact of life across the globe, looking back at an American application of this sad premise is in order.

Meet Orion Howe a thirteen-year-old who joined the 55th Illinois along with his brother, Lyston, and their father. At Vicksburg Orion was part of a hopeless May 1863 assault upon the Confederate lines. When the attack stalled Orion was sent back for much needed ammunition. En route Orion was wounded in his thigh but still suffered through to deliver the request for ammunition. For his efforts Orion Howe was awarded the Congressional Medal of Honor in 1896. Even in his old age Howe refused to accept his deeds during the Civil War as heroic. When asked to describe his wartime exploits by admirers Orion Howe generally said they "were most often embarrassing" and nothing "beyond what was expected of a soldier doing his duty." (Wisler 34)

Charley King of West Chester was only twelve when he joined the 49th Pennsylvania Volunteer Infantry Regiment. Charley served as a drummer boy and was part of the regiment's efforts during the Seven Days battles. One year and eight days after his enlistment Charley was on the field at Antietam where the bloodiest single day in American history was about to unfold. The 49th was held in reserve and had suffered only a few casualties from Confederate sharpshooters and stray artillery rounds. Unfortunately for Charley one of those Rebel shells struck him and grievously wounded him in the body. Charley was taken to the rear by some of his comrades where he was laid in a hospital. Charley King underwent great suffering from his wound and must have thought of his father and home so far away. Charley's father received word of his son's injury and rushed to Sharpsburg. When he arrived all he could do was return his son's shattered body home for burial. The youngest soldier to fall on the Antietam battlefield, Charley King was one of sea of Americans to perish in the Civil War.

On the Confederate side of the line readers of this fine book will encounter James Philip Carver who enlisted in Ector's Brigade of the Army of Tennessee at the age of seventeen. Known as JP and a member of the 32nd Texas dismounted cavalry young Carver was a willing soldier who saw some hard fighting. At Kennesaw Mountain JP suffered a terrible wound through his right lung. Surgeons removed a shattered rib but held out no hope for his recovery. Placed with the hopeless cases JP awoke in the night among a number of dead comrades. With great effort JP dragged himself to the surgeon's tent where he received assistance. James Philip Carver surprised his doctors and survived. He went home, lived through the end of the war, married, fathered thirteen children, and finally died in 1906.

The resilience of these young soldiers wearing blue and gray stands out as a testament to the courage of youth. The history of the boy soldiers of the Civil War is one that will move readers to their core. How sad it still seems although many decades have passed to think of these youths dressed in uniforms, formed in ranks, and killing and being killed. One can strain the mind to conjure up images of these callow youths who tried so hard to be grown up. Indeed, one of the best features of this touching book rests in the series of wonderful photographs of youthful combatants that are included. If you purchase this book take a few seconds to peer into those young faces. Then pause and reflect about children their age and the things they should have been doing in their playful youth. Finally, consider the reality of their service and what they actually saw & did during the Civil War.

Conclusion

The Civil War changed the lives of the children it encountered. In some cases the youngest American citizens emerged from the war as orphans. In other instances fathers returned home but never were quite the same. Widowed mothers struggled to make ends meet. Siblings who had boldly volunteered to fight for causes they little understood remained missing in parts unknown. Homes that had been the whole world for youngsters lay burned and shattered. The passing of the armies often meant an end to a way of life. Whatever the ultimate effect the Civil War shaped the lives of its youthful survivors in long-term ways. In realizing the enormous influence that war's grim hands can play in children's lives we should take heed. War is the ultimate act of human violence. It changes everything that touches. Even "just" wars leave maimed, saddened, dead, and traumatized children in their wake. Therefore, we should be cautious in turning to war too easily. The stakes are high in such instances for everyone but perhaps most of all for the children of the world.

Sources

Scotti Cohn, *Beyond Their Years: Stories of Sixteen Civil War Children.*
   Guilford, Connecticut: The Globe Pequot Press, 2003.

James Marten. *Children for the Union: The War Spirit on the Northern Home Front.* Chicago, IL: Ivan R. Dee Press, 2004.

Emmy E. Werner. *Reluctant Witnesses: Children's Voices from the Civil War.*
   Boulder, CO: Westview Press, 1998.

G. Clifton Wisler, *When Johnny Went Marching: Young Americans Fight the Civil War*, Harper Collins Publishers, 2001

9

Fanny Kemble's Rebellions

Fanny Kemble was one of the most renowned actresses of the mid-19th century. The daughter of a theater owner and performer, Fanny came from a long line of stage stars. Fanny Kemble's ability to capture the essence of Shakespearean dialog was a talent so pronounced that once, when she was touring the United States and performing in Boston, college attendance at Harvard fell off so sharply on the afternoons of her matinees that the faculty threatened to cancel all classes. Additionally, Fanny was a noted beauty of her era and a woman whose charms captivated men such as a young Robert E. Lee and Henry James. Fanny also demonstrated talent as a writer and ultimately published a series of biographical and fictional works. Yet, despite her talents, artistry, and allure, Fanny Kemble was destined to live a life fraught with anguish. She also was to become more famous for her writings about slavery and marriage than for her prowess on stage.

It is the fascinating and mercurial life of Fanny Kemble that in many ways is representative of some of the issues confronted by women in American society during the Civil War era. While Fanny Kemble's life was unusual it also contained two themes that were very representative of the age within which she lived and the fate of women of her time. First, Fanny Kemble, who was a bright and independent woman, encountered many conflicting emotions about the subject of marriage in a male-dominated age. In this vital social relationship Kemble found both love and despair as she struggled to maintain her independence at a time when women were generally seen as passive possessions of the men they wedded. Second, in an ironic twist of fate, Fanny Kemble grew to become a talented writer who opposed slavery but lived a married life with a man who owned a vast antebellum plantation staffed by over 1,000 slaves. Both of these subjects warrant some further study and analysis as they lead to inextricably connected results as well as a microcosm of woman's rights during the Civil War era.

Marriage in the 19th century was an institution best suited for submissive women and dominant men. A woman's primary role in society was to be a capable mother and spouse. Most women were viewed as having value primarily in the domestic roles that had traditionally been crafted for them. Fanny Kemble was a free spirit with an artistic temperament. She worked for a living and earned a considerable salary for her starring roles. A romantic minded individual it seemed alien to her to submit herself completely to the will of a single man. However, when she met the wealthy landowner named Charles Butler, Fanny put aside her doubts about the institution of marriage and set her cap for him. Fanny was warned by an independent minded aunt that, "While you remain single…and choose to work, your fortune is an independent and ample one; as soon as you marry, there's no such thing." (46-47) However, despite this warning and her own liberated nature, Fanny chose to marry a man who, in later years, she came to despise.

    Young wives of Fanny's day and age were advised in books such as Caroline Gillman's *Recollections of a Southern Matron* that, "The three golden threads with which domestic happiness is woven (are) to repress a harsh answer, to confess a fault, and to stop (right or wrong) in the midst of self-defense, in gentle submission." (77-78) Fanny Kemble, with her uniquely strong willed personality, was ill suited for such passivity. Quickly, her love for her husband transformed into a sense of enslavement. Fanny came to refer to Charles as "her lord and master" and rebelled against his authority. (82) In the long run this led to several separations and eventual divorce. In the short run Fanny became increasingly dissatisfied with married life and the responsibilities it entailed.

    When Fanny Kemble thought about a woman's lot in marriage she felt anger and frustration. At one time she wrote, "There is no justice in the theory, that one rational creature is to be subservient to another." (96) Marriages based upon inequality were anathema to Fanny who felt that the broader society overlooked many innate traits that women possessed as well as men. In Fanny's words, "We are not all made up of affections—we have intellects—and we have passions—and each and all should have their objects and their spheres of actions, or the creature is maimed." (153) When confronted by her husband's demands for obedience Fanny responded in this manner, "It is not the law of my conscience to promise implicit obedience to a human being, fallible like myself, and who can by no means relieve me of the responsibility of my actions before God." (153)

In the end this conflict of values doomed Fanny's marriage. In later years, when she contemplated the human cost that marriage sometimes exacted from women, Fanny mused, "I think that the women who have contemplated *any* equality between the sexes have almost all been unmarried." (236) Her divorce set Fanny free of a yoke that she felt stymied not only her spirit but also those of many American women. Still, although there was emancipation in her divorce, Fanny paid a great price for her freedom. As part of her divorce settlement Fanny yielded custody of her two daughters to Charles. She also lost a substantial amount of her income as he claimed a portion of her inheritance and stage earnings as his own under the laws of that era. Fanny gained her liberation but paid a stiff price for it.

A second area of Fanny's life that bears looking at with some care is that of her writing. The publication in 1863 of Fanny's *Journal of a Residence on a Georgian Plantation* in many ways marked a high point in her life. Originally written in 1839 Fanny's *Journal* began as a diary she kept during the year she spent with her husband living on his Georgian plantation. While ensconced on the Butler plantation Fanny had a first hand look at the *Peculiar Institution*. This glimpse of slavery confirmed Fanny's long-standing hatred of any institutions that set one person in control of another. Seeing the Butler slave cabins, watching pregnant women forced to work in the fields, seeing a girl whipped for a minor offense, and observing the numbing poverty and ignorance of slaves left a bitter taste in Fanny's mouth. When Fanny paid slaves for their work or complained to her husband about the owning of other people he chided her for what he saw as hypocrisy. Charles reminded Fanny that, " The act of marrying a slave owner made her also a slave owner; and her support as well as mine was derived from the product of slave labour." (128)

In order to both catalog the realities of slavery as well as to purge her own soul of responsibility Fanny crafted her *Journal*. Written at a time when slave narratives and abolitionist literature had a niche in the literary and political marketplace, Fanny's work was previewed and accepted by a publisher. However, the fierce opposition of her husband to its publication stymied Fanny's efforts. Charles categorically forbade Fanny to publish the *Journal*. Countless arguments ensued and this factor weighed heavily upon Fanny's family. Charles also withheld letters addressed to Fanny from potential publishers and forced her to return an advance payment for her book's publication. Eventually, Fanny succumbed to her husband's pressure and yielded. Later, after her divorce, Fanny was once again precluded for a period of years from publishing this book.

Only the passage of time, the sun-setting of part of her divorce agreement, and the coming of the Civil War allowed Fanny to publish what was to become her signature work.

      Fanny's work was widely praised in the North as an accurate and enlightening account of Southern life. Her book was, of course, bitterly attacked by Southerners both during and after the war. Ironically, the publication of Fanny Kemble's chronicle of slavery was most fiercely opposed by one of her own daughters, Francis, who ultimately returned to the Butler plantation after the war and ran it. Sadly, Fanny's writings resulted in permanent damage to her relationship with Francis and contributed to her feelings of loss. Yet, Fanny's record of Georgian slave holding has served as a vital record of antebellum life that has been used as a resource by historians for many years.

      In many ways Fanny Kemble stands out as a unique spirit living in an age ill suited to her needs. A woman who craved independence in an age of female dependency Fanny struggled to find her place in the sun. Plagued by marital unhappiness, ineffectiveness as a parent, and financial woes Fanny Kemble bore numerous "crosses" during her life. Conversely, Fanny was able to establish herself as a noted artist, wrote several successful books, toured the world, and fought for her rights and those of others. Ultimately, Fanny waged a war for independence that succeeded. However, that war, much like the Civil War fought by her fellow Unionists, was won at great personal cost. Looking at Fanny Kemble's life leaves the observer with an image of the tempestuous world of a woman who sought self-expression but was dogged by oppression. How many other women of her time felt the way Fanny Kemble did and lived their lives of quiet and not so quiet desperation? In what ways can the lessons gleaned from Fanny Kemble's experiences be applied to our own day-and-age?

Source

Catherine Clinton, Fanny *Kemble's Civil Wars,* New York, NY: Oxford University
   Press, 2000.

10

Mary Loughborough's Cave Life in Vicksburg

"Although I did not leave Jackson on the night of the 15th piping and dancing, yet it was with a very happy heart and very little foreboding of evil that I set off with a party of friends for a pleasant visit to Vicksburg." (Loughborough, 7) In this way did Mary Loughborough describe her decision to seek asylum from General Grant's advancing Union Army in April 1863. Little did this wife and mother realize that she would remain in a besieged city until its surrender nearly three months later. At Vicksburg, Mary Loughborough, and many other southern civilians, experienced a type of warfare that is shocking even to contemporary students of American history. Forced to literally live underground in the face of ongoing Federal bombardment, Mary Loughborough and the residents of Vicksburg, Mississippi felt the hard hand of war in a way that was exceptional even by Civil War standards. Mrs. Loughborough's story is one that is instructive not only as a personal history but also as a symbol of one type of civilian experience created by America's Civil War.

Interestingly enough, Mary Webster Loughborough was born in New York City in 1837. Her family migrated to Missouri where, in that divided state, they adopted southern sympathies. In 1859, at the age of twenty-two, Mary Webster became the wife of St. Louis attorney James Loughborough. Mary then entered into domestic life with no idea that in only a few short years her nation would be at war with itself.

In 1862 Mary's fortunes took a turn for the worse. Faced with Confederate defeats in Missouri and northern Arkansas, Mary and her family were forced into refugee status. Mrs. Loughborough began to follow her husband from place to place where he served as a Confederate staff officer. As time passed and Mary and her young daughter attempted to remain as close as possible to Mr. Loughborough. During the Loughborough's travels near the front lines their pathway came closer and closer to Vicksburg. By April of 1863 the incursion of Grant's forces south of Vicksburg and in the area of Jackson forced Mary and her family to flee. They elected to move to Vicksburg where her husband was serving on General Pemberton's staff. Thus began a compelling part of Mary Loughborough's life.

Among the many things that Mary Loughborough did while residing in Vicksburg was maintain a journal. Later, after the city was surrendered and Mary relocated to St. Louis, she shared her writings with friends and family. They were so impressed by both the content and style of Mary's journal that they enjoined her to publish it. In 1864 Mary submitted it to publisher in New York City who promptly put it in print. The book was titled *My Cave Life In Vicksburg* and, in accordance with the morality of the time that frowned upon women writers, the author was described as "By A Lady." In 1881 *My Cave Life* was reprinted to a large audience. Presently, the story of Mary Loughborough's experiences during the siege of Vicksburg can be purchased in a paperback version disseminated by the Vicksburg and Warren County Historical Society and Vicksburg National Military Park. Any serious student of the Vicksburg Campaign and the lives of civilians living in that embattled city would be remiss in overlooking the written record of this plucky woman.

One fascinating aspect of Mary Loughborough's writing is the uniform humanity of her words. Although Mary had been forced from her family home by the tides of war and that her husband was in combat against the Union hosts, Mary Loughborough records no malice towards her "enemies." This fact is doubly surprising when one considers the fact that those selfsame enemies indirectly made great efforts to harm or kill Mary and her loved ones. Yet, despite this fact, Mary described Union troops in a compassionate manner. For example, during her stay in Vicksburg Mary volunteered time at military hospitals. There, Mrs. Loughborough ministered to both Confederate and Union casualties. When she described this work in her journal she demonstrated no difference in terms of her feeling tone toward the well being of either Yanks or Rebs. At one point Mary recorded her thoughts after spending time at one of the hospitals assisting a Federal prisoner who ultimately perished, "What soul in the land but has felt and witnessed this grief—this unavailing sorrow for the brave and untimely dead? I thought of the letter from the sorrowing one in Iowa, whose son, a prisoner, I had nursed, receiving with the last breath words for the distant; unconscious mother; of her sorrow in writing of him in his distant grave; of her pride in him, her only son. How many in the land could take her hand and weep over a mutual sorrow! And in the hospital wards, men, who still hold the name of Americans, together were talking of battles, prisoners, and captors, when each told the other of acts of bravery performed on hostile fields, and took out pictures of innocent babes, little children, and wives, to show each other, all feeling a sympathy and interest in the unknown faces." (12-13)

In Mary Loughborough's view the Civil War was a clash between brethren that made very little sense. Even though Union men were trying to defeat a cause in which she not only believed but also had a vast personal stake, Mary did not come to the view that her nation's opponents were evil or miscreants. Rather, throughout Mary Loughborough's work she described war as the culprit. It was war, and the human drive to engage in it, that Loughborough saw as the great evil and not one cause versus another. At one point Mary defined war as "a species of passionate insanity." (13) It was this form of "insanity" that was to shape Mary's life in Vicksburg, a city that she came to sense was "like resting near a volcano." (14)

Another factor that made Mary Loughborough's written record of the Vicksburg siege so compelling was her talent as a writer. On the one hand, Mary Loughborough did a splendid job of capturing the details of everyday life in a community visited by artillery bombardment, infantry attacks, gunboat salvoes, and limited rations. Yet, during that time of duress, Mary also caught a poet's touch when she depicted the historic events happening around her. An example of this literary bent on Mary's part is her partial description of the fiery sinking of a Federal transport ship during Grant's daring and successful attempt to run his fleet past the powerful Vicksburg fortifications at night, "The lurid glare form the burning boat fell in red and amber light upon the house, the veranda, and the animated faces turned toward the river— lighting the white magnolias, paling the pink crape myrtles, and bringing out in bright distinctness the railing of the terrace, where drooped in fragrant wreaths the clustering passion vine: fair and beautiful, but false, the crimson, wavering light." (18)

In reading these words one can almost see the combination of beauty caused by the terror of warfare. But, later in the same section of her journal Mary Loughborough asked, "Did this smooth, deceitful current of the glowing waters glide over forms loved and lost to the faithful ones at home?" (19) All through her war record Mary Loughborough never lost touch with the innate tragedy that the Civil War was not only for her nation but even more significantly for those individual family pieces that accrued the suffering that was the detritus of a brutal conflict.

During her time in Vicksburg Mary directly observed the most horrible aspects of war. She saw artillery shells smash into people's homes. She experienced the tragic killing or maiming of white and black children in her cliffside neighborhood. Confederate soldiers who showed kindness to her family were blown apart in plain sight of Mary. In the hospitals where she labored Mary encountered the broken and declining victims of wounds and illness. But, even though the hard hand of war forced Mary Loughborough to see and hear of things she would never have dreamed of prior to the war, she maintained a strong love of her fellow man. Perhaps one reason was her religious faith which was such an all encompassing factor not only in Mary Loughborough's life but also those of so many of her contemporaries.

In her journal Mrs. Loughborough consistently turned to God to succor her and her loved ones. These references are not self-centered or selfish in nature. Rather, when Mary Loughborough wrote about her faith one can almost sense the vibrancy of it. On a day when she had seen some terrible things Mary sat down at night and wrote the following words, "Oh, this night time, this starlit, clear, and most pure heaven before us! Does not one see oneself more clearly, when looking upward with the ever-undefined emotion that we feel when gazing at the heavens at night?—does not our own unworthiness, our soul's need of a Saviour, come to us as our conscience, overcoming the callousness of the day and the world, whispers to us of many derelictions of our duty?" In Mary's world, faith and a belief in God's purposeful nature helped her to survive the siege not only physically but spiritually as well.

Ultimately, like so many Vicksburg residents, Mary was forced out of the house she was living in to a cave that her husband had procured for her. During the siege of Vicksburg Union army and naval guns maintained a fairly continuous bombardment of the city. In order to survive this bombardment many Vicksburg civilians chose to go underground and live a mole-like existence. However, even having a cave to live in did not guarantee survival.

Mary Loughborough, her daughter, and the family slaves all came near death during various Union artillery onslaughts. On one occasion Mary described a fairly typical bombardment and the way she and her family lived through it, "I shall never forget my extreme fear during the night, and my utter hopelessness of ever seeing the morning light. Terror stricken we remained crouched in the cave, while shell after shell followed each other in quick succession. I endeavored by constant prayer to prepare myself for the sudden death that I was almost certain awaited me. My heart stood still as we heard the reports from the guns, and the rushing and fearful sound of the guns, and the rushing and fearful sound of the shell as it came toward us. As it neared, the noise became more deafening; the air was full of the rushing sound; pains darted through my temples; my ears were full of confusing noise; and, as it exploded the report flashed through my head like an electric shock, leaving me in a quiet state of terror the most painful that I can imagine—cowering in a corner, holding my child to my heart—the only feeling of my life being the choking throbs of my heart, that rendered me almost breathless. As singly they fell short, or beyond the cave, I was aroused by a feeling of thankfulness that was of short duration. Again and again the terrible fright came over us in the night." (56-57)

This fearful night was but one of many such experiences Mary and her family suffered during the siege. On one occasion a Federal shell flew into the Loughborough's cave home. As Mary held a blanket in front of a visitor in a useless attempt at protection her slave, George, grabbed the shell and threw it out of the cave. Fortunately, the shell's fuse was defective or Mary's account might never have been written.

In other places in Mary Loughborough's journal she described the lethal effects that the Union artillery rounds had. Mary was fortunate indeed to survive unscathed and see her husband and daughter do so as well. Certainly the precautions that the Loughborough's took were a part of the reason for their survival but fate played a hand as well. In several instances Mary was saved by unpredicted twists of fate. One day Mary was sewing near the entrance to her cave. Then, she moved away to retrieve an article she had forgotten only to turn around and see that, "a Minie ball came whizzing through the opening; passed my chair, and fell beyond it. Had I been still sitting, I should have stopped it." Mary went on to note, "Conceive how speedily I took the chair into another part of the room, and sat in it!" (120-121)

But, despite Mary's good fortune, Vicksburg was a place of death and destruction. Throughout her book Mary Loughborough described the "sad news of a Vicksburg day." (91) On a daily basis Mary and her daughter saw the terrible violence of a city under assault. Families saw their children blown to bits by enemy guns. In later years Mary would look back on those memories and say, "The screams of the women of Vicksburg were the saddest I have ever heard." (131) Occasionally Mary would also hear the pain filled screams of horses, mules, and cows that had been smashed by artillery rounds. All around Mary was death and loss which led her to write, "How very sad this life in Vicksburg!—how little security can we feel, with so many around us seeing the morning light that will never more see the night!" (81)

On July 4th the underfed and outmatched Confederate garrison of Vicksburg, Mississippi surrendered to General Grant's Army of the Tennessee. Mary Loughborough's husband survived the siege and, although he continued to serve in the Confederate Army until the war's end, lived to see peace. After the war the Loughborough's moved to Little Rock, Arkansas where Mary's husband worked as a railroad official until his death in 1876. Living as a widow with four children to support Mary Loughborough relied upon her gifts as a writer to maintain her family. Mary authored several books and edited the *Southern Ladies Journal,* a monthly magazine. Mary passed away on August 26, 1887 at the age of fifty but her experiences at Vicksburg lived on in the form of her memoir.

In the words of Mary Loughborough students of Civil War history encounter a clear and pure voice. Mary's journal is not only a valuable primary source resource but also the heartfelt chronicle of a decent woman who became caught up in the machinery of war. Despite the horrors that Mary experienced first hand she maintained her perspective on life and death. One can only feel a sense of respect for a person who could live through what Mary Loughborough did and yet close her book with the following poignant words, "Vicksburg, with her terraced hills—with her pleasant homes and sad memories, passed from my view in the gathering twilight—passed, but the river flowed on the same, and the stars shone out with the same calm light! But the many eyes—O Vicksburg!—that have gazed on thy terraced hills—on thy green and sunny gardens—on the flow of the river—the calm of the stars—those eyes! How many thou hast closed on the world forever!" (145-146)

Source

Loughborough, Mary W. *My Cave Life In Vicksburg.* Vicksburg, MS: Vicksburg &
    Warren County Historical Society, 2003. \

11

Women Spies of the Civil War

Looking at her work as a Confederate spy young Belle Edmondson once wrote in her diary, "Tis a risk, yet we can accomplish nothing without great risk at times." (Caravantes 95) In fact, the work of being a Civil War spy involved both great risk and the potential for an untimely death. Yet, despite the inherent danger in espionage a number of women took up that clandestine role in order to serve the cause of their choice. The story of some of these intrepid and daring women is one of the more colorful aspects of civilian life during a war that went a long way toward establishing the nature of modern American history.

During the course of the Civil War intelligence services as we now know of them existed in a rather rudimentary state. The need to know what an opponent is planning or carrying out has been an important aspect of warfare since before the dawn of recorded history. In the American Civil War both the North & South used agents to secretly uncover important information about their enemies. In an age when women were supposed to be demure and controlled it was somewhat shocking to imagine a lady carrying out such nefarious work. However, despite the social stigma there were women who chose to plunge ahead and serve their country in the best way that they could. In a few cases a written record remains intact that details the spy work of these unusual women. In looking at the careers of a few of these female spy masters one comes away with a vivid impression of both their bravery and the risks they were willing to expose themselves to.

In looking back at some of the female spies of the Civil War a number of names come to mind. Among those figures was Elizabeth Van Lew of Richmond Virginia. Elizabeth Van Lew grew up in the heart of what was to become the Confederate capital. Still, despite this upbringing Miss Van Lew retained a staunch opposition to the institution of slavery. Educated in Philadelphia Elizabeth Van Lew came to believe that, "From the time I knew right from wrong it was my sad privilege to differ in many ways from the…opinions and principles of my locality." (Kane 233) Those differences led Van Lew to oppose both slavery and secession while choosing to become a spy for the Union.

Living in Richmond Elizabeth Van Lew made no secret of her support of the Union cause. Often Elizabeth would travel to Libby Prison where she brought food to some of the Federal prisoners ensconced there. On these visits of mercy Elizabeth Van Lew came to realize how miserable the condition of the Union prisoners was. In her August 10, 1861 journal entry Elizabeth described the terrible sights that greeted her at Libby Prison, "Sad day. Three prisoners died. The only medical attention these unfortunates get is what Mother and I give them. It is not enough. No one should see the sights I have seen. Men with limbs missing, forced to live in the filthiest of conditions. Our mare has a cleaner stall to sleep in." (Caravantes 80-81)

Seeing the men who fought for the cause she believed in treated in this inhumane manner may have contributed to Elizabeth Van Lew's decision to become a spy. At any rate Van Lew began to smuggle notes and messages in and out of Libby. To accomplish this secret activity Elizabeth Van Lew made use of a warming pan that contained a hidden compartment. Every time she visited the prison she brought in letters, instructions, and information while she exited with intelligence notations from the prisoners. In this way Van Lew became a valuable source of intelligence information gleaned from Confederate prison guards, officers, and other Rebel supporters who were overheard by the Yankee prisoners.

In another twist one of Elizabeth's freed slaves, Mary Elizabeth Bowser, became an employee in the household of President Jefferson Davis. Elizabeth Bowser had been sent north by the Van Lew's to be educated in a proper manner. Upon her return to Richmond her work at the Jefferson house became a valuable conduit of information that was passed on by Elizabeth Van Lew to her contacts in the Union. In this way Elizabeth Van Lew's influence and ability to spy for the Union cause extended into the Confederate White House.

During the war years Elizabeth Van Lew lived with the constant scorn of her Confederate neighbors. In order to offset this dislike and avert suspicion Elizabeth adopted an eccentric demeanor. She behaved in a strange manner that earned her the sobriquet of "Crazy Bet." (Caravantes 81) But, despite her efforts at concealment Elizabeth Van Lew lived with the certainty that her capture could occur at any time.

A *New York Times* article written after the war noted, "there was not a moment during those four years when Lizzie Van Lew could hear a step behind her on the street without expecting to have someone tap her on the shoulder and say, 'You are my prisoner.'" Perhaps it was this level of commitment to the Union cause that prompted General Grant to say to Elizabeth over tea, "You have sent me the most valuable information received from Richmond during the war." (Furguson 230)

Fortunately for Elizabeth Van Lew her espionage work was never discovered until the Union had won the war. Afterwards, Elizabeth was temporarily rewarded for her spy work by being given a series of civil service jobs. However, Elizabeth's spying left her permanently ostracized from Richmond society. Looking around her home town Elizabeth wrote in her journal in 1889, "I live—and have lived for years—as entirely distinct from the citizens as if I were plague stricken…Rarely, very rarely, is our doorbell ever rung by any but a pauper, or those desiring my service." (Ryan 126)

Elizabeth Van Lew died on September 25, 1900, at the age of eighty-two and was buried in Richmond's Shockhoe Hill Cemetery. Her tombstone bears an epitaph that Van Lew probably would have appreciated and understood, "She risked everything that is dear to man—friends, fortune, comfort, health, life itself, all for one absorbing desire of her heart—that slavery might be abolished." (Weinert 34)

While Elizabeth Van Lew risked all social standing as well as her very life for the Union Rose Greenhow chose to live in Washington D.C. while spying for the Confederacy. Among the female spies of the Civil War perhaps no one was more audacious than Rose Greenhow. Amazingly, Greenhow made no secret of her strong southern sympathies. At the outset of the war she publicly declared, "I am a Southern woman, born with Revolutionary blood in my veins." (Kane 19) But, despite these declarations Rose Greenhow was able to become intimate with a number of powerful Union soldiers and government officials. From these personal relationships Rose Greenhow received valuable intelligence information that she promptly passed on to Confederate officials.

An example of the magnetism that Rose Greenhow must have possessed was her relationship with Senator Henry Wilson of Massachusetts. Wilson was a powerful senator and chairman of the Senate Military Affairs Committee. The good senator from Massachusetts was also madly in love with Rose Greenhow. Wilson wrote torrid love letters to Rose Greenhow in which he declared, "You will know that I love you and will sacrifice anything." (Bakeless 10) In another letter Wilson stated, "Tonight, at whatever cost I will see you…I will be with you tonight, and then I will tell you again and again that I love you." (Bakeless 10)

Although Henry Wilson was never charged with any complicity in Greenhow's espionage work he surely betrayed relevant information that found its way into the hands of Confederate representatives. In this act of passionate indiscretion Senator Wilson was not alone. In fact, Rose Greenhow had a series of valuable liaisons with powerful Washingtonians each of which offered some actual or potential sources of intelligence data. Greenhow made no bones about her use of all her "charms" to worm her way into the confidence of the men she tempted. Indeed it was recorded that Rose Greenhow used "every capacity which God endowed" her with in pursuit of vital information for the southern cause. (Kane 28)

Perhaps the greatest intelligence boom that Rose Greenhow discovered was linked to the Confederate victory at First Bull Run. Through her connections and physicality Greenhow uncovered vital information about Federal troop movements prior to that battle. Just prior to the Bull Run fight Greenhow sent the following coded message to Confederate General Beauregard, "McDowell has certainly been ordered to advance on the sixteenth. ROG" (Papanek 27) This information assisted the Confederates to respond more promptly to Federal dispositions that they might otherwise have been able to. As a result Bull Run became a humiliating Union defeat. Afterwards Rose Greenhow received an anonymous message from the Confederate government, "Our President and our General direct me to thank you. We rely upon you for further information. The Confederacy owes you a debt." (Papanek 27)

Eventually Rose Greenhow's spying drew attention and suspicion to her. Famed detective Allen Pinkerton was assigned to observe Greenhow's home and movements. Over time Pinkerton became convinced that Greenhow was a spy. After patiently staking out the Greenhow residence Pinkerton finally raided it. Although Rose Greenhow was able to either swallow or dispose of incriminating evidence she could not stop the Federal government from placing her under house arrest. But even that action did not stop Rose Greenhow from continuing her espionage work.

While under house arrest Rose Greenhow still was able to continue her spying. Greenhow smuggled coded notes out with visitors, posted color-coded messages in needlework or flags she displayed in her windows, and tossed notes out to agents as they walked past the premises.

Ultimately Greenhow was discovered and sent to the Old Capital Prison where she was kept for a year. After finally refusing to sign an oath of allegiance Rose and several other suspected spies were sent south into the Confederacy. There, Rose Greenhow was received by President Jefferson Davis who told her, "But for you, there would have been no Bull Run." (Leonard 43) Emboldened by this reinforcement Rose Greenhow determined to continue her work for the Confederacy.

After spending time in Europe Greenhow decided that she had to return to the South. She boarded a British blockade-runner, the *Condor*, and sailed for America. In her possession was $2,000 in gold coin that was intended for the purchase of arms for the Confederate army. Unfortunately for Greenhow a Union warship caught up with the *Condor* at the mouth of the Cape Fear River near Wilmington, North Carolina. Fearing capture Greenhow cajoled the captain of the *Condor* to allow her to launch a lifeboat and head for shore with several companions. Despite high seas Greenhow was determined to avoid capture and potential execution as an unrepentant Confederate agent. In those stormy seas Greenhow's boat capsized. With the weight of her gold coins that were hidden in her dress Rose Greenhow was dragged down into the sea and drowned. Subsequently her body washed up on shore and was discovered the following day. The money that she possessed ultimately did end up in the hands of the Confederate government but her life was over. Greenhow was buried in Wilmington and her marble grave marker reads, "Mrs. Rose O'N.

Greenhow, a bearer of dispatchs (sic) to the Confederate Government." (Kane 67)

If the death of Rose Greenhow seems tragic, the near execution of Pauline Cushman has all the elements of high drama. At the start of the Civil War Pauline Cushman was making her living as an actress. A staunch Union sympathizer, Cushman was approached by Federal officials and enticed to begin working as a spy. In order to earn the trust of Confederate supporters Pauline was convinced that she would have to make a public display of her alleged Southern perspective. In order to gain the false confidence of Confederates Pauline chose to announce her rebellious leanings at a stage performance in Louisville, Kentucky. On the night of her performance Cushman stepped to the middle of the stage in the middle of the play, raised a glass in hand, and yelled, "Here's to Jeff Davis and the Southern Confederacy. May the South always maintain her honor and her rights!" (Young 237)

Pauline Cushman's surprise announcement was met with vibrantly divided emotions. Union supporters fired her and ridiculed her Rebel tendencies. Conversely, Cushman's ploy worked as she was accepted as a loyal Confederate by Southern officials. Their acceptance set the stage for the commencement of Pauline Cushman's espionage endeavors.

For several years Pauline Cushman toured the south performing on stage, interacting with leaders, and consistently smuggling intelligence data back north. Among the people Cushman was able to become close to were Confederate officers, local politicians, and military advisors. At the same time Cushman was ridiculed and disowned by the Northern press as well as past friends who saw her as a traitor to the Union cause.

Over time suspicion was cast upon Cushman's efforts. At one point the minions of General Nathan Bedford Forrest detained her. Forrest had his men bring Cushman to him and greeted her in the following manner, "Miss Cushman, I'm glad to see you. You're pretty sharp at turning a card, but I think we've got you on this last shuffle, and I've made up my mind not to part with you during the war." (Sarmiento 2253)

Cushman was then taken to the headquarters of Forrest's superior, General Braxton Bragg. In General Bragg's presence Pauline Cushman was questioned. After the interrogation Bragg informed Pauline Cushman about her potential fate if found guilty of spying, "If found guilty you will be hanged." (Sarmiento 286) Cushman begged Bragg to shoot her rather than a death by hanging and commented, "General, come now! I don't think I'd be either useful or ornamental dangling at the end of a rope." (Sarmiento 288)

After speaking with General Bragg, Pauline Cushman was then detained and subsequently questioned by Colonel McKinstry, provost marshal at Bragg's headquarters. After a prolonged session of questions and answers McKinstry was heard to say, "That woman is the very devil, and would almost convince one that black is white!" (Sarmiento 297) Pauline was then closely confined as the Confederates continued to investigate her doings. During the time of her confinement Pauline Cushman unsuccessfully attempted to win the trust of her jailers in the hope that they would allow her to escape. Sadly for Cushman this ploy failed and she was ultimately found guilty of spying. As General Bragg had promised, Pauline's sentenced was death by hanging.

By the grace of good fortune Pauline Cushman was spared the hangman's rope as Federal troops advanced into the area where she was being held. Cushman's Rebel jailors left her behind as they fled from the advancing Yankees. Shaken and depressed, Cushman gratefully accepted her salvation at the hands of the forces for which she had secretly worked for two years.

In 1864 Cushman published her wartime spying escapades in a biography appropriately titled *The Thrilling Adventures of Pauline Cushman.* At that time Cushman also began a tour of theatrical performances based upon her adventures. This lifestyle continued into the 1870's as Pauline performed and orated with her own life as the subject matter on stages as far west as California. Eventually Pauline gave up acting and began to work as a seamstress. On December 2, 1893 Pauline's San Francisco landlady found her unconscious in her room. Apparently Cushman had either accidentally or intentionally taken an overdose of morphine, a narcotic to which she had become addicted. Later that day Cushman succumbed to heart failure brought on by her overdose. Four days later Cushman was given a full military funeral at the National Cemetery in Presidio, California.

Although Pauline Cushman's name has not been definitively connected with any specific Union victory, her espionage efforts were greatly appreciated by her government. Also, despite the growing hyperbole that Cushman included in her stage plays about her exploits, it cannot be denied that she took her life in her hands when she worked as a Union spy. Therefore, it is quite probably fair to state as the *New York Times* did on May 28, 1864, "among the women of America who have made themselves famous since the opening of the rebellion, few have suffered more or rendered more service to the Federal cause than Pauline Cushman, the female scout and spy." (Leonard 58)

While Pauline Cushman was literally risking her neck for the Federal cause, Belle Boyd was working equally hard to subvert it. Boyd first comes to attention on the 4th of July in 1861. On that day Federal soldiers who two days prior had occupied Boyd's hometown of Martinsdale, Virginia attempted to force entry into her home. One drunken Union sergeant and several of his men managed to push their way into the Boyd home intent upon raising a Federal flag from the roof top. Mrs. Boyd yelled at the soldiers, "Men, every member of this household will die before that flag is raised over us." (Hergesheimer 244) The sergeant then cursed Mrs. Boyd and ended up scuffling with her. Belle Boyd came upon this discordant scene and, thinking her mother was in danger, pulled out a revolver. Later Belle recalled what came next, "I could stand it no longer…my blood was literally boiling in my veins; I drew out my pistol and shot him. He was carried away mortally wounded and soon after expired."(Hergesheimer 244)

Surprisingly, Federal officials found Belle's actions to be justifiable homicide and she was not charged with a crime. However, this intrusion into the sanctity of the Boyd home steeled Belle to carry out what she had longed to do—spy for her beloved Confederacy.

Over the following months Belle Boyd used whatever opportunities presented themselves to her to acquire and pass on valuable intelligence. In Boyd's own words, "Whatever I heard I regularly and carefully committed to paper, and whenever an opportunity offered I sent my secret dispatch to some brave officer in command of the Confederate troops." (Leonard 27) Amazingly, even though Belle Boyd was less than subtle about her spying she was never apprehended and charged with espionage. Time and again, Boyd was allowed to travel throughout the South by Federal officers who often issued her passes to go back and forth across enemy lines. It seems that Boyd's charisma and youth worked in her favor and charmed the Yankees whom she so righteously despised.

On one occasion in 1864 Boyd returned to her hometown of Martinsburg and asked for & received a pass to Richmond from a Union provost marshal. While on the train en route to the Confederate capital Belle Boyd granted an interview to a reporter working for the *New York Tribune*. The reporter later wrote, "She pleads guilty to nearly all charges against her, as far as they refer to conveying information to the enemy, carrying letters and parcels form the rebels within our lines to those without, and performing acts of heroic daring worthy of the days of the Revolution." (Bakeless 153-54)

In the summer of 1862 Belle Boyd was detained and temporarily imprisoned. In prison her Yankee jailers were unable to successfully prove their accusations against Boyd. Frustrated, the Union officers offered to release Boyd if she consented to swearing a loyalty oath to the Federal government. In response to this offer Belle flatly declared, "I hope that when I commence the oath of allegiance to the United States Government, my tongue may cleave to the roof of my mouth; and that if I ever sign one line that will show (that) I owe the United States Government the slightest allegiance, I hope my arm may fall paralyzed by my side." (Stern 106)

Without evidence, Belle had to be released. Following her imprisonment Belle Boyd persisted in her smuggling and spying for the remainder of the war. In 1864 Boyd was sent to London with secret dispatches for the British government. Once in London Belle married and remained there as the Confederacy fell to defeat. Boyd continued to live in Britain until 1866 where she wrote a two-volume account of her wartime adventures and experiences.

In 1866 Boyd returned to the United States as the then President Andrew Johnson had signed into law a Proclamation of Amnesty for former Confederates. Now widowed Boyd remarried in 1869. Unfortunately Boyd's second marriage, although it produced four children three of whom survived to adulthood, ended in divorce. After marrying a third time Belle Boyd commenced a theatrical career wherein she performed orations & performances based upon her Civil War adventures. Interestingly enough Belle Boyd chose to end those performances with a stirring declaration, "One God, One Flag, One People Forever." (Caravantes 45)

On June 10, 1900 Belle Boyd died of a heart attack. She had lived for Fifty-six years and had conducted an adventuresome existence. At the end Boyd's funeral expenses were paid by members of the woman's auxiliary of the Grand Army of the Republic, a Union veteran's organization. At her gravesite four Union veteran's helped to lower Belle Boyd's casket into the earth. In this odd way Belle Boyd's life, so much of which had been dedicated to the cause of secession, ended on a note of unity.

For Belle Boyd, Pauline Cushman, Rose Greenhow, and Elizabeth Van Lew the causes they supported were so powerful that they drew them into the maelstrom of espionage and danger. These four women had varying degrees of success and impact as spies. They were radically different personalities. Their spying machinations took their own unique forms. However, what they held in common was a willingness to take great risks for a cause they wholeheartedly believed in. In the end, the Confederacy that Belle Boyd and Rose Greenhow faded into non-existence. The Union cause supported by Pauline Cushman and Elizabeth Van Lew prevailed. But what is of some interest is the fact that win or lose those four women continue to hold a special place in the history of civilian efforts during the Civil War. Those intrepid women put aside the traditional lot of females in their era and took up the gauntlet of challenge that war thrust their way. For these and other reasons their work as Civil War spies stands out as adventuresome, brave hearted, and noteworthy.

Sources

Bakeless, John. *The War Between the Spies.* New York, NY: J.B. Lippincott Co., 1970.

Caravantes, Peggy. *Petticoat Spies: Six Women Spies of the Civil War.* Greensboro, NC:

Morgan Reynolds, 2002.

Furguson, Ernest B. *Ashes to Glory: Richmond at War.* New York, NY: Alfred A.
    Knopf, 1996

Hergesheimer, Joseph. *Swords and Roses.* New York, NY: Alfred A. Knopf, 1929.

Kane, Harnett T. *Spies for the Blue and Gray.* Garden City, NY: Hanover House, 1954.

Leonard, Elizabeth D. *All the Daring of the Soldier: Women of the Civil War Armies.*
    New York, NY: W.W. Norton & Co., 1999.

Papanek, John L., (ed.). *Spies, Scouts and Raiders: Irregular Operations.* Alexandria,
    VA: Time-Life, 1985.

Ryan, David D., (ed.). *A Yankee Spy in Richmond: The Civil War Diary of "Crazy Bet"*
    Van Lew. Mechanicsburg, PA: Stackpole Books, 1996.

Sarmiento, F.L. *Life of Pauline Cushman: The Celebrated Union Spy and Scout.*
    New York, NY: John W. Lovell Co., 1890.

Stern, Philip Van Doren. *Secret Missions of the Civil War.* New York, NY: Bonanzo
    Books, 1959.

Weinert, Richard P. "Federal Spies in Richmond." *Civil War Times Illustrated 3*
    (February 1965): 28-37.

Young, Agatha. *The Women and the Crisis: Women of the North in the Civil War.*
    New York, NY: McDowell, Oblensky, 1959.

12

Louisa May Alcott's Life & Times

When a listing of memorable 19th century American books is drafted, it inevitably includes Louisa May Alcott's domestic masterpiece *Little Women*. Written just after the Civil War, *Little Women* remains one of the most approachable, warm, and touching literary works of that era. Written by a bright, determined, and stouthearted woman of that day and age, *Little Women* stands out as a testament to the human spirit that typified an era within which the very soul of the nation was torn asunder. However, what can easily be forgotten is that the story contained within the pages of *Little Women* was one closely based upon the real life experiences of its author. Those same experiences continue to serve as vivid testimony to what coming of age in the mid-19th century meant not only for Louisa May Alcott but also for many other Americans.

Born in 1832 in Germantown, Pennsylvania, Louisa May Alcott was blessed by parents whose non-mainstream values assisted in her eventual rise to literary fame. Bronson and Abigail Alcott were abolitionists, Transcendentalists, social reformers, and liberal ideologues. As Louisa's parents began to raise a family they also honed a belief system that was to exert tremendous influence upon her life and works. The Alcott family believed in humane & comprehensive female education. They opposed slavery both in the human bondage form it took in the antebellum south as well as the wage slavery experienced by northern mill and factory workers. Louisa's parents frequently moved their family in pursuit of dreams based upon a philosophy that emphasized equality, freedom, independence, education, and service to others.

In her childhood Louisa May Alcott grew up being educated by her somewhat flamboyant and mercurial father and a mother who could be both loving and high strung. Louisa lived in many homes with her family and spent time on communally run utopian farms such as Fruitland. In that and similar settings, the Alcott family banded together with several other like-minded couples and attempted to eke out an agrarian living that exploited neither man nor beast. In many ways this rural lifestyle seems similar to the humble lives of pseudo-socialist societies or the efforts of the still existing Quakers and Amish.

Living in a family where learning, education, and reflection were stressed, Louisa May Alcott struggled with a spirit that tended toward fieriness. The Alcott's kept journals that other family members could read and place written comments within. On all too many occasions Louisa's childhood and adolescent journal entries center upon her personal faults. Sometimes alongside Louisa's self-critical entries would appear a more soothingly philosophical note from her mother, who her children referred to as "Abba." In Louisa May Alcott's journal we meet a turbulent but good-hearted spirit. On those pages a reader encounters a physically and mentally active girl who loved to run across fields, walk in the woods, provoke her sisters, study the falling leaves, and strive to improve herself.

Indeed these linked concepts of personal self-improvement and reflection were to remain cornerstone elements of Louisa May Alcott's life and writing. In her youthful journal one can also meet an impulsive soul who, after a particularly serious tantrum, was once gently chided by her mother with the following notation, "I was grieved at your selfish behavior this morning, but also greatly pleased that you bore so meekly father's reproof of it. I know that you will have a happy day after the storm. Keep quiet, read, walk, but do not talk much till all is peace again."(Meigs 88-89) On a more mellow day Abba praised Louisa, "I have observed all day your patience with baby, your obedience to me, your kindness to all." (Meigs 88) This process of sharing and the refinement of behavior and attitudes typified the family life of the Alcott's.

As Louisa May Alcott became a young woman she could look back on a young life filled with unusual opportunities. Henry David Thoreau tutored Louisa. Miss Alcott's circle of acquaintances included Ralph Waldo Emerson and his family. The Alcott's came in close contact with members of the abolitionist cause as well as Underground Railroad operatives. These formative experiences helped craft Louisa May Alcott's belief system and core values. In this fashion Louisa became a staunch opponent of slavery and could not grasp how human beings could see their brethren as mere chattel. Louisa also deeply felt the need to serve others while striving to assist in the support of her often financially strapped family. Louisa's search for self-expression via her work led her, in turn, to become a teacher, traveling companion, and tutor. In her spare time Louisa wrote short stories and essays. Simultaneous to Miss Alcott's search for herself, her beloved homeland was inexorably sliding toward the great cataclysm of civil war.

While grand national events were playing out Louisa May Alcott continued to go about the daily business of living. When she took up the challenge of earning a living as a teacher she found it to be a difficult charge but also one that she was quite good at. Still, it was in her writing that Louisa May felt she best expressed her inner talents. From her adolescence on into adulthood Louisa May Alcott strove to capture her emotions, beliefs, and thoughts in print. Childhood plays, youthful newspapers, short stories of adventure, sensational tales, and romantic renderings typified Louisa's early efforts as a writer. As the time of the Civil War neared, Louisa had seen several of her works published in various journals and magazines. However, Louisa was yet to find her true literary voice. On one occasion in that period Louisa's father sent some of his daughter's short stories to a noted editor. That man's verdict was swift and cutting, "Tell Louisa to stick to her teaching. She is never going to be a writer." (Meigs 86) Fortunately, Louisa did not take that criticism fully to heart and later demonstrated a noteworthy skill with her pen.

The coming of the Civil War awakened in the heart of Louisa May Alcott a strong desire to serve her nation and its citizenry. Louisa put aside her work as a teacher and writer and strove to craft some form of worthy service. For years the Alcott's had predicted an internecine conflict spurred on by the evils of slavery. Now it had arrived and Louisa greeted its coming with a whirlwind of emotion, "I've often longed to see war, and now I have my wish. I long to be a man; but as I can't fight, I will content myself with working for those who can." (Johnston 139) On that note, Louisa commenced to sew clothing for soldiers, minister to their families, and seek out any and all opportunities to assist the cause she so stridently believed in. But still, despite all her labors for the Union, she felt ill at ease with her contributions.

In her diary Louisa wrote, "The blood of the Mays is up. I must go." (Meigs 110)

As Louisa pondered what service she could better provide, no clear options came to mind. Trapped in a society where the work open to women was very limited it was fair for Louisa to become frustrated. All through this period of personal searching Louisa came back to one central point, "I want something to do." (Alcott 3) Finally, the idea of volunteering as a nurse became a self-evident one. With a goal in mind Louisa May Alcott successfully gained an assignment as a volunteer nurse in Washington. With a true vocation in mind Louisa May set out for the nation's capital to serve the soldiers who risked all for the noble cause she believed in.

In December 1862 Louisa May Alcott arrived in Washington City and began her tenure as a nurse at Union Hotel Hospital in nearby Georgetown. There, Louisa May was to experience all the sadness that warfare's terrible toll could create. As a nurse Louisa dedicated herself to helping the poor, battered, bruised, bloody, torn, and sickened men who came under her charge. As a volunteer nurse Louisa wrote letters home to loved ones dictated by men too battered, sick, or damaged to take pen in hand themselves. Some of those letters were the final contact beloved family members ever had with their departed kindred spirits. In the hospital wards Louisa tended to men's bandages and soothed the fevered brows of lads who tossed and turned in their illness. Feverish soldiers cried out in their troubled sleep for loved ones who were not present and Louisa spoke to them and quieted their fears. This time at Georgetown touched Louisa to the core and shaped much of her later literary work.

While serving at Georgetown Louisa wrote extensive letters home to her family that included long depictions of her nursing experiences. These "dispatches" were to become the basis for Louisa May Alcott's popularly successful publication when they were later compiled and printed as *Hospital Sketches*.

Written anonymously and with pseudonyms for the characters and the hospital itself, *Hospital Sketches* became a nearly instant "hit." First serialized in a journal this slim volume then became a very successful book. That success became a catalyst for some of Louisa May's later writing as well as being an honest description of the realities of a Civil War hospital. Within the one hundred or so pages of this little book Louisa May Alcott revealed not only her writing talents but also a soul that was quite striking.

In *Hospital Sketches* Louisa May shares her initial impressions and insecurities when she first arrived at the hospital, "Hurly-burly House, ma'am!" called a voice, startling me from my reverie, as we stopped before a great pile of buildings, with a flag flying before it, sentinels at the door, and a very trying quantity of men lounging about. My heart beat rather faster than usual, and it suddenly struck me that I was very far from home." (Alcott 24)

Very soon after arriving at "Hurly-burly House" Louisa was summoned to help with a load of wounded who were coming directly from the battlefield at Fredericksburg where they had fought with both bravery and futility. Once they arrived Louisa was shaken by their appearance, "I paused to take a breath and a survey. There they were! "our brave boys," as the papers justly call them, for cowards could hardly have been so riddled with shot and shell, so torn and shattered, nor have borne suffering for which we have no name, with an uncomplaining fortitude, which made one glad to cherish each like a brother." (Alcott 27-28)

As the wounded members of General Ambrose Burnside's defeated Army of the Potomac flowed into her ward Louisa May took hold of herself and plunged into the work at hand, "Round the great stove was gathered the dreariest group I ever saw—ragged, gaunt, and pale, mud to the knees, with bandages untouched since put on days before; many bundled up in blankets, coats being lost or useless; and all wearing that disheartened look that proclaimed defeat, more plainly than any telegram of the Burnside blunder. I pitied them so much, I dared not speak to them, though, remembering all they had been through since the fight at Fredericksburg, I yearned to serve the dreariest of them all." (Alcott 28-29)

Over time this type of activity would become almost second nature to Louisa May Alcott. But, despite the frequency with which she came in contact with human suffering, its proximity did not dull Louisa's compassionate nature. Indeed, it was Alcott's strong sense of empathy for her patients that led her to see the army doctors as unnecessarily impersonal and cold in their attitude toward their patients. This personal detachment led even the finest doctor Louisa May Alcott served with to see his patients as interesting science projects rather than fathers, husbands, brothers, or friends to others. At one point Louisa writes about this paradoxical thinking, "The more intricate the wound, the better he liked it. A poor private, with both legs off, and shot through the lungs, possessed more attractions for him than a dozen generals, slightly scratched in some "masterly retreat;" and had anyone appeared in small pieces, requesting to be put together again, he would have considered it a special dispensation." (Alcott 36-37)

Death was a frequent companion of Louisa May Alcott during her time at "Hurly-burly House." Each time she was called upon to see the passing of a soldier it touched Louisa's heart. On the first instance of seeing a soldier boy die Louisa pondered on the setting where a unique life had ended, "It seemed a poor requital for all he had sacrificed and suffered, —that hospital bed, lonely even in a crowd for there was no familiar face for him to look his last upon; no friendly voice to say, Good bye; no band to lead him gently down into the Valley of the Shadow; and he vanished, like a drop in that Red Sea upon whose shores so many women stand lamenting." (Alcott 35-36)

But even among so many deaths some individual ones stood out in Louisa's memory. On one occasion she stood quietly by as a father observed the passing of his son, " To me the saddest sight I saw in that sad place, was the spectacle of a gray-haired father, sitting hour after hour by his son, dying from the poison of his wound. The old father, hale and hearty; the young son, past all help, though one could scarcely believe it; for the subtle fever, burning his strength away, flushed his cheeks with color, filled his eyes with luster, and lent a mockery of health to face and figure, making the poor lad comelier in death than in life." (Alcott 85)

In *Hospital Sketches* readers of the Civil War era were afforded a first-hand glimpse into the sometimes cruel life on a ward in a military hospital. In the pages of this slim and compelling volume readers saw the sights that troubled Louisa's dreams. In those same pages they also encountered the men who stoically accepted loss, disability, and even death as their lot. Through its earnest sincerity and writing style *Hospital Sketches* became a solid success for its author. Still, while thousands perused the pages penned by Louisa May Alcott, those same words nearly led to her own death.

While fulfilling her duties as a nurse Louisa May Alcott became deathly ill with typhoid. For several weeks Louisa's life hung in the balance as she fought her illness. Fortunately, Louisa recovered from her disease although it did cost her all of her long and lustrous hair. Louisa's father traveled to Washington and took his daughter back home to Concord, Massachusetts. After one hard month of service, Louisa May Alcott returned home to be where she was nursed to recovery within the fabric of her loving family. Still, even though she had worked for only a short time as a nurse, what Louisa May Alcott observed in that month cast a spell upon much of the remainder of her life.

After the ending of the Civil War, Louisa May dedicated her writing to the telling of a simple story for girls. Those efforts were to blossom into *Little Women*, a novel that captured the moral values of its epoch. In *Little Women* we meet the fictional Marsh family, a literary version of the Alcott's. In the moving pages of this classic readers encountered the very substance of Louisa May Alcott's life. When the fictional Beth gently dies we are watching a recreation of Louisa's feelings when her own sister, Elizabeth, succumbed to the aftereffects of scarlet fever. The maternal star of the book, Marmy, is a paper and pencil version of Abba. The tempestuous Jo Marsh is Louisa to a tee. Readers who purchased *Little Women* entered the world of both the Marsh's and the Alcott's. After reading this moving book they left it changed for the better. Values such as generosity, service, compassion, reflection, and responsibility flow throughout *Little Women* like a river of honesty. Those values were also at the core of Louisa May Alcott and her family. In many ways those same values were also typical of elements of broader American ethics of the Civil War era.

In her later years Louisa May Alcott continued her writing career. Alcott published numerous books inclusive of several continuations of the Marsh saga. Louisa also traveled and worked as an educator. Upon the death of May, one of her younger sisters, Louisa was placed in charge of her young niece, Lulu. As an adoptive parent Louisa May dedicated herself to the successfully caring for her niece and found fulfillment in this maternal role. Yet, despite this loving dip into the world of parenthood and domesticity, Louisa May Alcott remained single until her death.

Although she had several suitors in her lifetime, Louisa May Alcott preferred a life of freedom and independence. At one point Louisa recorded her belief that, "I put in my list all the busy, useful, independent spinsters I know, for liberty is a better husband than love to many of us." (Johnston 167) In her solitary life Louisa felt like a "happy millionaire" dependent upon no other person for her sustenance. (Johnston 167)

Years passed and, in 1877, Louisa's beloved Abba died. Then, on March 4, 1888, so too did Bronson Alcott. Interestingly enough, just two days later, Louisa May Alcott also died. Over the years since the close of the Civil War Louisa had prospered but never fully recovered form the effects of her bout with typhoid fever. Like so many other Civil War "veterans," Louisa May Alcott's life was cut short due to the travails and suffering inherent in warfare.

It is all too easy to forget that famous personages form the past were also living, breathing human beings just like ourselves. In Louisa May Alcott one can see a famous writer with an illustrious literary pedigree. One can also look back and consider the life of a brave and passionate woman who not only wrote books that remain moving to this day but also placed her life on the line for the cause that touched her soul. Louisa May Alcott had hopes and dreams, fears, and foibles, & a vibrant personality. At times she behaved in a moral and ethical manner that continues to ring true in the pages of her books. At other moments in her life Louisa May acted in a childish and argumentative fashion. To put it simply—Louisa May was a real person with gifts and deficits like everyone else. In her life and work we are blessed to be able to recreate some of the elements of her spirit. As a volunteer nurse, writer, loving daughter, and moral friend Louisa May Alcott represented a person that would have been fascinating to know. She also typified the values and morals of the era in which she lived. In studying the course of this one woman's life one can discern themes that were typical of the years that encompassed the gravest challenge ever faced by Louisa May Alcott's homeland. Louisa was a child of the Civil War and a participant in the tragedy and resurrection that conflict embodied. She was one memorable atom in the structure of her day and age.

Sources

Alcott, Louisa May. *Hospital Sketches.* Bedford, MA: Applewood Books, 1993.

Johnston, Norma. *Louisa May: The World and Works of Louisa May Alcott.*
    New York, NY: Beech Tree Books, 1991.

Meigs, Cornelia. *Invincible Louisa: The Story of the Author of Little Women.*
    New York, NY: Little, Brown & Company, 1995

13

A Gentrified View of Plantation Life

The primary reason that the Civil War even occurred was slavery. In our own times the concept of the owning of human beings seems bestial. Yet, in the antebellum United States it was not only legal but also commonplace. The paradox of Americans publicly declaring their love of freedom & independence while simultaneously holding millions of African-Americans in bondage seems almost too hypocritical to believe. But, in 1861 many Americans, particularly but not solely in the South, saw no contradiction between holding dear their revolutionary heritage while at the same time dealing in human flesh & blood.

In looking back at the Civil War era it may be beneficial to make a closer examination of how southern plantation folk justified their lifestyle. After the war, and particularly in the final two decades of the 19th century, a host of memoirs, compilations of letters, diaries, and other publications came to the fore each of which had something to say about the Civil War and its meaning. One particularly impactful genre of these post-war writings was that of the military or civilian story of the "lost cause." Typically, "lost cause" books told the story of how the Confederacy represented a noble endeavor based upon principles akin to those held dear to the hearts of the "Founding Fathers." In these sorts of publications the defeated South no longer stood for the evils of slavery but rather a wholesome land of knights, cavaliers, civility, and peaceful coexistence among the races. For "lost cause" writers the Civil War was a national tragedy that could have been avoided if only the endemic nature of the gentle southern culture had been respected. Instead, overly aggressive and profit driven "Yankees" swooped in with little understanding of the nature of slavery or the society which was built upon it. In many ways Margaret Mitchell's romantic novel of the South, *Gone With the Wind*, is a more modern version of this mindset.

In reality, life in the ante bellum South was far from a peaceful kingdom of grace & understanding. Over four million African-Americans were held in the South as slaves. While the conditions of servitude widely varied across slave owners, there can be little doubt that the very nature of human bondage was cruel, dehumanizing, and brutal. Still, even years after the war many southerners held onto the notion that there was something essentially noble about the style of life maintained in the slave-owning Confederacy. A prime example of that mindset was Parthenia Antoinette Hague, a woman who took pen in hand twenty-five years after the Civil War to describe her own romantic notion of both the "lost cause" and the mellow society that carried it out.

Born on November 19, 1839 Parthenia Antoinette Hague was the daughter of a slave owner in rural Georgia. As a young adult in the 1850's Parthenia Hague traveled to Alabama to teach school on plantations located near Eufaula. There, ensconced among the slave owning agriculturalists, teaching the children of privileged families, Parthenia Hague became steadily more convinced of the justness of the ante bellum way of life. Years later, as a woman in her fifties, Parthenia Hague composed a wartime memoir titled *A Blockaded Family: Life In Southern Alabama During the Civil War*.

In that book Hague traced the day-to-day minutia that marked life in a rural part of the Confederacy that suffered both invasion and isolation due to Federal military successes. Much of Parthenia Hague's writing dealt with in-depth descriptions of how household tasks were completed in a region that had a steadily decreasing amount of access to materials & resources. Page after page of Hague's book detailed the intricacies of dying cloth without commercial dies, making clothing from homespun fabrics, dipping candles, weaving cloth, and generally using ingenuity to allow her neighbors to survive. In this way Parthenia Hague served the cause of social history well in that she left behind a clearly delineated & literate image of a lifestyle that is long gone. However, beneath the surface of her words Parthenia Hague also displayed the sectarian attitudes that led to the Civil War and exacerbated the dire elements of racism that plagued not only 19th century America but our own age as well.

In reading Parthenia Hague's memoir one comes away with a clearer understanding of the belief system that could have allowed otherwise intelligent and Christian people to possess their fellow men, women, and children and plunge a nation into bloody war in defense of that right. In Parthenia Hague's mind the election of Abraham Lincoln as a Republican President of the United States represented just cause for the secession that ensued, "Need there be any wonder that, when a political party, with no love in its heart for the Southern white people, came into power, a party which we believed felt the people of the South were fit only for the pikes hidden at Harper's Ferry, we should have cried out, "What part we in David? To your tents, O Israel." It is cheering to know that our deeds and intentions have one great Judge, who will say, "Neither do I condemn thee." (Hague 3-4)

For Parthenia Hague the act of secession, even twenty-five years after the war's conclusion, was utterly justified simply because the Republican Party in 1861 was anti-slavery. It made no difference to Hague that most Republican leaders, inclusive of Lincoln, were not intent upon the immediate abolition of slavery. No, what probably would have resulted in lieu of Civil War would have been another in a series of politically constructed compromises such as were featured in the 1850's. However, we shall never know that as the firing on Fort Sumter in April 1861 brought about a cataclysm that was to spread sorrow and blood across the land.

Even retrospectively Parthenia Hague remained fixed on her belief that the Civil War was a defensive one waged by a just South. Hague distrusted northerners and recounted how, in the pre-war years, they had behaved in a way that could leave southerners nothing but suspicious of their actions, "I remembered a temperance lecturer from one of the New England States, who came to our settlement and who was kindly received and warmly welcomed into our Southern homes. There was nothing too good for this temperance lecturer from the far North. He was given earnest and attentive audiences, with never a thought that in the guise of a temperance reformer his one sole purpose was to make a secret survey of our country, to ascertain which settlements were most populated with slaves, for the already maturing uprising of the blacks against the whites." (4-5)

In the mind of Parthenia Hague such an abolitionist could never have understood the fact that, "We were happy and contented, both master and slave." (119) Indeed, rather than the image of slavery that northerners such as Harriett Beecher Stowe created in works like *Uncle Tom's Cabin;* Hague's version of slavery is a far different one. Hague's south is a world wherein, even during the low point of the war when resources were stretched thin, whites treated their slaves in a benign manner. In Hague's own words, "During the war when bacon was very scarce, it often happened that the white household would deny themselves meat to eat, so as to give to the slaves, as they had to toil in the field." (120) Hague held onto this mythology despite the fact that after the war many former slaves stated a preference for death rather than a return to slavery.

Parthenia Hague's memoir was laced with anecdotes that smack of a romantic imagery associated with knightly plantation owners and comfortable black serfs. At one point Hague recounted the wedding of a young slave girl on a nearby plantation. Parthenia assisted the girl's owner in dressing and preparing her for the wedding ceremony. As Hague and her friend, Winnie, labored on behalf of the slave bride she had an almost religious feeling about the proceedings, "With flowers scattered all around, our laps and hands full, we twined the wreath for the negro girl, the bride elect for the evening. When twilight had deepened into darkness, the bride was called into your room to make ready for the marriage. When fully robed in her wedding garment, she was inspected by each and every member of the household, and judged to be quite *au fait.* But Winnie pulled off her own watch and chain, together with her bracelets, and with these further adorned the bride. She was married in the wide hall of her master's house, for having been raised in the house almost from her cradle, her marriage taking place in one of the cabins was not to be thought of." (8)

Such a description of a slave wedding can almost seem beautiful. What Hague's romanticized depiction leaves out is the all too obvious reality of how marriages and general sexual demeanor evolved in slave owning regions of the nation. What Hague ignored, or chose to ignore, was the fact that slave marriages had no legal status. Children of a slave mother belonged to her owner even if their father was a freedman. The frequency of rape committed by slave owners on their "property" was quite high as was the incidence of children fathered by owners amongst their slaves. Yet, despite the fact that these realities were broadly known in the South, Parthenia Hague chose to leave her readers with a blissful image of two privileged white women benignly helping an innocent slave girl on the evening of her wedding. There is something almost nauseating about this form of selective memory as it leads to a misunderstanding of what history really was made of.

One answer to the question of how could Parthenia Hague, an otherwise intelligent person, appear to be so blind to the dehumanizing aspects of slavery, rests in her personal racial attitudes. Hague was not subtle in depicting her impressions of blacks whom she sincerely believed benefited from slavery. At one point in her narrative while discussing the ingenuity that allowed white southerners to hold out for so long against the overwhelming forces arrayed against them, she revealed a great deal of her core beliefs concerning slaves, "I often wonder how we were so quickly able to adapt ourselves to the great changes rendered necessary by our modes of life during the blockade. But be it remembered that the Southerners who were so reduced and so compelled to rely entirely upon their own resources belonged to the Anglo-Saxon race, a race which, despite all prating about "racial equality," has civilized America. The reflection to which memory gives rise when I recall war times in the South is this, "blood will tell." (97)

Given this belief in the innate inferiority of the slaves, it was only a small step to coalesce into a creed that made the whites the rightful "caretakers" of the lowly blacks. It was the duty of the slave owners to care for their "property" in a compassionate but firm manner. Once released from this civilizing grip, liberated slaves quickly fell prey to lower impulses or, as Hague noted, "We felt no fear of the slaves. The idea of any harm happening through them never for one instant entered our minds…But now, not for my right hand would I be situated, as I was that April night of 1865. Now it would by no means be safe, for experience is showing us that in any section where the negro forms any very great part of the population, white men or women are in danger of murder, robbery, and violence." (153)

Conversely, the nature of white southerners shines from the very pages of Hague's work like a bright beacon of virtue. In Hague's wondrous Southland, "many had engaged in work purely as a matter of choice, there were none, even the wealthiest, who had not been taught that labor was honorable, and who had very clear ideas of how work must be done; so when our misfortunes came, we were by no means found wanting in any of the qualities that were necessary for our changed circumstances." (14)

In Parthenia Hague's worldview these industrious and noble southerners pulled together during the war and created an egalitarian society based upon shared burdens. Looking back at the ultimately unsuccessful & costly war, Hague still held a soft spot in her heart for this shared effort, "Ah, those stormy days of our convulsed country had their guileless pleasures, as well as sorrows! We were drawn together in a closer union, a tender feeling of humanity linking us all together, both rich and poor; from the princely planter, who could scarce get off his wide domains in a day's ride, and who could count his slaves by the thousand, down to the humble tenants of the log-cabin on rented or leased land." (107-108)

Facing shortages of all sorts Hague's noble southerners made the best of life and pitched in with all they had. Even when things looked dark the southerners hunkered down and made the best of things, "We were being led in a way we knew not: and like the humble woman of the cottage, we even made merry over our inevitable privations and inconveniences. Indeed, we grew so accustomed to them that they scarcely seemed privations." (110)

When untidy details linked to poor conduct on the part of southerners pop up, Hague is always ready with an answer. For example, the terrible plight of Union prisoners of war at places such as Andersonville in Georgia troubled Hague. But, even the horrible fact of 13,000 deaths in the twelve months that Andersonville was open did not strike Hague as a southern culpability. No, the Union deaths at Andersonville were not the result of poor conduct on the part of southerners. In Hague's schema, those men died because of Federal advances that made supplying not only prisoners but also all of the South nearly impossible. Rather than accepting the horrors of Andersonville as a reality to learn from, Parthenia Hague boldly stated, "When the great book of remembrance" is opened to view, on its pages white and fair the North will surely see, not that the South would not, but that the South could not, better feed the Northern prisoners." (135)

In reality, the world that Parthenia Antoinette Hague recreates in her memoir was one that never really existed. While there certainly were kind slave owners they were not the norm. If slave existence was so benign why was it that, once Federal armies penetrated the south, so many slaves fled their owners and followed the blue clad soldiers? For Hague it was the fact that the Yankees "decoyed" the slaves with false promises and then abandoned them that explained this phenomenon—but that explanation simply does not wash.

Likewise, where Hague saw an egalitarian society within which every white person valued labor and excelled in a multiplicity of things, the reality was that the Confederacy was a stratified and nearly feudal society. Not only slaves, but also poor whites, were trapped in a generational web of poverty and subservience to a planter class. Thousands of southerners died in the Civil War defending the slave owning rights of a wealthy upper crust. Ironically, the slaves whom Hague took such great pains to paint as incapable fortunates who were well cared for by their masters were owned by only a small minority of southerners. Similarly, it was the every same slave owners who could be excluded from conscription and military service because of their slave property. The reality of southern life was a far cry from the propagandistic wordings of Parthenia Hague's propagandistic work.

Ultimately, the society that nurtured Parthenia Hague was ground to dust by the advancing forces of the Union. Eufaula was visited by Yankee troops who showed little mercy when it came to foraging, burning, and looting. Hague was shocked by such uncivil behavior and lamented how "a match would be applied, and the labor of years would swirl up in smoke." (155) Yet, what Hague misses in this thought is that the labor": she is referencing was slave labor wrung from bonded human beings who had no control over their own lives. This is the missing piece throughout Parthenia Hague's memories of the war years and what followed.

In the end, the defeat of the Confederacy was a bitter blow to Hague and other members of the ruling oligarchy of the ante bellum south. Looking back at the start of the war Hague recalled, "What a change from 1861, when all were so buoyant and full of fiery patriotism, with never a thought of being overcome! Now our cause was lost, all our homes more or less despoiled, the whole South seemingly almost hopelessly ruined, every little town and village garrisoned by the troops who had overcome us by great odds...Yet all our great and sore afflictions, I found only cheerfulness and Christian resignation at the end of those troublesome war times, and the hope that we might yet rise above our misfortunes." (175-176)

But, when you look more closely at even such seemingly humane words a drop of doubt emerges. Parthenia Hague, and all too many southern apologists for slavery, painted a picture that misrepresented both what the war was about and why it was fought. What was a "lost cause" to people like Parthenia Hague, was a war of liberations for abolitionists and millions of African-Americans. A paternalistic image of slavery that Hague projected clashed with the historically documented brutalization that typified slavery in America. No, the world that Parthenia Hague penned, and which was splashed across movie screens with Rhett Butler and Scarlet O'Hara was fiction from the start. In this way Parthenia Hague typified the southern gentry who fought a war to defend their lifestyle, were utterly defeated, and then rose again upon a foundation of racism and oppression. It is only one small step from the words of Parthenia Hague to the lynch mob's noose and a world of degradation in the name of white racial superiority. If you are searching for the realities of slavery and the meaning of the Civil War you are unlikely to find it in the works of slavery's apologists and those who benefited the most from the south's "Peculiar Institution."

Source

Hague, Parthenia Antoinette. *A Blockaded Family: Life In Southern Alabama During the*
    Civil War. Lincoln, NE: University of Nebraska Press, 1991.

14

Harriet Jacobs' Life as a Slave

While Parthenia Hague described slavery from the outside looking in, the world of Harriet Jacobs was that of a slave full of all the realities entailed by that term. In 1861, after having escaped from her owner in North Carolina, Harriet Jacobs set down in print the course of her life as a slave. Jacobs' book was one of a series of "slave narratives" that appeared on the literary scene in the years leading up to the Civil War. Printed in support of the abolitionist cause, these "slave narratives" contained the firsthand experiences of men and women who had been property of southern slave owners. These stories shed an ugly light on the institution of slavery and were consistently debunked by southerners both at the time of their publication and for decades after the war. However, the course of history has proven books such as Harriet Jacobs' *Incidents In the Life of a Slave Girl* to have the ring of truth. In looking at slavery from the perspective of one of its captives a fair minded person comes away with a vastly different view of the "Peculiar Institution" than that purported to be true by its supporters.

Harriet Jacobs was born in 1813 on the property of a slave owning family in rural North Carolina. In her early childhood years Harriet lived with her parents and was shielded from the realities of her existence as chattel. In fact the first words of Harriet Jacob's memoir reveal the fact that, "I was born a slave; but I never knew it till six years of happy childhood had passed away." (Jacobs 8) Indeed, living with her parents in a beautiful area of the country young Harriet appeared to have a blissful life ahead of her. She looked at her family as one that was normal and that would protect her. In regards to her parents Harriet's youngest memories were not unlike those of children who were not raised as slaves, "They lived together in a comfortable home; and, though we were all slaves, I was so fondly shielded that I never dreamed that I was a piece of merchandise, trusted to them for safe keeping, and liable to be demanded of them at any moment." (8)

Harriet's family was fortunate in that their mistress was a benevolent and kind person. Despite the legal and societal strictures against it, Harriet's mistress sat her down and actually instructed her in literacy. Years later Harriet could still recall these teaching sessions, "While I was with her, she taught me to read and spell; and for this privilege, which so rarely falls to the lot of a slave, I bless her memory." (11) Unfortunately, in a changing circumstance that was all too common in the lives of slaves, the death of this kind mistress was followed by a drastic change in the quality of life for Harriet Jacobs, her family, and other slaves on their plantation home.

    Upon the death of the Jacobs' mistress their ownership descended to less angelic members of that gentry family. In short order Harriet's parents died and she was transferred to the care of her maternal grandmother. This saintly figure reared Harriet but could not completely protect her form the ill favors of changing ownership. In fact, Harriet became painfully aware of her lot in life as a slave and bitterly resented it. Symbols of her servitude troubled Harriet and made her bondage even more onerous. For example, the new owners, Mr. & Mrs. Flint, provided Harriet with some simple clothing and, despite the annual gift, all Harriett could see in these poor hand-me-downs were material examples of her property status, "I have a vivid recollection of that linsey-woolsey dress given me every winter by Mrs. Flint. How I hated it! It was one of the badges of slavery." (13)

    In another cruel twist, Harriet's grandmother had been promised her freedom upon the death of her old mistress. When that sad event transpired, the new owners refused to acknowledge this long-standing promise. Instead, the new master, Dr. Flint, chose a different pathway. As Harriet recorded, Dr. Flint approached Harriet's grandmother and informed her "under the existing circumstances, it was necessary she be sold." (13) Fortunately, the fact of the late mistress' pledge was widely known in the local community and Harriet's grandmother was a respected slave. Therefore, at the auction only one person bid on Harriet's grandmother and purchased her for the low price of fifty dollars. After the sale this benign soul then manumitted Harriet Jacobs' grandmother and helped her establish herself in her own home near to the site of her former slavery.

As Harriet grew into a young teenager she began to mentally catalogue the inhumanities that slavery bred. Before her eyes Harriet Jacobs observed acts by slave owners that remain shocking even to this day. At one point Harriet observed a slave auction where a mother was being sold separately form her children. That memory remained with Harriet Jacobs for the remainder of her life, "On one of these sale days, I saw a mother lead seven children to the auction-block. She knew that *some* of them would be taken from her; but they took *all*. The children were sold to a slave trader, and their mother was bought by a man in her own town. Before night her children were all far away. She begged the trader to tell her where he intended to take them; this he refused to do. How *could* he, when he knew he would sell them, one by one, wherever he could command the best price? I met the mother in the street, and her wild, haggard face lives to-day in my mind. She wrung her hands in anguish and exclaimed, "Gone! All gone! Why *don't* God kill me?" I had no words wherewith to comfort her. Instances of this kind are of daily, yea, of hourly occurrence." (17)

Not only did Harriet see mothers separated from their children but also the way in which some older slaves were treated. These elderly slaves had served their masters and mistresses for long years. Yet, in some cases, when they were at a retirement point, their owners saw them as no longer valuable property. Much like a worn out old chair, these relics were cast out onto the waste heap of humanity. At one point Harriet described just such an occurrence, "Slaveholders have a method, peculiar to their institution, of getting rid of *old* slaves, whose lives have been worn out in their service. I knew an old woman, who for seventy years faithfully served her master. She had become almost helpless, from hard labor and disease. Her owners moved to Alabama, and the old black woman was left to be sold to any body who would give twenty dollars for her." (17)

As the harsh and brutal truth of her condition registered in Harriet's mind she began to simmer. Harriet Jacobs came to hate her owners and, in particular, Dr. Flint.
At some point Harriet became keenly aware of the fact that, "O, how I despised him! I thought how glad I should be if some day when he walked the earth, it would open and swallow him up, and disencumber the world of a plague." (18)

Perhaps this hatred, combined with the natural resilience that Harriet Jacobs possessed, allowed her to withstand the vicissitudes of a slave's life. Harriet's single brother, Benjamin, was a strong-willed person as well. Eventually, that strength of character caused Benjamin to flee his slavery and successfully head north. In Harriet's mind, her brother's character and her own personality were sources of strength in a world where a thinking person held in perpetual bondage might well go mad. This internal battle between the need to temper actions, emotions, and speech while simultaneously kindling the sparks of humanity that were necessary to persevere, was a source of some thought for Harriet, "I was not unconscious of the beam in my own eye. It was the very knowledge of my own shortcomings that urged me to retain, if possible, some sparks of my brother's God-given nature. I had not lived fourteen years in slavery for nothing. I had felt, seen, and heard enough, to read the characters, and question the motives, of those around me. The war of my life had begun; and though one of God's most powerless creatures, I resolved never to be conquered. Alas, for me!" (19)

The final lament in the above statement was all too tragic and realistic. Harriet Jacobs's persistence in terms of efforts to remain a whole person and not a mere laboring appendage to her master's will, would both support and tax her in her years as a slave. Slaves, regardless of their inner capacities, could not control their very lives. They were subject to rigorous and sometimes barbaric treatment on the part of their owners. Like any "livestock" slaves could be under the control of a kindly or sadistic master. Early in her memories Harriet Jacobs could recall an example of the type of "correction" that was sometimes used by slave owners, "When I had been in the family a few weeks, one of the plantation slaves was brought to town, by order of his master. It was near night when he arrived, and Dr. Flint ordered him to be taken to the workhouse, and tied up to the joist, so that his feet would just escape the ground. In that situation he was to wait until the doctor had taken his tea. I shall never forget that night. Never before, in my life, had I heard hundreds of blows fall, in succession, on a human being. His piteous groans and his, "O, pray don't massa," rang in my ears for months afterwards. There were many conjectures as to the cause of this terrible punishment. Some said master accused him of stealing corn; others said the slave had quarreled with his wife, in presence of the overseer, and had accused his master of being the father of her child. They were both black, and the child was very fair." (15)

This type of torture was not an isolated incident in Harriet Jacobs' life. Capricious cruelty could result from petty offenses, slovenly work, or actual or suspected enforced sexual dalliances with white owners that came to the attention of frustrated plantation mistresses. In one case Harriet Jacobs recalled seeing one such unfortunate female slave whose punishment was the result of the anger of her mistress over a recent childbirth, "I once saw a young slave girl dying after the birth of a child nearly white. In her agony she cried out, "O Lord come and take me!" Her mistress stood by, and mocked at her like an incarnate fiend. "You suffer, do you?" she exclaimed. "I am glad of it. You deserve it all, and more too." (15)

As Harriett entered into her puberty and began to assume the aspect of a young woman, she too fell prey to the sexual predation that was an all too common and disreputable element of slavery. Shortly after her fifteenth birthday, Harriet Jacobs began to be the object o Dr. Flint's attention in a way that was altogether inappropriate, "But I now entered my fifteenth year—a sad epoch in the life of a slave girl. My master began to whisper foul words in my ear. Young as I was, I could not remain ignorant of their import. I tried to treat them with indifference or contempt. My master's age, my extreme youth, and the fear that his conduct would be reported to my grandmother made him bear this treatment for many months. He was a crafty man and resorted to many means to accomplish his purposes…My master met me at every turn, reminding me that I belonged to him, and swearing by heaven and earth that he would compel me to submit to him." (26-27)

For the remainder of her time on the plantation, Harriet Jacobs was a fixation in the mind of Dr. Flint. Time and again Flint threatened, cajoled, promised, and attempted to force his sexual attentions upon Harriet. Eventually, in order to dissuade Dr. Flint form continuing in this perverse tact, Harriet became the mistress of a neighboring white man. From this liaison Harriet was to bear two children and create a barrier to Dr. Flint's desire to have her. Sadly however, the fact that Harriet was a mother was also a means whereby the Flint's could exert pressure upon her to do whatever they wished, as they were the owners of her children.

In describing the Flints, Harriet Jacobs presented an image of people who through the possession of other human beings were afforded an opportunity to inflict their basest behavior upon their fellow creatures. Slave masters were able to indulge their lowest desires & appetites with women who could do virtually nothing to defend themselves. On the surface ante bellum southern society bore a patina of civility. But beneath that façade was a far different reality. In Harriet Jacobs' words, "The secrets of slavery are concealed like those of the Inquisition. My master was, to my knowledge, the father of eleven slaves. But did the mothers dare to tell who was the father of their children? Did the other slaves dare to allude to it, except in whispers among themselves? No, indeed! They knew too well the terrible consequences." (32)

The sad reality was that on all too many plantations a slave owner's legitimate and enslaved children mingled together but faced far different futures. On one occasion Harriet Jacobs observed one such slave master's white and mixed race children playing together. Seeing this circumstance Harriet contemplated upon the different pathways those linked half-siblings would follow, "I once saw two beautiful children playing together. One was a fair white child: the other was her slave, and also her sister. When I saw them embracing each other, and heard their joyous laughter, I turned sadly away from the lovely sight. I foresaw the inevitable blight that would fall on the little slave's heart. I knew how soon her laughter would be changed to sighs. The fair child grew up to be a still fairer woman. From childhood to womanhood her pathway was blooming with flowers, and overarched by a sunny sky. Scarcely one day of her life had been clouded when the sun rose on her happy bridal morning…How had those years dealt with her slave sister, the little playmate of her childhood? She, also, was very beautiful; but the flowers and sunshine of love were not for her. She drank the cup of sin, and shame, and misery, whereof her persecuted race are compelled to drink." (28)

In her writings Harriet Jacobs did acknowledge the fact that not all slave owners were demons. There were some decent people who, through economic necessity or culture mores, maintained slaves but did so in a compassionate fashion.

However, despite the existence of such decent slave owners, Harriet Jacobs had learned that they were the exception and not the rule, "I could tell of more slaveholders as cruel as those I have described. They are not exceptions to the general rule. I do not say there are no humane slaveholders. Such characters do exist, notwithstanding the hardening influences around them. But they are "like angles' visits—few and far between." (44)

Living in a society wherein people dominated other human beings in such a complete manner was damaging to all concerned. While the slaves suffered all the ignominy of servitude, their masters were debased by the side effects of such absolute power. In a sense, slavery caused a dual corruption of both the enslaved and the slave owner. Looking back on her years as a slave Harriet Jacobs pondered the holistic corruption that slavery bred, "You may believe what I say; for I write only that whereof I know. I was twenty-one years in that cage of obscene birds. I can testify, from my own experience and observation, that slavery is a curse to the whites as well as to the blacks. It makes the white fathers cruel and sensual; the sons violent and licentious; it contaminates the daughters, and makes the wives wretched. And as for the colored race, it needs an abler pen than mine to describe the extremity of their sufferings, the depth of their degradation." (46)

In such a painful world it might only be expected that Harriet Jacobs would seek to find an escape route. However, having two young children and no great financial wherewithal, it was difficult for Jacobs to carry out an escape. Given these barriers, and the constant threats that Dr. Flint leveled at her children, it was to be expected that periodically Harriet Jacobs fell into a morose state. At one point Harriet was tending to her son who was ill. In that context Jacobs looked at her child, contemplated his future and that of her daughter, and came to a terrible conclusion, "As the months passed on my boy improved in health. When he was a year old, they called him beautiful. The little vine was taking deep root in my existence, though its clinging fondness exerted a mixture of love and pain. When I was most sorely oppressed I found a solace in his smiles. I loved to watch his infant slumbers; but always there was a dark cloud over my enjoyment. I could never forget that he was a slave. Sometimes I wished that he might die in infancy." (54)

Consider the nature of a society within which mothers would contemplate the deaths of their children as better alternatives when compared to a life of slavery. This is not the beatific imagery of slavery's apologists who maintained the mythology of the contented slaves. No, this is the desperate and anguished cry of human beings reduced to the status of possessions yet still encompassing all the emotions that people hold so dear.

But, how could a society that proclaimed Christian values allow such perfidy to exist?

One interesting aspect of Harriet Jacobs slave narrative is the role that religion played in the relationship between masters and slaves. A devout believer in her own right, Harriet Jacobs was quick to point out both the hypocrisy of this position as well as the way in which religion was used as a tool of the oppressive slaveholders. Preachers were sent to minister to the slaves but their message was generally one that encompassed a submissive brand of faith. One such sermon remained etched in Harriet Jacobs' memory and featured the following homily, "You must forsake your sinful ways, and be faithful servants. Obey your old master, and young master—your old mistress, and your young mistress. If you disobey your earthly master you offend your heavenly Master. You must obey God's commandments. When you go from here, don't stop at the corners of the street to talk, but go directly home, and let your master and mistress see that you have come." (60)

In light of such patently propagandistic preaching, and the real life degradation built into slavery, it was little wonder that Harriet Jacobs passed a much different judgment on slave society than did such ministers. In Harriet's opinion the religiosity of the ante bellum south was a far cry from the ministerial words noted above, "There is a great difference between Christianity and religion at the south. If a man goes to the communion table, and pays into the treasure of the church, no matter if it be the price of blood, he is called religious. If a pastor has offspring by a woman not his wife, the church dismisses him, if she is a white woman; but if she is colored, it does not hinder his continuing to be their good sheppard." (64)

Eventually, events evolved to a point wherein Harriet Jacobs could no longer stand to remain a slave. First, she fled her master and mistress & went into hiding in a small crawlspace in her grandmother's house. Amazingly, Harriet remained undiscovered in that location for seven years. In those years she spent the lion's share of her time secluded in a cramped attic area. Periodically she descended to exercise and speak with her grandmother. But, for most of the time, Harriet Jacobs' life was bounded by the slanting roof and mice infested domain created for her as a safe haven.

After the torturously slow passage of those long years of seclusion Harriet Jacobs was physically atrophied but still mentally resilient. Sensing the probability of discovery Harriet was smuggled north by kind hearted supporters. There in Philadelphia, Boston, and primarily New York City, Harriet Jacobs established a furtive lifestyle. Over time, and with the support of compassionate souls both white and black, Harriet was able to reunite with her brother and her two children. Harriet, and her children, were eventually purchased from their former owners by a third party. The Jacobs were then emancipated and, at last, could breathe easier without the fear of capture and re-enslavement under the cruel provisions of the Fugitive Slave Law. The coming of the Civil War provided even more authenticity to Harriet Jacob's sense that she no longer belonged to anyone save herself.

At one point while she was unsure of her ability to orchestrate the liberation of her daughter, Harriet Jacobs wrote about the fear she held so close to her heart regarding her child's potential life as a slave. With both great emotion and cutting realism Harriet wrote, "How earnestly I prayed that she might never feel the weight of slavery's chain, whose iron entereth into the soul." (68) With good fortune, audacity, courage, and intelligence Harriet Jacobs was able to create a liberated future for her children and herself. She then bowed to the requests of abolitionist friends who enjoined her to tell her story so that other people could better understand the debasement that slavery was. In telling that tale Harriet Jacobs offered a true-to-life view of the terrible nature of slavery in America. Harriet Jacobs' portrait of slaveholders and their culture certainly differed form the picture painted by many southerners. That honest rendering of slavery's essential evil was vital in 1861 when it was written and remains so now in an age when racial hatred still mars all too many aspects of human society.

Source

Jacobs, Harriet. *Incidents In the Life of a Slave Girl.* Mineola, NY:
    Dover Publications, Inc., 2001.

15

"Dear Emma": Letters To & From the Homefront

People of flesh and blood just like any person you may know fought the Civil War. The soldiers who marched off to war proudly wearing their uniforms of blue, gray, or shades of brown left behind loved ones who mourned their absence, feared for their well being and longed for their safety. At home, while the soldiers marched, fought, and died family members carried on the daily tasks involved in everyday life. Women nursed their babies in the absence of the infant's father. Wives girded their loins and took on the previously "manly" tasks of planting crops, managing home finances, and handling business matters. All across the North and the South lives went on—not quite the same—but nevertheless constantly moving ahead despite the drums of war.

In many ways life is basically about relationships. If you stop and think about what matters in life you probably will think about people more than things. Material goods are part of a safe & happy life. It is difficult to imagine happiness in the face of starvation and want. However, it may be even more difficult to imagine true happiness in the absence of caring relationships. The American Civil War—like wars before and after It—shattered literally millions of relationships. No conflict that claimed over 630,000 lives and maimed hundreds of thousands of other men, could possibly avoid these destructive ramifications. Each death or disabling wound claimed not only the recipient but also a web of others who were involved in that soldier's welfare. As the 17th century English cleric and writer John Donne once wrote, "The death of any man diminishes me, for I am involved in mankind. So, send not to see for whom the bell tolls, for it tolls for thee." The truth of that classic line is borne out when people take the time to look at the human effects that war's grim impact has upon the loving relationships of its participants.

In order to grasp the human cost of the Civil War one can quote statistics and manage data in order to pinpoint the enormity of suffering that accrued from that conflict. Such a macrocosmic approach to empathy development certainly can be a powerful tool. The tremendous number of casualties suffered in the Civil War is ample evidence of the grieving that the American nation withstood during those violent years. Yet, such an approach may be too statistical and sanitized to really understand the way in which every single one of the men killed in the Civil War left a gaping hole in the web of life of all those with whom he once lived, loved, worked, and remained.

Another way of trying to convey the emotional debt that the Civil War exacted is to look at single relationships and how they were fundamentally altered by the experience of war. One such relationship was that developed by two New Jersey residents. In the courting, wooing, and love held between these two common yet unique people, readers may find an even deeper understanding of what war does to people than any facts or figures can convey. These two people are Emma Randolph and Walter G. Dunn and their story is one that remains universal in its lessons.

In 1862 Walter Dunn enlisted in the 11th New Jersey. Like so many of his contemporaries, Dunn did not expect to participate in a war that would ultimately nearly grind his nation into ruin. Dunn marched off with the rest of the 11th with a sense of purpose but also in possession of a secret. Just prior to his departure, Dunn had pledged to maintain an ongoing correspondence with a young woman who had caught his fancy. That young lady, Emma Randolph, was attractive and thoughtful. While Walter and Emma had no clear-cut understanding or engagement they did enjoy one another's company. Hence, a correspondence was struck up and maintained. Every week or so Walter and Emma would sit down, take pen in hand, and scribe out the events of their days. These letters came to be penultimately important to both of them. Indeed, the importance of the letters was so self-evident that they saved most of them. Years later, in a fortuitous turn of events, those letters were unearthed and compiled in a book form. Their content traces both the evolution of a loving relationship as well as the dire cost that war can charge those who cross its path.

For Walter Dunn active service in the field was short lived but eventful. Dunn had only been in service for a few months when his unit, along with the bulk of the Army of the

Potomac, ventured into the Virginia wilderness. Under the audacious but ultimately fumbling command of General Joe Hooker, the Union troops marched into the region near Chancellorsville. There, amidst the roots, branches, scrub, and forest of that wild countryside Walter and his comrades were soundly trounced by General Lee's legions. In the course of the battle Walter was shot through the lungs with the ball deflecting up and finally lodging in his right shoulder.

Walter was fortunate to survive so dreadful a wound. He lived in an age when medical care was fairly primitive and it is somewhat amazing that he could live through a severe wounding. However, he did and was ultimately evacuated to a military hospital in Baltimore, Maryland. There, during his convalescence, Walter began to write to Emma. Those letters served as a means of communicating with his home and the future that he had some inkling might be so important for him.

Initially, Walter's letters speak of non-threatening subjects. Often, in these initial letters, Walter mentions the state of his health. For example, in one of his first letters Walter catalogs the nature of his wound and the treatment prescribed by his attending physician, "My shoulder is nearly well. I have found the ball and am waiting on the Surgeon's motion to have it extracted. He says that it is in a very critical place and that it would not be safe to cut it out now but thinks that in course of time it will work nearer the surface. It is behind the shoulder." (Bailey & Cottom, p., 8)

Life in the hospital was fairly grim for Walter. In the first few months he often writes Emma about the illnesses that claim some of the residents of his ward. One patient suffers from a spreading infection and must decide whether or not to have his foot amputated. In the end the soldier agreed to the amputation. Walter, who was recovered sufficiently to act as a hospital orderly, assisted in the surgery. He described it in the following manner, "They have taken up two arteries in his foot and tied them to keep him from bleeding to death. I think that if you had seen me when the doctors were performing the operation you would have thought that I was a butcher, I was so covered with blood." (10)

On another occasion Walter encountered the spouse of a patient who had recently died. That meeting left an indelible impression upon young Dunn and he shared it with Emma, "A few days ago one of our patients died and about an hour afterward his wife came to see him. I never saw a woman so struck with disappointment as she was when I told her that he had just died. She was out of employment in the city where she lived and the Surgeon in charge gave her employment here as a nurse." (10)

As the weeks passed Walter began to describe some emerging feelings he had for the eighteen-year-old Emma. Walter, being just nineteen himself, was relatively inexperienced in amorous affairs and his initial caution in describing any feelings to Emma was quite natural. Yet, by the late fall of 1863 Walter felt he could lift the veil over his emotions a bit. In one letter he hinted at his deepening attitude while also reassuring Emma that their correspondence meant a great deal to him "It is not my desire for any means to cease corresponding with you, the reading of your letters is a source of great pleasure, I only wished to give you to understand that if it was your desire, that I would not be burdensome. Instead of your letters being without interest as you said you supposed they were, they have been the right reverse and I should feel it a great loss to loose (sic) such a correspondence as you have been for over one year." (18)

This sort of hinting at the feelings he was developing continued for a few more weeks. Then, shortly before Christmas in 1863, Walter became bolder, "Em, we have been corresponding as you will admit for a considerable over a year and now I want you to tell me frankly if you had any other object in view in wishing our correspondence to continue, more than merely a correspondence of friendship." (22)

Interestingly enough, although Emma's response must have been encouraging as the correspondence continued and deepened, there is no record as to what it exactly was. Walter destroyed Emma's letters in the summer of 1864 when the forces of Jubal Early moved north. While Early's troops were delayed at Monocacy and ultimately stymied near Washington, Walter felt certain that they would head toward Baltimore. He feared that such a turn of events might leave Emma's letters in the hands of invading Confederates. Therefore, Walter chose to burn them rather than risk their forfeiture. While this action may seem somewhat impulsive, and certainly is regrettable from a historian's standpoint, who can truly understand the stress and anxiety that led Walter Dunn to destroy his treasured letters. Nevertheless, following that series of unfortunate events, Walter religiously preserved Emma's letters. That act allows modern readers to see the evolution of one relationship gripped by the passage of armies.

One quality that shines through in these letters is the elemental morality of these two people. Both Walter and Emma were young. Yet, despite their youth, they were willing to bear the burdens of separation and fear that war bred. Likewise, both of these young people were able to see beyond their own selfish needs. At one point Walter was in line for a furlough. This gift of time would allow Walter to return home and see both his family and his sweetheart. Yet, when he knew another soldier's needs, Walter undertook an act of sacrifice that is worth mentioning. In Walter's own words, "I could have had my furlough and been home ere this but I let a young man go in my place who received a letter that his mother was quite sick and as I have had one furlough which he has not, I thought that it would be doing as I would be done by, to let him go first." (31)

As time passed and Walter and Emma's love and future plans deepened, their separation became more saddening to both of them. One trait that maintained the morale of both of these young people was their deep and abiding religious faith. In the summer of 1864 Walter touched upon this theme of belief in one of his letters, "But we must be content and not complain, for whether in ill or good health we must remember that all comes from the hand of an All Wise Providence and our trials and afflictions here are to show us, our frailty and weakness and fit us, more perfectly, for a happy hereafter. May they not be without effect." (58)

Emma also tried to be stoic in her demeanor. Surely the absence of her beloved fiancée was a burden for her to maintain. Also, while Walter was not in the front lines, he was in constant pain from his wound and exposed to the dreadful miasmas of a military hospital. Yet, Emma often notes "but the longest day will have an end."
(82) But, there were moments in Emma's letters when her sadness is hinted at. In October of 1864 she wrote, "Oh how I miss you Walt. You dont (sic) know.
You cant (sic) half imagine. My feelings compel me to close. I hope your prayers will soon be answered for I'm tired of this, but I

endeavor to endure to the end, for I know "tis all for the best"" (128)

Walter too fell into emotional doldrums at times. He missed seeing and touching his future wife. In response to the sadness felt by Emma Walter wrote, "Dear Emma you said that you missed me very much, you cannot miss me any more than I do you, that is impossible. I have dreamed about you several times since I have returned and oh, such pleasant dreams. I only wish that I might realize them soon. If you were only here tonight I could tell you how much I miss you, not only with words but with my actions as I have a keen desire for a good hug, but that is impossible under the circumstances." (132)

It is not too difficult to imagine how sad some days were for these two young lovers. In an age when all too many families were receiving notice of sons lost on battlefields, in prison camps, and on sick beds, it certainly was not improbable that Walter might not make it home. Similarly, many of Emma's letters touch upon her own recurring illnesses and the deaths of neighbors at the hands of disease. There were no guarantees that Walter and Emma's long distance courtship would blossom into full flown nuptials. Perhaps such thoughts were darkening Emma's thoughts when she penned the following closing to one of her letters, "My feeling(s) compel me to stop. Oh how I wish you was coming up to see me tonight, but never mind spaces there is between us and how far apart. I think of you always, and remember you as my own Dearest Friend, the one I expect to find "True as the Stars." I have confidence that such you will prove. Good night. Please write soon to your own true and still loving." (136)

One fear that Emma often refers to is the thought that Walter would succumb to some form of respiratory malady. Emma realized that Walter's grievous wound from the Chancellorsville Battle had damaged his lungs. His visits back to New Jersey when he actually secured a furlough were grand but he was still weakened by his injuries. On several occasions Emma enjoins Walter to try to avoid soldiers ill with breathing disorders. At one point in this correspondence Emma advises Walter as per how to recover from a heavy cold that he reported to her. Emma goes on to caution Walter thusly, "Now I feel as though I ought to caution and give you a little advice, for I am anxious about you.

Be verry (sic) careful of your own self Dear Walt, for remember there is a mortgage on you. Will you? Do not expose your self more than is necessary for if you have got such a strong constitution, nothing will help to restore if after once it is gone." (163)

As is true of all elements of life and existence, time passes and things change. Slowly the war years passed. Events rolled by inclusive of great battles, the surrender of Lee's army, the assassination of President Lincoln, the passing of Union armies along the streets of Washington in the Grand Review, and the disbanding of the mighty hosts that fought the Civil War. Along with these momentous events came smaller but no less important ones. One such happening that surely caused no great media stir was the returning of Private Walter Dunn to his New Market, New Jersey home in July of 1865.

Once home, Walter and Emma wasted very little time in wedding. On September 19, 1865 Walter and Emma were married at New Market's Seventh Day Baptist Church. The young couple, having limited means, moved in with Emma's parents in Plainfield, New Jersey. There, Walter secured work although his profession remains unknown. Sadly, the ravages of war had left a mark on Walter. The weakened lungs that Emma had worried about were to be his downfall. In January of 1866 Walter became quite ill. His disease settled into his lungs and, after a twelve-week illness, Walter died on April 16, 1866. (248)

Not long after the death of her twenty-two-year-old husband, Emma gave birth to a daughter. The child was named Mary Emma Dunn but her birth drained Emma. Shortly after Mary Emma's birth Emma became ill and died on August 20, 1866. At Emma's funeral service the presiding minister mentioned that she had gone on to "that eternal world of joy, where now we doubt not, she has been welcomed by her Saviour, and where too she has joined the company of her dear companion, among the blood-washed throng." (248)

Less than a single month later the infant Mary Emma Dunn also died. The child's death was recorded in the *Seventh Day Baptist Recorder* with the following commentary, "the last light of the family has expired. Father, mother, and child are now numbered with the dead. They are, we have good reason to hope, an unbroken family in the kingdom of heaven." Whatever one's belief structure may be, it could be justly surmised that, "A war that had already claimed more than six hundred thousand lives, had claimed three more." (248)

In the end, the joined lives of Walter and Emma Dunn, as well as their infant daughter, were incredibly brief. Looking back at their letters to and from the homefront readers are touched by the joys and pain that young love can give birth to. Walter and Emma experienced a courtship that possessed all the elements of drama that emerging love can bear. Over time, they came to fall in love. Across a great distance they maintained a jointed love that harbored the possibility of future bliss. However, time and circumstance had other plans for these young folks. They survived the war but not unscathed. The hopes they nurtured across three years of correspondence fell into dust and ashes when confronted by the hard realities of wartime injury and illness in an era when disease was a grim reaper.

In Walter and Emma Dunn modern students of the Civil War can get in touch with the human face of that conflict. The young Dunn's were in no way dissimilar to countless thousands of other people who yearned for a loving life but realized that hopes could be crushed by war. There was a "mortgage" placed upon the happiness of these young people. In a seemingly inscrutable manner the principal and interest on that loan were collected far too soon. But, in recounting the story of Walter Dunn and Emma Randolph Dunn one can virtually touch the human cost of the Civil War, and all wars that are waged. In that way these poignant writings broaden not only one's understanding of the Civil War but also the human condition as well.

Source

Judith A. Bailey & Robert I. Cottom (eds.), *After Chancellorsville: The Civil War*
   Letters Of Private Walter G. Dunn & Emma Randolph, Baltimore, MD: Maryland
   Historical Society, 1998.

The Faded Stone

The marker rested in an old part of the cemetery.
Rain and time had worn away much of the lettering.
The passing of days & years left it tilted and sunken.
The passerby stopped and looked down.
Here rested a soldier of days gone by.
Was he a kind and decent man?
Did he have a wife and child?
How was his body brought to this final resting place?
Beneath the sod his humble remains still rest.
Whatever earthly sins or worthy deeds are long over.
He wore the coat of blue as so many others did.
On some far off field he fell.
Killed by a brother clad in gray or butternut.
Now, all that remains is the slanting and faded stone.
Each life gone by has a history.
Rascals & cowards—saints and stalwarts—they all served in turn.
The faded stones and weathered monuments are more than bric-a-brac.
Each stone represents a life once lived—hopes & dreams—fears & courage.
In pausing at the old stone we look both backwards and forwards.
Each of us is mortal—we will have our final moment.
Pay heed to the sacrifice of those who went before.
In those old stones and faded memories resides our connection to the past.
This single soldier's marker symbolizes the time he lived and our mortality.
Take heed—remember—then walk away to ponder our comings and goings.
Those who served in those long gone days have had their day—what will our legacy be?

GMR—4/3/05

www.ingramcontent.com/pod-product-compliance
Lightning Source LLC
Chambersburg PA
CBHW071424150426
43191CB00008B/1036